Collins

Student Book, Foundation 2

Approved by AQA

# NEW GCSE MATHS
# AQA Modular
## Matches the 2010 GCSE Specification

**Brian Speed • Keith Gordon • Kevin Evans • Trevor Senior**

# CONTENTS

## RECALL

## UNIT 3: GEOMETRY AND ALGEBRA

# INTRODUCTION

Welcome to Collins New GCSE Maths for AQA Modular Foundation Book 2. The first part of this book covers the Recall content you will have learnt in your Unit 1 and Unit 2 exams. You will also need some content covered in this section for your Unit 3 exam. The second part covers the content that is specific for Unit 3.

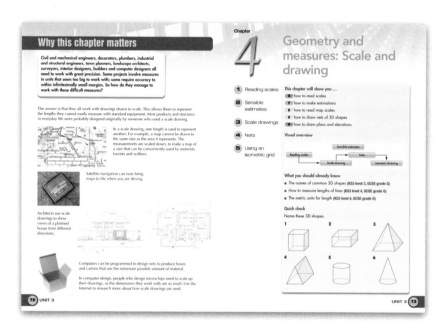

## Why this chapter matters

Find out why each chapter is important through the history of maths, seeing how maths links to other subjects and cultures, and how maths is related to real life.

## Chapter overviews

Look ahead to see what maths you will be doing and how you can build on what you already know.

## Colour-coded grades

Know what target grade you are working at and track your progress with the colour-coded grade panels at the side of the page.

## Use of calculators

Questions when you must or could use your calculator are marked with an 📱 icon. Explanations involving calculators are based on the *Casio fx-83ES*.

## Grade booster

Review what you have learnt and how to get to the next grade with the Grade booster at the end of each chapter.

## Worked examples

Understand the topic before you start the exercise by reading the examples in blue boxes. These take you through questions step by step.

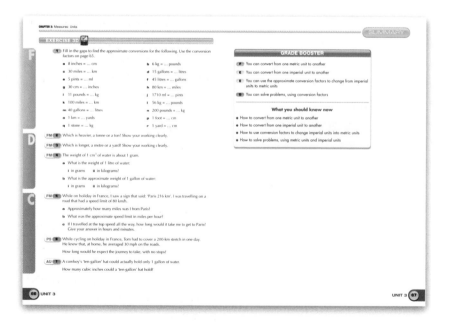

# Functional maths

Practise functional maths skills to see how people use maths in everyday life. Look out for practice questions marked **FM**.

There are also extra functional maths and problem-solving activities at the end of every chapter to build and apply your skills.

## New Assessment Objectives

Practise new parts of the curriculum (Assessment Objectives AO2 and AO3) with questions that assess your understanding marked **AU** and questions that test if you can solve problems marked **PS**. You will also practise some questions that involve several steps and where you have to choose which method to use; these also test AO2. There are also plenty of straightforward questions (AO1) that test if you can do the maths.

## Exam practice

Prepare for your exams with past exam questions and detailed worked exam questions with examiner comments to help you score maximum marks.

## Quality of Written Communication (QWC)

Practise using accurate mathematical vocabulary and writing logical answers to questions to ensure you get your QWC (Quality of Written Communication) marks in the exams. The Glossary and worked exam questions will help you with this.

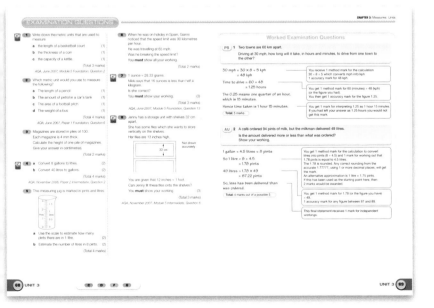

# Why this chapter matters

Technology is increasingly important in our lives. It helps us do many things more efficiently than we could without it.

Modern **calculators** take away the need to perform long calculations by hand. They can help to improve accuracy – but a calculator is only as good as the person using it. If you press the buttons in the wrong order when doing a calculation then you will get the wrong answer. That is why learning to use a calculator effectively is important.

The earliest known calculating device was a **tally stick**, which was a stick with notches cut into it so that small numbers could be recorded.

In about 2000 BC the **abacus** was invented in Eygpt.

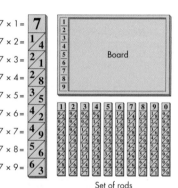

Set of rods

Abacuses are still used widely in China today and they were used widely for almost 3500 years, until John Napier devised a calculating aid called **Napier's bones**.

These led to the invention of the **slide rule** by William Oughtred in 1622. These stayed in use until the mid-1960s. Engineers working on the first ever moon landings used slide rules to do some of their calculations.

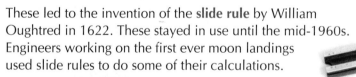

In the mid-sixteenth century the first **mechanical calculating machines** were produced. These were based on a series of cogs and gears and so were too expensive to be widely used.

The first **electronic computers** were produced in the mid-twentieth century. Once the transistor was perfected, the power increased and the cost and size decreased until the point where the average scientific calculator that students use in schools has more computing power than the first craft that went into space.

# Number: Using calculators

**1** Basic calculations and using brackets

**2** Using a calculator to add and subtract fractions

**3** Using a calculator to multiply and divide fractions

## This chapter will show you ...

to  how to use a calculator effectively

## Visual overview

Basic calculations (+, −, ×, ÷) → Inputting fractions → Calculating with fractions

## What you should already know

- How to add, subtract, multiply and divide with whole numbers, fractions and decimals **(KS3 level 5, GCSE grade E)**
- How to simplify fractions and decimals **(KS3 level 3, GCSE grade G)**
- How to convert improper fractions to mixed numbers or decimals and vice-versa **(KS3 level 4, GCSE grade F)**
- The rules of BIDMAS/BODMAS with decimals **(KS3 level 5, GCSE grade E)**

## Quick check

1 Complete these calculations. Do not use a calculator.

  **a** $48 + 89$    **b** $102 - 37$    **c** $23 \times 7$    **d** $336 \div 8$

  **e** $3.6 + 2.9$    **f** $8.4 - 3.8$    **g** $3 \times 4.5$    **h** $7.8 \div 6$

2 **a** Convert these mixed numbers into improper fractions.

    **i** $2\frac{2}{5}$    **ii** $3\frac{1}{4}$    **iii** $1\frac{7}{9}$

  **b** Convert these improper fractions into mixed numbers.

    **i** $\frac{11}{6}$    **ii** $\frac{7}{3}$    **iii** $\frac{23}{7}$

3 Work these out without using a calculator.

  **a** $2 + 3 \times 4$      **b** $(2 + 3) \times 4$

  **c** $6 + 4 - 3^2$      **d** $6 + (4 - 3)^2$

4 Work these out without using a calculator.

  **a** $\frac{2}{3} + \frac{3}{4}$      **b** $\frac{1}{5} + \frac{2}{7}$

  **c** $\frac{4}{5} - \frac{1}{4}$      **d** $2\frac{1}{3} - 1\frac{2}{5}$

# 1.1 Basic calculations and using brackets

**This section will show you how to:**
- use some of the important keys, including the bracket keys, to do calculations on a calculator

**Key words**
brackets
equals
function key
key
shift key

Most of the calculations in this unit are carried out to find the final answer of an algebraic problem or a geometric problem. The examples are intended to demonstrate how to use some of the **function keys** on the calculator. Remember that some functions will need the **shift key** SHIFT to make them work. When you have **keyed** in the calculation, press the **equals** key = to give the answer.

Some calculators display answers to fraction calculations as fractions. There is always a key to change this to a decimal. In examinations, an answer given as a fraction or a decimal will always be acceptable unless the question asks you to round to a given accuracy.

Most scientific calculators can be set up to display the answers in the format you want.

**EXAMPLE 1**

These three angles are on a straight line.

To find the size of angle $a$, subtract the angles 68° and 49° from 180°.

You can do the calculation in two ways.

$180 - 68 - 49$ or $180 - (68 + 49)$

Try keying each calculation into your calculator.

**180 − 68 − 49**

[1] [8] [0] [−] [6] [8] [−] [4] [9] [=]

The display will show 63.

**180 − (68 + 49)**

[1] [8] [0] [−] [(] [6] [8] [+] [4] [9] [)] [=]

Again, the display should show 63.

It is important that you can do this both ways.

You must use the correct calculation or use **brackets** to combine parts of the calculation.

A common error is to work out $180 - 68 + 49$, which will give the wrong answer.

You will learn more about angles in Chapter 8.

**FM** Functional Maths **AU** (AO2) Assessing Understanding **PS** (AO3) Problem Solving

**EXAMPLE 2**

Work out the area of this trapezium,
where $a = 12.3$, $b = 16.8$ and $h = 2.4$.

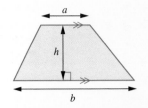

To work out the area of the trapezium,
you use the formula:

$$A = \frac{1}{2}(a + b)h$$

Remember, you should always substitute into
a formula before working it out.

> You will learn more about
> areas of shapes in
> Chapter 6.

$$A = \frac{1}{2}(12.3 + 16.8)2.4$$

Between the brackets and the numbers at each end there is an assumed
multiplication sign, so the calculation is:

$$\frac{1}{2} \times (12.3 + 16.8) \times 2.4$$

Be careful starting. $\frac{1}{2}$ can be keyed in lots of different ways:

- As a division

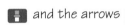

    0.5

- Using the fraction key and the arrows

     and the arrows

    The display should show $\frac{1}{2}$.

Key in the full calculation, using the fraction key:

The display should show $34.92$ or $\frac{873}{25}$.

Your calculator has a power key $x^\blacksquare$ and a cube key $x^3$.

**EXAMPLE 3**

Find the value of $4.5^3 - 2 \times 4.5$.

Try keying in:

`4` `.` `5` `x³` `−` `2` `×`

`4` `.` `5` `=`

The display should show **82.125** or $\dfrac{657}{8}$ .

> You often have to work out calculations like this in trial and improvement questions.
> You will learn more about trial and improvement in Chapter 2.

Most calculations involving circles will involve the number π (pronounced 'pi'), which has its own calculator button `π` .

> You will learn a lot more about π and circles in Chapter 9.

The decimal value of π goes on for ever. It has an approximate value of 3.14 but the value in a calculator is far more accurate and may be displayed as 3.1415926535 or π.

**EXAMPLE 4**

Work out:  **a**  $\pi \times 3.2^2$  **b**  $2 \times \pi \times 4.9$

Give your answers to 1 decimal place.

**a**  Try keying in:

`π` `×` `3` `.` `2` `x²` `=`

The display should show **32.16990877** or $\dfrac{256}{25}\pi$. (Convert this to a decimal.)

This is 32.2 to 1 decimal place.

**b**  Try keying in:

`2` `×` `π` `×` `4` `.` `9` `=`

The display should show **30.78760801** or $\dfrac{49}{5}\pi$. (Convert this to a decimal.)

This is 30.8 to 1 decimal place.

## EXERCISE 1A

Use your calculator to work out the following.

Try to key in the calculation as one continuous set, without writing down any intermediate values.

**1** Subtract these sets of numbers from 180.

   **a** 54, 81        **b** 21, 39, 68        **c** 51, 34, 29

**2** Subtract these sets of numbers from 360.

   **a** 68, 92        **b** 90, 121, 34        **c** 32, 46, 46

**3**  **a** Subtract 68 from 180 and divide the answer by 2.

   **b** Subtract 46 from 360 and divide the answer by 2.

   **c** Subtract 52 from 180 twice.

   **d** Subtract 39 and 2 lots of 64 from 360.

**4** Work these out.

   **a** $(10 - 2) \times 180 \div 10$

   **b** $180 - (360 \div 5)$

**5** Work out:

   **a** $\dfrac{1}{2} \times (4.6 + 6.8) \times 2.2$

   **b** $\dfrac{1}{2} \times (2.3 + 9.9) \times 4.5$

**6** Work out the following and give your answers to 1 decimal place.

   **a** $\pi \times 8.5$

   **b** $2 \times \pi \times 3.9$

   **c** $\pi \times 6.8^2$

   **d** $\pi \times 0.7^2$

**FM 7** At Sovereign garage, Jon bought 21 litres of petrol for £21.52.

At the Bridge garage he paid £15.41 for 15 litres.

At which garage is the petrol cheaper?

**D**

**AU** **8** A teacher asked her class to work out $\dfrac{2.3 + 8.9}{3.8 - 1.7}$.

Abby keyed in:

`(` `2` `.` `3` `+` `8` `.` `9` `)` `÷` `3` `.` `8` `−` `1` `.` `7` `=`

Bobby keyed in:

`2` `.` `3` `+` `8` `.` `9` `÷` `3` `.` `8` `−` `1` `.` `7` `=`

Col keyed in:

`(` `2` `.` `3` `+` `8` `.` `9` `)` `÷` `(` `3` `.` `8` `−` `1` `.` `7` `)` `=`

Donna keyed in:

`2` `.` `3` `+` `8` `.` `9` `÷` `(` `3` `.` `8` `−` `1` `.` `7` `)` `=`

They each rounded their answers to 3 decimal places.

Work out the answer each of them found.

Who had the correct answer?

**PS** **9** Show that a speed of 31 metres per second is approximately 70 miles per hour.

You will need to know that 1 mile $\approx$ 1610 metres.

**10** Work the value of each of these, if $a = 3.4$, $b = 5.6$ and $c = 8.8$.

a $abc$

b $2(ab + ac + bc)$

**11** Work out the following giving your answer to 2 decimal places.

a $\sqrt{(3.2^2 - 1.6^2)}$

b $\sqrt{(4.8^2 + 3.6^2)}$

**12** Work these out.

a $7.8^3 + 3 \times 7.8$

b $5.45^3 - 2 \times 5.45 - 40$

**12** **RECALL**

# Using a calculator to add and subtract fractions

**This section will show you how to:**
- use a calculator to add and subtract fractions

**Key words**
fraction
improper fraction
key
mixed number
proper fraction
shift key

In this lesson, questions requiring calculation of **fractions** are set in a context linked to other topics, such as algebra or geometry.

You will recall from Chapter 2 in Book 1 that a fraction with the numerator bigger than the denominator is called an **improper fraction** or a *top-heavy fraction*.

You will also recall that a **mixed number** is made up of a whole number and a **proper fraction**.

For example:

$$\frac{14}{5} = 2\frac{4}{5} \text{ and } 3\frac{2}{7} = \frac{23}{7}$$

## Using a calculator with improper fractions

Check that your calculator has a fraction key. Remember, for some functions, you may need to use the **shift key** .

To **key** in a fraction, press ▯.

Input the fraction so that it looks like this SHIFT.

$\frac{9}{5}$ or $9 \lrcorner 5$

Now press the equals key = so that the fraction displays in the answer part of the screen.

Pressing shift and the key S⇔D will convert the fraction to a mixed number.

$1 \lrcorner 4 \lrcorner 5$

This is the mixed number $1\frac{4}{5}$.

Pressing the equals sign again will convert the mixed number back to an improper fraction.

- Can you see a way of converting an improper fraction to a mixed number without using a calculator?

- Test your idea. Then use your calculator to check it.

## Using a calculator to convert mixed numbers to improper fractions

To input a mixed number, press the shift key first and then the fraction key .

Pressing the equals sign will convert the mixed number to an improper fraction.

- Now key in at least 10 improper fractions and convert them to mixed numbers.

- Remember to press the equals sign to change the mixed numbers back to improper fractions.

- Now input at least 10 mixed numbers and convert them to improper fractions.

- Look at your results. Can you see a way of converting a mixed number to an improper fraction without using a calculator?

- Test your idea. Then use your calculator to check it.

---

**EXAMPLE 5**

A water tank is half full. One-third of the capacity of the full tank is poured out.

What fraction of the tank is now full of water?

The calculation is $\frac{1}{2} - \frac{1}{3}$.

Keying in the calculation gives:

The display should show $\frac{1}{6}$.

The tank is now one-sixth full of water.

---

**RECALL**

**EXAMPLE 6**

Work out the perimeter of a rectangle $1\frac{1}{2}$ cm long and $3\frac{2}{3}$ cm wide.

> You will learn more about perimeters of shapes in Chapter 6.

To work out the perimeter of this rectangle, you can use the formula:

$$P = 2l + 2w$$

where $l = 1\frac{1}{2}$ cm and $w = 3\frac{2}{3}$ cm.

$$P = 2 \times 1\frac{1}{2} + 2 \times 3\frac{2}{3}$$

Keying in the calculation gives:

| 2 | × | SHIFT | ▦ | 1 | ▶ | 1 | ▼ | 2 | ▶ |

| + | 2 | × | SHIFT | ▦ | 3 | ▶ | 2 | ▼ | 3 | ▶ | = |

The display should show $10\frac{1}{3}$.

So the perimeter is $10\frac{1}{3}$ cm.

**EXERCISE 1B**

**1** Use your calculator to work these out. Give your answers as fractions.

Try to key in the calculation as one continuous set, without writing down any intermediate values.

**a** $\dfrac{3}{4} + \dfrac{4}{5}$      **b** $\dfrac{5}{6} + \dfrac{7}{10}$      **c** $\dfrac{4}{5} + \dfrac{9}{20}$

**d** $\dfrac{3}{8} + \dfrac{9}{25}$      **e** $\dfrac{7}{20} + \dfrac{3}{16}$      **f** $\dfrac{5}{8} + \dfrac{9}{16} + \dfrac{3}{5}$

**g** $\dfrac{9}{20} - \dfrac{1}{12}$      **h** $\dfrac{3}{4} - \dfrac{7}{48}$      **i** $\dfrac{11}{32} - \dfrac{1}{6}$

**j** $\dfrac{4}{5} + \dfrac{9}{16} - \dfrac{2}{3}$      **k** $\dfrac{7}{16} + \dfrac{3}{8} - \dfrac{1}{20}$      **l** $\dfrac{3}{4} + \dfrac{2}{9} - \dfrac{3}{11}$

**D**

**2** Use your calculator to work these out. Give your answers as mixed numbers.

Try to key in the calculation as one continuous set, without writing down any intermediate values.

**a** $4\frac{3}{4} + 1\frac{4}{5}$

**b** $3\frac{5}{6} + 4\frac{7}{10}$

**c** $7\frac{4}{5} + 8\frac{9}{20}$

**d** $9\frac{3}{8} + 2\frac{9}{25}$

**e** $6\frac{7}{20} + 1\frac{3}{16}$

**f** $2\frac{5}{8} + 3\frac{9}{16} + 5\frac{3}{5}$

**g** $6\frac{9}{20} - 3\frac{1}{12}$

**h** $4\frac{3}{4} - 2\frac{7}{48}$

**i** $8\frac{11}{32} - 5\frac{1}{6}$

**j** $12\frac{4}{5} + 3\frac{9}{16} - 8\frac{2}{3}$

**k** $9\frac{7}{16} + 5\frac{3}{8} - 7\frac{1}{20}$

**l** $10\frac{3}{4} + 6\frac{2}{9} - 12\frac{3}{11}$

**3** A water tank is three-quarters full. Two-thirds of a full tank is poured out.

What fraction of the tank is now full of water?

**4**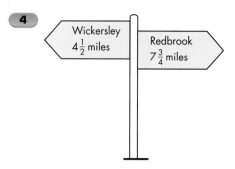

**a** What is the distance between Wickersley and Redbrook, using these roads?

**b** How much further is it to Redbrook than to Wickersley?

**C**

**AU 5** Here is a calculation.

$$\frac{3}{25} + \frac{7}{10}$$

Imagine that you are trying to explain to someone how to use a calculator to do this.

Write down what you would say.

**6** There are the same number of boys and girls in a school.

Because of snow $\frac{4}{5}$ of the boys are absent and $\frac{5}{12}$ of the girls are absent.

What fraction of the students are present?

**PS** **7** **a** Use your calculator to work out $\frac{18}{37} - \frac{23}{43}$.

     **b** Explain how your answer tells you that $\frac{23}{43}$ is greater than $\frac{18}{37}$.

**AU** **8** Jon is working out $\frac{9}{32} + \frac{5}{7}$ without using a calculator.

He adds the numerators and the denominators to get an answer of $\frac{14}{39}$ which is not correct.

     **a** Use a calculator to work out the correct answer.

     **b** Work out $\frac{14}{39} - \frac{9}{32}$ on your calculator.

     **c** Work out $\frac{14}{39} - \frac{5}{7}$ on your calculator.

     **d** Explain why your answers to parts **b** and **c** show that $\frac{14}{39}$ is a fraction between $\frac{9}{32}$ and $\frac{5}{7}$.

**AU** **9** **a** Choose two other fractions to add together.

     Write down the incorrect answer that Jon would get.

     Repeat the steps of question **6** for these fractions.

     **b** Is Jon's answer between your two fractions?

**AU** **10** To work out the perimeter of a rectangle the following formula is used.

     $P = 2l + 2w$

Work out the perimeter when $l = 5\frac{1}{8}$ cm and $w = 4\frac{1}{3}$ cm.

**PS** **11** A shape is rotated 90° clockwise and then a further 60° clockwise.

What fraction of a turn is needed to return it to its original position?

Give both possible answers.

# Using a calculator to multiply and divide fractions

**This section will show you how to:**
- use a calculator to multiply and divide fractions

**Key words**

fraction

key

shift key

In this lesson, questions requiring calculation of **fractions** will be set in a context linked to other topics such as algebra or geometry. Remember, for some functions, you may need to use the **shift key** SHIFT .

**EXAMPLE 7**

Work out the area of a rectangle of length $3\frac{1}{2}$ m and width $2\frac{2}{3}$ m.

The formula for the area of a rectangle is:

area = length × width

You will learn more about perimeters of shapes in Chapter 6.

**Keying** in the calculation, where length = $3\frac{1}{2}$ and width = $2\frac{2}{3}$ gives:

[ SHIFT ] [ ▤ ] [ 3 ] [ ▶ ] [ 1 ] [ ▼ ] [ 2 ] [ ▶ ] [ × ]

[ SHIFT ] [ ▤ ] [ 2 ] [ ▶ ] [ 2 ] [ ▼ ] [ 3 ] [ ▶ ] [ = ]

The display should show $9\frac{1}{3}$.

The area is $9\frac{1}{3}$ cm².

**EXAMPLE 8**

Work out the average speed of a bus that travels $20\frac{1}{4}$ miles in $\frac{3}{4}$ hour.

The formula for the average speed is:

$$\text{average speed} = \frac{\text{distance}}{\text{time}}$$

You will learn more about distance, speed and time in Chapter 5.

Use this formula to work the average speed of the bus, where distance is $20\frac{1}{4}$ and time is $\frac{3}{4}$.

Keying in the calculation gives:

The display should show 27.

The average speed is 27 mph.

---

**EXERCISE 1C**

**1** Use your calculator to work these out. Give your answers as fractions.

Try to key in the calculation as one continuous set, without writing down any intermediate values.

**a** $\frac{3}{4} \times \frac{4}{5}$

**b** $\frac{5}{6} \times \frac{7}{10}$

**c** $\frac{4}{5} \times \frac{9}{20}$

**d** $\frac{3}{8} \times \frac{9}{25}$

**e** $\frac{7}{20} \times \frac{3}{16}$

**f** $\frac{5}{8} \times \frac{9}{16} \times \frac{3}{5}$

**g** $\frac{9}{20} \div \frac{1}{12}$

**h** $\frac{3}{4} \div \frac{7}{48}$

**i** $\frac{11}{32} \div \frac{1}{6}$

**j** $\frac{4}{5} \times \frac{9}{16} \div \frac{2}{3}$

**k** $\frac{7}{16} \times \frac{3}{8} \div \frac{1}{20}$

**l** $\frac{3}{4} \times \frac{2}{9} \div \frac{3}{11}$

**2** The formula for the area of a rectangle is:

area = length × width

Use this formula to work the area of a rectangle of length $\frac{2}{3}$ m and width $\frac{1}{4}$ m.

**3** Each of the steps on a ladder is $\frac{1}{5}$ m high. Ben needs to climb 3 m to fix the shed roof. How many steps will he go up the ladder?

**AU 4** **a** Use your calculator to work out $\frac{3}{4} \times \frac{9}{16}$.

**b** Write down the answer to $\frac{9}{4} \times \frac{3}{16}$.

**D**

**C**

**AU** **5** **a** Use your calculator to work out $\frac{2}{3} \div \frac{5}{6}$.

**b** Use your calculator to work out $\frac{2}{3} \times \frac{6}{5}$.

**c** Use your calculator to work out $\frac{4}{7} \div \frac{3}{4}$.

**d** Write down the answer to $\frac{4}{7} \times \frac{4}{3}$.

**6** Use your calculator to work these out. Give your answers as mixed numbers.

Try to key in the calculation as one continuous set, without writing down any intermediate values.

**a** $4\frac{3}{4} \times 1\frac{4}{5}$

**b** $3\frac{5}{6} \times 4\frac{7}{10}$

**c** $7\frac{4}{5} \times 8\frac{9}{20}$

**d** $9\frac{3}{8} \times 2\frac{9}{25}$

**e** $6\frac{7}{20} \times 1\frac{3}{16}$

**f** $2\frac{5}{8} \times 3\frac{9}{16} \times 5\frac{3}{5}$

**g** $6\frac{9}{20} \div 3\frac{1}{12}$

**h** $4\frac{3}{4} \div 2\frac{7}{48}$

**i** $8\frac{11}{32} \div 5\frac{1}{6}$

**j** $12\frac{4}{5} \times 3\frac{9}{16} \div 8\frac{2}{3}$

**k** $9\frac{7}{16} \times 5\frac{3}{8} \div 7\frac{1}{20}$

**l** $10\frac{3}{4} \times 6\frac{2}{9} \div 12\frac{3}{11}$

**7** The formula for the area of a rectangle is:

area = length × width

Use this formula to work out the area of a rectangle of length $5\frac{2}{3}$ metres and width $3\frac{1}{4}$ metres.

**8** The volume of a cuboid is $26\frac{3}{4}$ cm$^3$. It is cut into eight equal pieces.

Work out the volume of one of the pieces.

**9** The formula for the distance travelled is:

distance = average speed × time taken

Work out how far a car travelling at an average speed of $36\frac{1}{4}$ mph will travel in $2\frac{1}{2}$ hours.

**10** Glasses are filled from litre bottles of water.

Each glass holds $\frac{1}{2}$ pint.

1 litre = $1\frac{3}{4}$ pints.

How many litre bottles are needed to fill 10 glasses?

**PS** **11** The ribbon on a roll is $3\frac{1}{2}$ m long. Joe wants to cut pieces of ribbon that are each **FM** $\frac{1}{6}$ m long.

He needs 50 pieces.

How many rolls will he need?

## GRADE BOOSTER

**D** You can use BIDMAS/BODMAS to carry out operations in the correct order

**D** You can use a calculator to add, subtract, multiply and divide fractions

**C** You can use a calculator to add, subtract, multiply and divide mixed numbers

### What you should know now

● How to use a calculator effectively, including the brackets and fraction keys

**1** Ahmed uses $\frac{2}{3}$ of a litre of milk each day.

He buys milk in 2-litre bottles.

What is the least number of bottles that he needs to buy for one week?

You **must** show your working.

*AQA, Foundation, Module 3, June 2009, Question 18*

 **2** A train travels 350 miles in $4\frac{3}{4}$ hours. Work out the average speed of the train in miles per hour.

 **3** A painter has 40 litres of paint.

The paint is in 2.5-litre tins.

How many tins of paint does he have?

 **4** The diagram shows a trapezium.

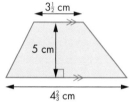

Work out the area of the trapezium.

**Hint**: Area $= \frac{1}{2}(a + b)h$

 **5** Matt counts 40 strides as he walks 30 m.

**a** How long is each stride?

**b** How many strides would he take if he walked 75 m?

**c** He decides that to get enough exercise he will do 3000 strides.

How far will he need to walk?

**6** **a** A parallelogram has base $7\frac{1}{2}$ cm and perpendicular height $7\frac{1}{2}$ cm.

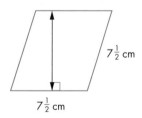

Work out the area.

**Hint**: Area of a parallelogram = base × perpendicular height

**b** The perimeter of the parallelogram is $35\frac{1}{2}$ cm.

How long is one of the sloping sides?

 **7** Calculate $\dfrac{5.6 \times 7.8}{4.3 - 2.1}$

**a** Write down your full calculator display. (1)

**b** Write your answer to part **a** to 1 decimal place. (1)

(Total 2 marks)

*AQA, Higher, Module 3, June 2008, Question 1*

 **8** Calculate $\sqrt{8.17^3 + 4.39^2}$

**a** Give all the figures on your calculator display. (1)

**b** Give your answer to an appropriate degree of accuracy. (1)

(Total 2 marks)

*AQA, Specification A, Paper 2 November 2007, Question 1b*

 **9** Work out $\dfrac{21.6 \times 64}{35.1 + 9.57}$

**a** Write down your full calculator display. (1)

**b** Write your answer to 2 decimal places. (1)

(Total 2 marks)

*AQA, Higher, Module 3, June 2009, Question 1*

 **10** Work out as a decimal $\dfrac{4.6^2}{8.6 - 2.7}$

**a** Write down your full calculator display. (1)

**b** Write your answer to three significant figures. (1)

(Total 2 marks)

*AQA, Higher, Module 3, March 2008, Question 4*

 **11** **a** A cuboid has length $5\frac{1}{2}$ cm, width $3\frac{1}{2}$ cm and height 4 cm.

Work out the volume.

**Hint**: Volume of a cuboid = length × width × height

**b** The volume of a cuboid is 50 cm³

One edge is $2\frac{1}{2}$ cm long.

Work out a pair of possible lengths for the other edges.

C D

# Worked Examination Questions

**AU** **1** The perimeter of a rectangle is $32\frac{1}{2}$ cm.

Work out a pair of possible values for the length and the width of the rectangle.

Perimeter is 2 × length + 2 × width

Length + width = $32\frac{1}{2}$ ÷ 2

Length + width = $16\frac{1}{4}$ cm

Possible length and width are:

Length = 10 cm

Width = $6\frac{1}{4}$ cm

You get 1 mark for method for writing down the correct formula and completing the first step of the calculation.

You get a mark for an accurate calculation.

Any two values with a sum of $16\frac{1}{4}$ would score the final mark.

**Total:** 3 marks

**FM** **2** A driver is travelling 200 miles.

He sets off at 10 am.

He stops for a 20-minute break.

His average speed when travelling is $42\frac{1}{2}$ mph.

He wants to arrive before 3 pm.

Is he successful?

Time travelling = distance ÷ average speed

= 200 ÷ $42\frac{1}{2}$

= $4\frac{12}{17}$ or 4.7058 …

20 minutes = $\frac{1}{3}$ hour or 0.33

$4\frac{12}{17} + \frac{1}{3}$ or 4.7058 … + 0.33 …

= $5\frac{2}{51}$ hours 5.039 hours

10 am to 3 pm is 5 hours so he arrives after 3 pm

Substituting the correct figures into the formula gets 1 method mark.

This calculation gets 1 mark for method.

This answer gets 1 mark for accuracy.

A statement giving the correct conclusion from correct working would get 1 mark for quality of written communication.

**Total:** 4 marks

You have been asked by your Business Studies teacher to set up a jewellery stall selling beaded jewellery at an upcoming Young Enterprise fair. There will be 50 stalls at this fair (many of which will be selling jewellery) and it is expected that there will be 500 attendees.

You will be competing against every other stall to sell your products to the attendees, either as one-off purchases or as bulk orders. In order to be successful in this you must carefully plan the design, cost and price of your jewellery, to ensure that people will buy your products and that you make a profit.

## Getting started

Answer these questions to begin thinking about how beads can be used to make a piece of jewellery.

1 How many 6 mm beads are needed to make a bracelet?

2 How many 8 mm beads are needed to make an anklet?

3 How many 10 mm beads are needed to make a short necklace?

4 How many 10 mm beads are needed to make a long necklace?

5 You are asked to make a bracelet with beads of two different lengths. You decide to use 6 mm red beads and 8 mm blue beads. How many would you need if you used them alternately?

## How to make beaded jewellery

Beads are sold in different sizes and wire is sold in different thicknesses, called the gauge. To make a piece of jewellery the beads are threaded onto the wire.

**Step 1** Choose a gauge of wire and cut the length required.

**Step 2** Put a fastening on one end.

**Step 3** Thread on beads of different sizes in a pattern.

**Step 4** Put a fastener on the other end.

Your jewellery is now complete.

## Cost of materials

**Here are the costs of the raw materials that you will need to make your jewellery.**

| | |
|---|---|
| 6 mm beads | 10p each |
| 8 mm beads | 12p each |
| 10 mm beads | 15p each |
| 24-gauge wire | 10p per centimetre |
| 20-gauge wire | 8p per centimetre |
| Fasteners for both ends: 30p per item of jewellery | |

## Advice

For bracelets and anklets use 20-gauge wire.

For necklaces use 24-gauge wire.

Beads are available in three lengths: 6 mm, 8 mm and 10 mm.

Beads are available in three colours, green, blue and red.

## Your task

With a partner, draw up a business plan for your jewellery stall, to ensure you produce high quality beaded jewellery that will turn a good profit. In your plan, you should include:

- an outline of who you expect to buy your jewellery (your 'target market')
- a design for at least one set of jewellery that will appeal to your target market
- a list of all the materials you will need
- the cost of your designs
- a fair price at which to sell your jewellery
- a discounting plan for bulk orders, or if you must reduce your prices on the day
- an expected profit.

Use all the information given on these pages to create your business plan.

Be sure to justify your plan, using appropriate mathematics and describing the calculations that you have done.

Present your business plan as a report to the Young Enterprise committee.

| Standard lengths for bracelets and necklaces | |
|---|---|
| Bracelet | 17 cm |
| Anklet | 23 cm |
| Short necklace | 39 cm |
| Long necklace | 46 cm |

# Why this chapter matters

For thousands of years, people have tried to solve equations and express them in a symbolic or algebraic way.

| | |
|---|---|
| **1850 BC** | The Rhind Papyrus was written. This gave some insight into the mathematics used by the Ancient Egyptians. From this it was clear that they could solve linear equations in one unknown but they had no symbolism. Problems were solved verbally. |
| **1600 BC** | In Babylonia mathematicians developed arithmetic methods for solving equations involving squares but they still did not use symbols to represent unknowns. |
| **300 BC** | The Cairo Papyrus was written. By this time Egyptian mathematics had moved on to far more complex equations that are met in A level mathematics. They still did not have any symbolism and despite their advanced algebra they only used fractions with a numerator of 1 which made some of their working really difficult. |
| **250 AD** | The Greek mathematician, Diophantus, was the first to use a type of symbolism to solve equations although it was many centuries before the verbal method of solution disappeared. |
| **600 AD** | Hindu mathematicians were influenced by what the Greek mathematicians had done and did a large amount of work on astronomy. They developed the base 10 (decimal) system and were the first to use the number zero and solve problems using this number. They also introduced negative numbers at this time. |
| **1150 AD** | The Hindu mathematician, Bhaskara, was the first to realise that a number such as 9 has two square roots (3 and $-3$). Hindu mathematicians were the first to use symbols. |
| **1400 AD** | Arab mathematicians working in Spain improved the Hindu number and symbolic system into the algebraic notation we use today. |
| **1600 AD** | Once symbolism was established mathematics made great advances, with methods for solving complicated equations being found. |
| **1850 AD** | With an established method of recording mathematics in a concise form, European mathematicians moved into the world of abstract algebra which deals with concepts such as the square root of $-1$. (This is beyond GCSE mathematics.) |
| **Today** | You are starting to learn a branch of mathematics that has its origins 4000 years ago. |

# Algebra: Review of algebra

1. Basic algebra

2. Substitution using a calculator

3. Solving linear equations

4. Setting up equations

5. Trial and improvement

## This chapter will show you ...

- **F** how to use letters to represent numbers
- to **F** **E** how to solve linear equations with the variable on one side only
- **E** how to form simple algebraic expressions
- **E** how to simplify such expressions by collecting like terms
- **E** how to substitute numbers into expressions and formulae
- **D** how to factorise expressions
- **D** how to express simple rules in algebraic form
- **D** how to solve linear equations with the variable on both sides
- **C** how to solve equations using trial and improvement

## Visual overview

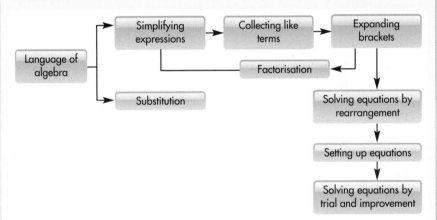

## What you should already know

- The BODMAS/BIDMAS rule, which gives the order in which you must do the operations of arithmetic when they occur together **(KS3 level 5, GCSE grade F)**

## Quick check

1 Write down the value of each expression.
   **a** $(10 - 2) \times 3$                     **b** $10 - (2 \times 3)$

2 Work out    $(6 - 3) \times (6 + 2 - 1)$

3 **a** Put brackets in the calculation to make the answer 21.
     $2 + 5 \times 3$
   **b** Put brackets in the calculation to make the answer 47.
     $2 + 5 \times 3 + 6$

This section will show you how to:

- recall the rules of algebra
- simplify algebraic expressions by multiplying terms
- simplify algebraic expressions by collecting like terms
- expand and simplify brackets
- factorise expressions
- substitute numbers into expressions and formulae

**Key words**

brackets
equation
expand
expand and simplify
expression
factor
factorisation
formula
like terms
simplify
substitution

Work through these examples to remind yourself of some of the algebra you will need for Unit 3.

---

**EXAMPLE 1**

State whether each of the following is an expression (E), an equation (Q) or a formula (F).

A: $x + 4 = 9$      B: $S = \dfrac{x}{9}$      C: $4x - 5y$

A is an equation (Q) as it can be solved to give $x = 5$.

B is a formula (F). This is the formula for the side of a square with a perimeter of $x$.

C is an expression (E) with two terms.

---

**EXAMPLE 2**

What is the perimeter and area of each of these squares?

   **a** side of 8 cm          **b** side of $x$ m

   **a** Perimeter = $4 \times 8 = 32$ cm

      Area = $8 \times 8 = 64$ cm$^2$

   **b** Perimeter = $4 \times x = 4x$ m

      Area = $x \times x = x^2$ m$^2$

---

**EXAMPLE 3**

Simplify:

**a** $2t \times 5t$        **b** $4t^2 \times t$        **c** $2t^2 \times 7t^3$

**a** $2t \times 5t = 10t^2$

**b** $4t^2 \times t = 4t^3$

**c** $2t^2 \times 7t^3 = 14t^5$

**EXAMPLE 4**

Simplify     $6a + 7b + 5c^2 + 2a - 3b + 2c^2$

Write out the expressions with like terms next to each other.

$6a + 2a + 7b - 3b + 5c^2 + 2c^2$

$= 8a + 4b + 7c^2$

**EXAMPLE 5**

Expand     **a** $3(2x + 7)$        **b** $2x(3x - 4y)$

**a** $3 \times 2x + 3 \times 7 = 6x + 21$

**b** $2x \times 3x - 2x \times 4y = 6x^2 - 8xy$

**EXAMPLE 6**

Expand and simplify     $6(2x + 5) - 3(3x - 1)$

$6(2x + 5) - 3(3x - 1) = 12x + 30 - 9x + 3$

$= 12x - 9x + 30 + 3$

$= 3x + 33$

**EXAMPLE 7**

Factorise the following expressions.

**a** $3x + 6$        **b** $4my + 12mx$        **c** $5kp - 10k^2p + 15kp^2$

**a** The common factor is 3, so $3x + 6 = 3(x + 2)$

**b** The common factor is $4m$, so $4my + 12mx = 4m(y + 3x)$

**c** The common factor is $5kp$, so $5kp - 10k^2p + 15kp^2 = 5kp(1 - 2k + 3p)$

**EXAMPLE 8**

The formula for the perimeter of a rectangle is $P = 2l + 2w$

Work out the perimeter when $l = 4.5$ cm and $w = 1.75$ cm

$P = 2(4.5) + 2(1.75) = 9 + 3.5 = 12.5$ cm

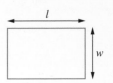

**EXERCISE 2A**

**1** Rex has $n$ marbles.

Stu has three times as many marbles as Rex.

Tamara has five more marbles than Rex.

Ursula has four fewer marbles than Rex.

Vic has six more marbles than Stu.

**a** How many marbles does each person have?

**b** How many marbles do they have altogether?

**2** My wife is 35 years old and I am $Y$ years old. How old will we be in $z$ years' time?

**3** Simplify each of the following expressions.

**a** $5 \times 4x$                                  **b** $3w \times w$

**c** $6h \times 3h$                                 **d** $5x + 7x$

**e** $6z - z$                                       **f** $4y^2 + 5y^2 - 2y^2$

**g** $3a + 7b + 8a - 2b$                     **h** $8x + 7 - 5x - 9$

**PS 4** My son is 24 years old. In 2 years' time he will be half as old as I am.

What age am I now?

**AU 5** The answer to $5 \times 6w$ is $30w$.

Write down two **different** expressions for which the answer is $30w$.

**PS 6** Alison has £1.25 and Helga has 90p more than Alison.

How much should Helga give to Alison so they both have the same amount?

**FM 7** Syd measures the length and width of a football field using a long stick $L$ and a short stick $S$.

He finds the length is $98L + 2S$ and the width is $52L + S$

**a** Work out the perimeter in terms of $L$ and $S$.

**b** Later he finds that the long stick is 90 cm and the short stick is 20 cm.

What is the actual perimeter of the football field?

Give your answer in metres.

**8** Find the value of the following expressions when a = 5, b = 3 and c = −4.

**a** $4a + 1$          **b** $6b - a$          **c** $a^2 + c^2$

**d** $ab$          **e** $3ac$          **f** $4ab - 3bc$

**9** State whether each of the following is an expression (E), an equation (Q) or a formula (F).

**a** $5x - 2$          **b** $A = s^2$          **c** $5x - 2 = 13$

**AU 10** $5x + 2y + 3x - 5y = 8x - 3y$

Write down two other similar but **different** expressions for which the answer is $8x - 3y$.

**FM 11** A taxi company uses the following rule to calculate their fares.

Fare = £3.50 plus £1.20 per kilometre

**a** How much is a journey of 3 kilometres?

**b** Frankie pays £8.30 for a taxi ride. How far was the journey?

**c** Mark knows that his house is 8 kilometres from town. He has £10.50.

Has he got enough for a taxi ride home?

**AU 12 a** Which of the following expressions are equivalent?

$3m \times 8n$      $2m \times 12n$      $4n \times 6m$      $m \times 24n$

**b** The expressions $\dfrac{x}{2}$ and $x^2$ are the same for only one positive value of $x$.

What is the value?

**13** Expand these expressions.

**a** $5(3 - m)$          **b** $3(2x + 7)$          **c** $x(x + 2)$

**d** $2m(5 - m)$          **e** $5s(s + 3)$          **f** $3n(m - p)$

**14** Factorise the following expressions.

**a** $18 - 3m$          **b** $6x + 12$          **c** $x^2 + 5x$

**d** $10m - m^2$          **e** $15s^2 + 3$          **f** $3n - pn$

**D**

**AU** **15** Find the missing terms to make these equations true.

    **a** $8x + 12y - \boxed{\phantom{0}} - \boxed{\phantom{0}} = 5x + 4y$

    **b** $3a - 5b - \boxed{\phantom{0}} + \boxed{\phantom{0}} = a - b$

**PS** **16** ABCDEF is an L-shape.

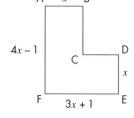

    AB = DE = $x$

    AF = $4x - 1$ and EF = $3x + 1$

    **a** Explain why the length BC = $3x - 1$.

    **b** Find the perimeter of the shape in terms of $x$.

    **c** If $x = 6$ cm what is the perimeter of the shape?

**PS** **17** A square and a rectangle have the same perimeter.

The rectangle has one side that is three times as long as the other.

The square has a side of 8 cm.

What are the dimensions of the rectangle?

**AU** **18** The formula for the area, $A$, of a square with side $x$ is $A = x^2$.

The formula for the area, $T$, of a triangle with base $b$ and height $h$ is $T = \frac{1}{2}bh$

Find **different** values of $x$, $b$ and $h$ so that $A = T$

**AU** **19** Kaz knows that $x$, $y$ and $z$ have the values 3, 6 and 9 but he does not know which variable has which value.

    **a** What is the maximum that the expression $x + 3y - 5z$ could be?

    **b** What is the minimum value that the expression $2x - y + 3z$ could have?

**FM** **20** A car costs £90 per day to rent.

Some friends decide to rent the car for five days.

    **a** Which of the following formulae would represent the cost per person if there are $n$ people in the car and they share the cost equally?

        $\dfrac{450}{5n}$                 $\dfrac{450}{n + 5}$                 $\dfrac{450}{n}$

    **b** Three friends rent the car.

When they get the bill they find that there is a special price for a five-day rental.

They each find it cost them £20 less than they expected.

How much does a five-day rental cost?

**21** Expand each of these expressions.

    **a** $4p^2(3p - q)$          **b** $5t^2(2t^2 + 7)$          **c** $5x(2x + 7y)$

    **d** $2m^2(5 - m^3)$          **e** $8s^3(s + 3t)$          **f** $6nm^2(m - n)$

**FM** **22** The local supermarket is offering £2 off a large box of chocolates. Madge wants four boxes.

    **a** If the normal price of one box is £$t$, write down the expressions below that represent how much it will cost Madge to buy four boxes.

         $4(t - 2)$          $4t - 1$          $4t - 4$          $4t - 8$

    **b** The original price of a box of chocolates was £8.50. How much will Madge actually pay?

**23** Expand and simplify the following expressions.

    **a** $5(4x + 1) + 3(x + 2)$                 **b** $4(y - 2) + 5(y + 3)$

    **c** $2(3x - 2) - 4(x + 1)$              **d** $5(2x + 3) + 6(2x - 1)$

    **e** $6x(2x - 3) + 2x(x + 4)$           **f** $3(4x^2 - 3) + x^2(5 + 2x)$

**24** Factorise the following expressions.

    **a** $9p^2 + 6pt$                      **b** $12mp - 8m^2$

    **c** $16a^2b + 4ab$                  **d** $4a^2 - 6a + 2$

    **e** $20xy^2 + 10x^2y + 5xy$       **f** $8mt^2 - 4m^2t$

**AU** **25** Darren wrote the following: $2(3x - 5) = 5x - 3$

Darren has made two mistakes.

Explain the mistakes that Darren has made.

> **HINTS AND TIPS**
>
> It is not enough to give the right answer. You must try to explain why Darren wrote 5 for $2 \times 3$ instead of 6.

**PS** **26** The expansion $3(x + 4) = 3x + 12$ can be shown by the diagram.

    **a** What expansion is shown in this diagram?

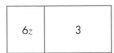

    **b** Write down an expansion that is shown on this diagram.

| 6z | 3 |
|----|---|
|    |   |

**FM 27** In Highville school there are 2000 students. One day a student returns from abroad with an infectious disease. The following day the student is off school. The following day three students are off school with the disease and then each day three times more students than the day before are off. How many days will it be before there are no students left in school?

**FM 28** A three-carriage train has $2f$ first-class seats and $2s$ standard-class seats.

A four-carriage train has $3f$ first-class seats and $3s$ standard-class seats.

On a weekday six three-carriage trains and three four-carriage trains travel from Bristol to Bournemouth.

**a** Write down an expression for the total number of first- and standard-class seats available during the day.

**b** On average in any day one-third of the first-class seats are used at a cost of £45. On average in any day four-fifths of the standard-class seats are used at a cost of £30.

How much money does the rail company earn in an average day on this route?

Give your answer in terms of $f$ and $s$.

**c** $f = 16$ and $s = 50$. It costs the rail company £30 000 per day to operate this route. How much profit or loss do they make on an average day?

**PS 29** A rectangle with sides 6 and $3x + 5$ has a smaller rectangle with sides 2 and $x - 2$ cut from it.

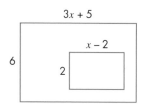

Work out the area remaining.

**FM 30** Five friends have a meal together. They each have a main course costing £7.25 and a desert costing £2.75.

Colin says that the bill will be $5 \times 7.25 + 5 \times 2.75$.

Kim says that she has an easier way to work out the bill as $5 \times (7.25 + 2.75)$.

**a** Explain why Colin and Kim's methods both give the correct answer.

**b** Explain why Kim's method is better.

**c** What is the total bill?

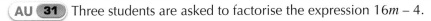
**AU** **31** Three students are asked to factorise the expression $16m - 4$.

These are their answers

| A | B | C |
|---|---|---|
| $2(8m - 2)$ | $4(4m - 1)$ | $8m\left(2 - \dfrac{1}{2m}\right)$ |

All the answers are accurately factorised but only one is the normally accepted answer.

**a** Which student gave the correct answer?

**b** Explain why the other two students' answers are not acceptable as correct answers.

**PS** **32** Explain why $7x - 9y$ cannot be factorised.

---

## 2.2 Substitution using a calculator

**This section will show you how to:**
- substitute numbers for letters in formulae and use a calculator to evaluate the resulting expression

**Key words**
brackets
calculator
formula
substitute

Although you have already **substituted** numbers into **formulae** in the previous exercise, you will meet harder examples where you will need to use a **calculator**.

Sometimes you need to work out the denominator of a fraction. You will need to use **brackets** to do this.

To find $w$ if $w = \dfrac{x}{y + z}$

and $x = 8$, $y = 2.3$ and $z = 4.1$

key into your calculator:

⟨8⟩ ⟨÷⟩ ⟨(⟩ ⟨2⟩ ⟨.⟩ ⟨3⟩ ⟨+⟩ ⟨4⟩ ⟨.⟩ ⟨1⟩ ⟨)⟩ ⟨=⟩

You should get the answer 1.25

Although the expression does not include brackets, you need to use them on your calculator.

Now try to work out the value of

$$\frac{4.7^2 - 5.2}{\sqrt{9.6 + 3.8}}$$

You will need to key into your calculator:

( 4 • 7 $x^2$ − 5 • 2 ) ÷ ( √ ( 9 • 6 + 3 • 8 ) ) =

You should get the answer 4.614 to 3 dp.

## EXERCISE 2B

**1** Where $A = 4t + h$, find $A$ when:

   **a** $t = 2.6$ and $h = 3.9$     **b** $t = 8.4$ and $h = 5.2$

   **c** $t = 0.8$ and $h = 2.2$

**2** Where $P = 5w - 4y$, find $P$ when:

   **a** $w = 3.6$ and $y = 2.7$     **b** $w = 6.2$ and $y = 4.9$

   **c** $w = 2.5$ and $y = 0.7$

**3** Where $A = b^2 + c$, find $A$ when:

   **a** $b = 2.4$ and $c = 3.6$     **b** $b = 1.7$ and $c = 3.8$     **c** $b = 0.5$ and $c = 2.75$

**4** Where $L = f^2 - g^2$, find $L$ when:

   **a** $f = 6.4$ and $g = 3.6$     **b** $f = 3.9$ and $g = 2.1$     **c** $f = 5.5$ and $g = 3.5$

**5** Where $T = P - n^2$, find $T$ when:

   **a** $P = 10$ and $n = 1.6$     **b** $P = 5.9$ and $n = 2.3$     **c** $P = 11.4$ and $n = 3.2$

**6** Where $A = 180(n - 2)$, find $A$ when:

   **a** $n = 5.8$     **b** $n = 3.9$     **c** $n = 6.4$

**7** Where $t = 10 - \sqrt{P}$, find $t$ when:

   **a** $P = 1.96$     **b** $P = 27.04$     **c** $P = 2.56$

**8** Where $W = v + \dfrac{m}{5}$, find $W$ when:

   **a** $v = 3.2$ and $m = 7.4$     **b** $v = 2.9$ and $m = 10.6$     **c** $v = -4.6$ and $m = 7.5$

> **HINTS AND TIPS**
>
> With modern calculators you can type in the calculation as it reads. For example, $(1.7)^2 + 3.8$
>
> 1 • 7 $x^2$ +
>
> 3 • 8 =

**FM 9** The formula for the electricity bill each quarter in a household is £7.50 + £0.07 per unit.

A family uses 6720 units in a quarter.

**a** How much is their total bill?

**b** The family pay a direct debit of £120 per month towards their electricity costs.

By how much will they be in credit or debit after the quarter?

**AU 10** $x$ and $y$ are different positive numbers.

Choose values for $x$ and $y$ so that the formula

$5x + 3y$

**a** evaluates to an odd number

**b** evaluates to a prime number.

> **HINTS AND TIPS**
>
> You will need to remember the prime numbers, 2, 3, 5, 7, 11, 13, 17, 19...

**11** Find the value of the following expressions when $x = 1.4$, $y = 2.5$ and $z = 0.8$.

**a** $\dfrac{3x + 4}{2}$ **b** $\dfrac{x + 2y}{z}$ **c** $\dfrac{y}{z} + x$

**FM 12** The formula for the gas bill each quarter in a household is £17.50 + £0.12 per unit.

A family uses 6250 units in a quarter.

**a** How much is their total bill?

**b** The family pay a direct debit of £220 per month towards their gas costs.

By how much will they be in credit or debit after the quarter?

**AU 13** $x$ and $y$ are different prime numbers.

Choose values for $x$ and $y$ so that the formula

$5x + 2y$

**a** evaluates to an even number **b** evaluates to an odd number.

**PS 14** Marvin hires a car for the day for £40.

He wants to know how much it costs him for each mile he drives.

Petrol is 98p per litre and the car does 10 miles per litre.

Marvin works out the following formula for the cost per mile, $C$, in pounds for $M$ miles driven.

$$C = 0.098 + \frac{40}{M}$$

**a** Explain each term of the formula.

**b** How much will it cost per mile if Marvin drives 200 miles that day?

# Solving linear equations

**This section will show you how to:**

● solve linear equations by rearrangement

**Key words**

do the same to both sides

inverse operations

rearrangement

solution

variable

Work through these examples to remind yourself how to solve equations.

---

**EXAMPLE 9**

Solve these equations.

**a** $x + 7 = 10$     **b** $5y = 30$     **c** $\dfrac{z}{3} = 5$

**a** Subtract 7 from both sides

$x + 7 - 7 = 10 - 7$

$x = 3$

**b** Divide both sides by 5

$\dfrac{5y}{5} = \dfrac{30}{5}$

$y = 6$

**c** Multiply both sides by 3

$3 \times \dfrac{z}{3} = 3 \times 5$

$z = 15$

**Note:** Remember to check your answers in the original equations

**a** $3 + 7 = 10$ ✓     **b** $5 \times 6 = 30$ ✓     **c** $15 \div 3 = 5$ ✓

---

**EXAMPLE 10**

Solve the following equations.

**a** $4x - 5 = 7$  **b** $\dfrac{y}{5} + 7 = 4$  **c** $\dfrac{z + 4}{3} = 5$

**a** Add 5 to both sides  $4x = 12$

Divide both sides by 4  $x = 3$

Check:  $4 \times 3 - 5 = 12 - 5 = 7$ ✔

**b** Subtract 7 from both sides  $\dfrac{y}{5} = -3$

Multiply both sides by 5  $y = -15$

Check:  $-15 \div 5 + 7 = -3 + 7 = 4$ ✔

**c** Multiply both sides by 3  $z + 4 = 15$

Subtract 4 from both sides  $z = 11$

Check:  $(11 + 4) \div 3 = 15 \div 3 = 5$ ✔

**EXAMPLE 11**

Solve the following equations.

**a** $2(x + 7) = 15$  **b** $4(y - 9) = 12$

**a** Expand the bracket  $2x + 14 = 15$

Subtract 14  $2x = 1$

Divide by 2  $x = \dfrac{1}{2}$

Check:  $2 \times \left( \dfrac{1}{2} + 7 \right) = 2 \times 7\dfrac{1}{2} = 15$ ✔

**b** Expand the bracket  $4y - 36 = 12$

Add 36  $4y = 48$

Divide by 4  $y = 12$

Check:  $4 \times (12 - 9) = 4 \times 3 = 12$ ✔

## EXAMPLE 12

Solve the following equations.

**a** $5x + 2 = 3x + 11$ **b** $6(x - 1) = 2x + 14$

**a** Rearrange the equations to get $x$ terms on one side and
number terms on the other $\qquad 5x - 3x = 11 - 2$

Collect terms $\qquad\qquad 2x = 9$

Divide by 2 $\qquad\qquad x = 4\dfrac{1}{2}$

Check: left-hand side $\qquad 5 \times 4\dfrac{1}{2} + 2 = 24\dfrac{1}{2}$

right-hand side $\qquad 3 \times 4\dfrac{1}{2} + 11 = 24\dfrac{1}{2} = $ left-hand side ✓

**b** Expand the brackets $\qquad 6x - 6 = 2x + 14$

Rearrange $\qquad\qquad 6x - 2x = 14 + 6$

Collect terms $\qquad\qquad 4x = 20$

Divide by 4 $\qquad\qquad x = 5$

Check: $\qquad 6(5 - 1) = 24, 2 \times 5 + 14 = 10 + 14 = 24$ ✓

## EXERCISE 2C

Solve the following equations.

**1 a** $x + 5 = 10$ **b** $y - 8 = 9$ **c** $4z = 30$ **d** $\dfrac{w}{5} = 10$

**2 a** $4x + 5 = 15$ **b** $3x - 7 = 23$ **c** $2x + 9 = 5$ **d** $6x - 5 = 10$

**e** $\dfrac{x}{4} + 7 = 12$ **f** $\dfrac{x}{3} - 9 = 11$

**3 a** $\dfrac{x + 2}{5} = 3$ **b** $\dfrac{x - 7}{6} = 2$ **c** $\dfrac{x + 3}{2} = 1$ **d** $\dfrac{x - 1}{8} = 5$

**4 a** $3(x + 7) = 12$ **b** $4(x - 1) = 6$

**c** $5(3x + 9) = 45$ **d** $3(2x - 7) = 12$

**5 a** $7x + 9 = 2x + 19$ **b** $4x - 8 = 3x + 7$

**c** $3x + 5 = 5x - 9$ **d** $3x - 1 = 6 - 4x$

**6 a** $3(x + 9) = x + 3$ **b** $4(2x - 1) = 3(x + 7)$

**c** $2(x + 8) + 3(x - 2) = x + 6$ **d** $5(x - 1) - 2(x - 7) = 4(x + 2)$

# Setting up equations

**This section will show you how to:**
- set up equations from given information and then use the methods already seen to solve them

**Key words**
equation
variable

**Equations** are used to represent situations, so that you can solve real-life problems.

---

**EXAMPLE 13**

A milkman sets off from the dairy with eight crates of milk each containing $b$ bottles. He delivers 92 bottles to a large factory and finds that he has exactly 100 bottles left on his milk float. How many bottles were in each crate?

The equation is:

$8b - 92 = 100$

$\quad 8b = 192$      (Add 92 to both sides.)

$\quad\quad b = 24$      (Divide both sides by 8.)

---

**EXAMPLE 14**

The rectangle shown has a perimeter of 40 cm.

Find the value of $x$.

The perimeter of the rectangle is:

$3x + 1 + x + 3 + 3x + 1 + x + 3 = 40$

This simplifies to $8x + 8 = 40$.

Subtract 8.          $8x = 32$

Divide by 8.         $x = 4$

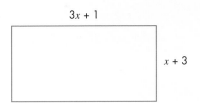

$3x + 1$

$x + 3$

**EXERCISE 2D**

Set up an equation to represent each situation described below. Then solve the equation. Remember to check each answer.

**PS** **1** A teacher asks her class to think of a number and add 3 to it.

I thought of 6 to start.

My final answer was 11.

   **a** What was Adrianne's final answer?

   **b** What was Benjy's original number?

**FM** **2** Four friends shared the cost, £M, of a meal.

Ken collected each person's share and took the money to the till.

At the till he produced a coupon for £5 without telling his friends.

Ken only paid £7 from his own pocket.

   **a** Which of the following equations represents this situation?

   $4M - 5 = 7$ $\qquad\qquad \dfrac{(M - 5)}{4} = 7$ $\qquad\qquad \dfrac{M}{4} - 5 = 7$

   **b** What was the cost, £M, of the meal?

**FM** **3** A carpet costs £12.75 a square metre. The shop charges £35 for fitting. The final bill was £137.

How many square metres of carpet were fitted?

**FM** **4** Moshin bought 8 garden chairs. When he got to the till he used a £10 voucher as part payment. His final bill was £56.

   **a** Set this problem up as an equation using $c$ as the cost in pounds of one chair.

   **b** Solve the equation to work out the cost of one chair.

**FM** **5** This diagram shows the traffic flow through a one-way system in a town centre.

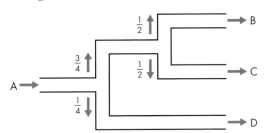

Cars enter at A and at each junction the fractions show the proportion of cars that take each route.

**a** 1200 cars enter at A. How many come out of each of the exits, B, C and D?

**b** If 300 cars exit at B, how many cars entered at A?

**c** If 500 cars exit at D, how many exit at B?

**FM** **6** A rectangular room is 3 m longer than it is wide.
The perimeter is 16 m.

Carpet costs £9.00 per square metre.

How much will it cost to carpet the room?

> **HINTS AND TIPS**
>
> Set up an equation to work out the length and width, then calculate the area.

**FM** **7** A man buys a daily paper from Monday to Saturday for $d$ pence. On Sunday he buys a Sunday paper for £1.80.
His weekly paper bill is £7.20.
What is the price of his daily paper?

**8** The diagram shows a rectangle.

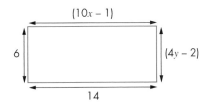

> **HINTS AND TIPS**
>
> Use the letter $x$ for the variable unless you are given a letter to use. Once the equation is set up solve it by the methods above.

**a** What is the value of $x$?

**b** What is the value of $y$?

**PS** **9** In this rectangle, the length is 3 cm more than the width.
The perimeter is 12 cm.

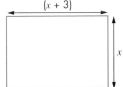

**a** What is the value of $x$?

**b** What is the area of the rectangle?

**10** Mary has two bags, each of which contains the same number of sweets. She eats four sweets. She then finds that she has 30 sweets left. How many sweets were there in each bag to start with?

**PS** **11** A boy is $Y$ years old. His father is 25 years older than he is. The sum of their ages is 31. How old is the boy?

**PS** **12** Another boy is $X$ years old. His sister is twice as old as he is. The sum of their ages is 27. How old is the boy?

**13** The diagram shows a square.
Find $x$ if the perimeter is 44 cm.

$(4x - 1)$

**PS** **14** Max thought of a number. He then multiplied his number by 3. He added 4 to the answer. He then doubled that answer to get a final value of 38. What number did he start with?

**15** The angles of a triangle are $2x$, $x + 5°$ and $x + 35°$.

**a** Write down an equation to show this.

**b** Solve your equation to find the value of $x$.

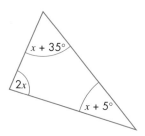

$x + 35°$

$2x$

$x + 5°$

**AU** **16** The diagram shows two number machines that perform the same operations.

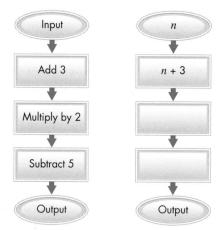

**a** Starting with an input value of 7 work through the left-hand machine to get the output.

**b** Find an input value that gives the same value for the output.

**c** Fill in the algebraic expressions in the right-hand machine for an input of $n$. (The first operation has been filled in for you.)

**d** Set up an equation for the same input and output and show each step in solving the equation to get the answer in part **b**.

**PS 17** A teacher asked her class to find three angles of a triangle that were consecutive even numbers.

Tammy wrote:

$$x + x + 2 + x + 4 = 180$$
$$3x + 6 = 180$$
$$3x = 174$$
$$x = 58$$

So the angles are 58°, 60° and 62°.

The teacher then asked the class to find four angles of a quadrilateral that are consecutive even numbers.

Can this be done? Explain your answer.

**FM 18** Mary has a large and a small bottle of pop. The large bottle holds 50 cl more than the small bottle.

From the large bottle she fills 4 cups and has 18 cl left over.

From the small bottle she fills 3 cups and has 1 cl left over.

How much pop does each bottle hold?

> **HINTS AND TIPS**
>
> Do the same type of working as Tammy for a triangle. Work out the value of $x$. What happens?

> **HINTS AND TIPS**
>
> Set up equations for both using $x$ as the amount of pop in a cup. Put them equal but remember to add 50 to the small bottle equation to allow for the difference. Solve for $x$, then work out how much is in each bottle.

## 2.5 Trial and improvement

**This section will show you how to:**

- use the method of trial and improvement to estimate the answer to equations that do not have exact solutions

**Key words**
comment
decimal place
guess
trial and
  improvement

Certain equations cannot be solved exactly. However, a close enough solution to such an equation can be found by the **trial and improvement** method. (Sometimes wrongly called the trial and error method.)

The idea is to keep trying different values in the equation to take it closer and closer to the 'true' solution. This step-by-step process is continued until a value is found that gives a solution that is close enough to the accuracy required.

The trial and improvement method is the way in which computers are programmed to solve equations.

**EXAMPLE 15**

Solve the equation $x^3 + x = 105$, giving the solution correct to one **decimal place**.

**Step 1** You must find the two consecutive whole numbers between which $x$ lies. You do this by intelligent guessing.

Try $x = 5$: $125 + 5 = 130$        Too high – next trial needs to be much smaller.

Try $x = 4$: $64 + 4 = 68$        Too low.

So you now know that the solution lies between $x = 4$ and $x = 5$.

**Step 2** You must find the two consecutive one-decimal-place numbers between which $x$ lies. Try 4.5, which is halfway between 4 and 5.

This gives $91.125 + 4.5 = 95.625$        Too small.

Now attempt to improve this by trying 4.6.

This gives $97.336 + 4.6 = 101.936$        Still too small.

Try 4.7 which gives 108.523.        This is too high, so the solution is between 4.6 and 4.7.

It looks as though 4.7 is closer but there is a very important final step.

**Step 3** Now try the value that is halfway between the two one-decimal-place values. In this case 4.65.

This gives 105.194 625.

This means that 4.6 is nearer the actual solution than 4.7 is, so never assume that the one-decimal-place number that gives the closest value to the solution is the answer.

The diagram on the right shows why this is.

The approximate answer is $x = 4.6$ to 1 decimal place.

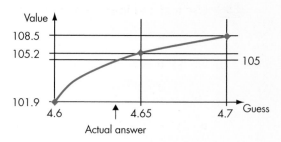

The best way to answer this type of question is to set up a table to show working. There will be three columns: **guess** (the trial); the equation to be solved; and a **comment** whether the value of the equation is too high or too low.

| Guess | $x^3 + x$ | Comment |
|---|---|---|
| 4 | 68 | Too low |
| 5 | 130 | Too high |
| 4.5 | 95.625 | Too low |
| 4.6 | 101.936 | Too low |
| 4.7 | 108.523 | Too high |
| 4.65 | 105.194625 | Too high |

## EXERCISE 2E

**1** Find the two consecutive *whole numbers* between which the solution to each of the following equations lies.

**a** $x^2 + x = 24$      **b** $x^3 + 2x = 80$      **c** $x^3 - x = 20$

**2** Copy and complete the table by using trial and improvement to find an approximate solution to:

$$x^3 + 2x = 50$$

Give your answer correct to 1 decimal place.

| Guess | $x^3 + 2x$ | Comment |
|-------|-----------|---------|
| 3 | 33 | Too low |
| 4 | 72 | Too high |

**3** Copy and complete the table by using trial and improvement to find an approximate solution to:

$$x^3 - 3x = 40$$

Give your answer correct to 1 decimal place.

| Guess | $x^3 - 3x$ | Comment |
|-------|-----------|---------|
| 4 | 52 | Too high |

**4** Use trial and improvement to find an approximate solution to:

$$2x^3 + x = 35$$

Give your answer correct to 1 decimal place.

You are given that the solution lies between 2 and 3.

**HINTS AND TIPS**

Set up a table to show your working. This makes it easier for you to show method and the examiner to mark.

**5** Use trial and improvement to find an exact solution to:

$$4x^2 + 2x = 12$$

Do not use a calculator.

**6** Find a solution to each of the following equations, correct to 1 decimal place.

**a** $2x^3 + 3x = 35$      **b** $3x^3 - 4x = 52$      **c** $2x^3 + 5x = 79$

**PS 7** A rectangle has an area of 100 cm². Its length is 5 cm longer than its width.

**a** Show that, if $x$ is the width, then $x^2 + 5x = 100$.

**b** Find, correct to 1 decimal place, the dimensions of the rectangle.

**8** Use trial and improvement to find a solution to the equation $x^2 + x = 40$.

**PS 9** A cuboidal juice carton holds $\frac{1}{2}$ litre (500 cm³).

The sides of the base are in the ratio 1 : 2.

The height is 8 cm more than the shorter side of the base.

Use trial and improvement to find the dimensions of the carton.

**HINTS AND TIPS**

Call the length of the side with 'ratio 1' $x$, write down the other two sides in terms of $x$ and then write down an equation for the volume = 500.

**C**

**AU** **10** A cube of side $x$ cm has a square hole of side $\dfrac{x}{2}$ and depth 8 cm cut from it.

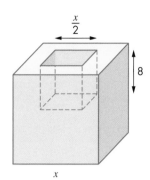

**HINTS AND TIPS**

Work out the volume of the cube and the hole and subtract them. The resulting expression is the volume of 1500.

The volume of the remaining solid is 1500 cm$^3$.

**a** Explain why $x^3 - 2x^2 = 1500$.

**b** Use trial and improvement to find the value of $x$ to 1 decimal place.

**PS** **11** Two numbers $a$ and $b$ are such that $ab = 20$ and $a + b = 10$.

Use trial and improvement to find the two numbers to two decimal places.

**HINTS AND TIPS**

Set up a table with three columns and headings $a$, $b = 10 - a$, $ab$.

## GRADE BOOSTER

**F** You can solve equations such as $5x = 15$ and $x + 9 = 12$

**E** You can solve equations such as $4x + 7 = 3$ or $\dfrac{x}{2} - 5 = 6$

**D** You can solve equations such as $\dfrac{x-2}{3} = 8$ or $3x - 8 = x + 7$

**D** You can set up equations from given information

**C** You can solve equations such as $4(x - 5) = 2x + 3$

**C** You can solve equations by trial and improvement

### What you should know now

- How to set up equations
- How to simplify and factorise expressions, and substitute numbers into expressions
- How to solve a variety of linear equations using rearrangement or 'doing the same thing to both sides'
- How to solve equations by trial and improvement

**1** Are the following statements true (T) or false (F)?

  **a**   $c$ multiplied by 3 is written as $3c$      (1)

  **b**   $d$ divided by 2 is written as $\dfrac{d}{2}$      (1)

  **c**   $a$ subtracted from $b$ is written as $a - b$      (1)

                             (Total 3 marks)

*AQA, June 2008, Paper 1 Foundation, Question 6*

**2**  **a**   Suki is playing a 'Think of a Number' game.

     What number does Suki think of?      (2)

  **b**   Tim is also playing a 'Think of a Number' game.

     Write down an expression in terms of $x$ for Tim's answer.      (2)

                             (Total 4 marks)

*AQA, June 2006, Paper 1 Intermediate, Question 5*

**3** Alan has some unknown weights labelled $a$ and $b$ and some 5 kg and 10 kg weights.

He finds that the following combinations of weights balance.

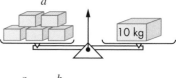

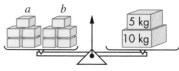

  **a**  **i**   Find the value of $a$.      (1)

      **ii**   Find the value of $b$.      (2)

  **b**   Alan also has some unknown weights. labelled $c$.

     He finds that      $5c + 2b = c + 6a$

     Find the value of $c$.      (4)

                             (Total 7 marks)

*AQA, November 2007, Paper 1 Intermediate, Question 10*

**4**  **a**   Simplify      $4c - c + 2c$      (1)

  **b**   Solve the equations

    **i**    $2x = 24$      (1)

    **ii**   $y - 9 = 11$      (1)

    **iii**   $\dfrac{z}{4} = 8$      (1)

    **iv**   $4w + 3 = 13$      (2)

                             (Total 6 marks)

*AQA, June 2006, Paper 1 Foundation, Question 17*

**5**  **a**   Simplify      $2x + 8 + 4x - 3$      (2)

  **b**   Solve the equation      $\dfrac{x}{3} = 5$      (1)

  **c**   Tom is investigating the two expressions

     $ab + c$ and $a(b + c)$

    **i**   He finds that both expressions have the same value when $a = 1$, $b = 3$ and $c = 4$

        Show that this is true.      (3)

    **ii**   Tom says that this means that

        $a(b + c) = ab + c$

        Explain why Tom is wrong.      (2)

                             (Total 8 marks)

*AQA, June 2006, Paper 1 Intermediate, Question 12*

**6** Ali is $x$ cm tall.

**a** Suki is 5 cm taller than Ali.

Write down an expression in $x$ for Suki's height. (1)

**b** Ali's sister is 2 cm shorter than Ali.

Write down an expression in $x$ for the height of Ali's sister. (1)

**c** Ali's father is twice as tall as Ali.

Write down an expression in $x$ for the height of Ali's father. (1)

**d** Darius has a height, in cm, given by the expression $2x - 65$

He is 115 cm tall.

Solve the equation

$2x - 65 = 115$

to find Darius's height. (2)

(Total 5 marks)

*AQA, June 2005, Paper 2 Foundation, Question 19*

**7** All areas in this question are in square centimetres.

Here is a rectangle of area $R$, a square of area $S$ and a trapezium of area $T$.

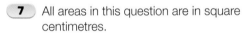

**a** The area of the shape below is given by $A = R + 2T$

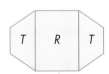

Find the value of $A$ when $R = 7.5$ and $T = 6.3$ (2)

**b** Here is a different shape.

**i** Write down an expression for the area of this shape. (1)

**ii** Which of the following is correct?

$3R = S$   $2R = S$   $R = 2S$   $R = 3S$ (1)

(Total 4 marks)

*AQA, November 2007, Paper 1 Intermediate, Question 5*

**8** Use the formula

$v = u + at$

to find the value of $v$ when $u = -10$, $a = 1.8$ and $t = 3.7$ (2)

(Total 2 marks)

*AQA, June 2005, Paper 2 Foundation, Question 24*

**9** Dean picks three numbers.

His first number is $y$.

His second number is five more than his first number.

**a** Write down his second number in terms of $y$. (1)

**b** His third number is double his first number.

Write down his third number in terms of $y$. (1)

**c** Write down an expression for the sum of the three numbers. (1)

**d** The sum of the three numbers is 77.

Form an equation and solve it to find the value of $y$. (3)

(Total 6 marks)

*AQA, June 2007, Paper 2 Intermediate, Question 6*

**10** Complete the following table. (3)

| $x = 8$ | $3x = 24$ |
|---------|-----------|
| $y = \ldots\ldots$ | $4y = 20$ |
| $3z = 12$ | $5z = \ldots\ldots$ |

(Total 3 marks)

*AQA, June 2007, Paper 1 Foundation, Question 19*

**11** Two car hire firms use different ways of charging for the hire of a car.

**a** Cheap Days uses this formula

$H = 50d + 120$

$H$ is the hire charge in pounds.

$d$ is the number of days the car is hired.

Work out $H$ when $d = 2$ (2)

**b** Cheap Miles uses this formula.

$$H = \frac{m + 750}{5}$$

$H$ is the hire charge in pounds.

$m$ is the number of miles the car travels.

Work out $m$ when $H = 200$ (2)

(Total 4 marks)

*AQA, June 2007, Paper 1 Intermediate, Question 10*

**12** Each expression in this wall is formed by adding the two supporting expressions from the row below.

For example

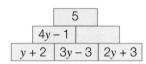

$x + 3 + 2x + 5 = 3x + 8$

Use the wall below to find the value of $y$. (3)

| 5 |
|---|
| $4y - 1$ |
| $y + 2$ | $3y - 3$ | $2y + 3$ |

(Total 3 marks)

*AQA, June 2008, Paper 2 Foundation, Question 24*

**13** Kerry is using trial and improvement to find a solution to the equation

$$8x - x^3 = 5$$

Her first two trials are shown in the table.

| $x$ | $8x - x^3$ | Comment |
|---|---|---|
| 2 | 8 | too high |
| 3 | −3 | too low |
|   |   |   |
|   |   |   |
|   |   |   |
|   |   |   |
|   |   |   |

Continue the table to find a solution to the equation.

Give your answer to one decimal place. (3)

(Total 3 marks)

*AQA, June 2007, Paper 2 Intermediate, Question11*

**14**  Use trial and improvement to find a solution to the equation

$$x^3 + 2x = 60$$

Give your answer to 1 decimal place.

You must show your working. (4)

(Total 4 marks)

*AQA, November 2007, Paper 2 Intermediate, Question 15*

# Worked Examination Questions

**PS 1** The angles of a quadrilateral are 73°, $2x°$, $3x°$ and 102°.

Find the value of the largest angle in the quadrilateral.

> The key word here is quadrilateral. You should know that the angles in a quadrilateral add up to 360°.

$3x + 2x + 102 + 73 = 360$

> Showing that you know that the sum of the angles equals 360 would get 1 method mark.

$5x + 175 = 360$

Largest angle = 111°

> Collecting terms together correctly would get 1 accuracy mark.

**Total: 3 marks**

> Solving the equation gives:
> subtracting 175 $\quad 5x = 360 - 175 = 185$
> dividing by 5 $\quad x = 37$
> Do not stop at this point as the question asks for the largest angle.
> This is the angle $3x°$, which is $3 \times 37 = 111°$.
> This gets 1 accuracy mark.

**2** Mark is $x$ years old.

Nell is eight years older than Mark.

Oliver is twice as old as Nell.

Given that their total age is 44, find Mark's age.

Nell: $x + 8$

Oliver: $2(x + 8)$

> Write down their ages in terms of Mark's age $x$.
> '8 years older' means an addition, so Nell's age is $x + 8$.
> 'Twice as' means multiply. Use brackets around Nell's age, as $2x + 8$ is wrong.
> This gets 1 method mark.

$x + x + 8 + 2(x + 8)$
$\quad = 2x + 8 + 2x + 16$
$\quad = 4x + 24$

> Write down the total of all the ages.
> Expand the brackets and collect terms.
> This gets 1 accuracy mark.

$4x + 24 = 44$

$4x = 20$

$x = 5$

Mark is five years old.

> Set up the equation and expand the brackets.
> Subtract 24, then divide by 4.
> Setting up the equation gets 1 method mark and solving it correctly gets 1 accuracy mark.

**Total: 4 marks**

**AU 3** The solution of the equation $3x + 7 = 4$ is $x = -1$.

Write down a **different** equation of the form $ax + b = 4$ for which the solution is also $x = -1$.

$4 \times -1 = -4$

> Start with a value for $a$, say 4, and work out $4 \times -1$.

$-4 + 6 = 2$

> Add a value, say 6.

So $4x + 6 = 2$ has a solution of $x = -1$

(There are many other possible answers.)

> Write down the equation.
> This gets 2 marks for independent working.

**Total: 2 marks**

In Chapter 10 of Book 1 you may have done a Functional Maths task called 'Walking using Naismith's rule'. As you are reviewing your basic algebra skills, now is a good time to revisit this task.

In 'Revisiting Naismith's rule' you will complete questions similar to those in Book 1. You will also investigate Naismith's rule in a new way, developing and extending your algebra skills in a familiar context.

## Naismith's rule

Naismith's rule is a rule of thumb that you can use when planning a walk to help you calculate how long it will take. The rule was devised by William Naismith, a Scottish mountaineer, in 1892.

The basic rule is:

Allow 1 hour for every 3 miles (5 km) forward, plus $\frac{1}{2}$ hour for every 1000 feet (300 m) ascent (height).

## Getting started

Use algebra to write Naismith's rule.
Now, use this rule to copy and complete the table below.

The table that you have completed shows the actual times taken by a school group as they did five different walks in five days. Use this information to work out the following.

- If the group had started at the same times and had the same breaks how long would the group have taken each day, according to Naismith's rule?

- Do you think Naismith's rule is still valid today? Explain your reasons.

| Day | Distance (km) | Time (minutes) | Time (hours/ minutes) | Height (m) | Start | Breaks |
|-----|------|------|------|------|------|------|
| 1 | 16 | | | 250 | 10.00 | 2 h |
| 2 | 18 | | | 0 | 10.00 | 1 h 30 m |
| 3 | 11 | | | 340 | 09.30 | 2 h 30 m |
| 4 | 13 | | | 100 | 10.30 | 2 h 30 m |
| 5 | 14 | | | 120 | 10.30 | 2 h 30 m |

## Your task

Use the internet to research the walking times of some of Britain's most famous walks. Produce a report that compares and contrasts Britain's most famous walks, such as Ben Nevis, Snowdon, Helvellyn and the Pennine Way. Your report should contain realistic guidance on how best to approach these walks, including:

- suggested day-by-day plans supported by mathematical evidence
- starting times
- places to rest
- how the walks will vary for walkers of different fitness levels
- how weather conditions could affect the walk and precautions that should be taken.

Using this information, evaluate how similar the walks are, and which walk would be the toughest for an average walker to complete.

# The usefulness of units

Simon Stevin was a Dutch mathematician. He was born in Bruges (now in Belgium) in 1584. He added greatly to the study of several areas of mathematics, including trigonometry and mechanics, the study of motion. He was also influential in the fields of geography, navigation, architecture and musical theory.

Simon Stevin has several other claims to fame.

- He invented a carriage with sails, a little model of which was preserved at Scheveningen until 1802. The carriage itself had been lost long before, but we know that in about 1600 Stevin, with Prince Maurice of Orange and 26 others, used it on the seashore between Scheveningen and Petten. It moved only by the force of the wind and, at its top speed, it was just a bit quicker than horses.

- He had the idea of explaining the tides by the attraction of the moon.

His greatest success, however, was a small pamphlet, first published in Dutch in 1585, in which he put forward the use of a decimal system for measurement throughout. He declared that the universal introduction of decimal coinage, measures and weights was only a question of time.

In the UK, we used imperial units such as, feet, inches, ounces and pounds for many years. Your grandparents will remember them well.

In the later part of the 20th century, the British Government started trying to ensure that we all use metric units here, as much as possible. This is now common practice, apart for the use of the mile.

The metric system is now predominantly used in the UK and most of the world, apart from the USA.

Road signs in the UK give distances in miles, but in Europe distances are given in kilometres.

## A brief history of the metric system

| 1585 | Simon Stevin suggested a decimal system for weights and measures. |
|------|------------------------------------------------------------------|
| 1790 | Thomas Jefferson proposed a decimal-based measurement system for the USA. A vote in the USA congress to replace the UK imperial system by a metric system was lost by just one vote. |
| 1795 | The metric system became the official system of measurement in France. |
| 1959 | The UK and USA redefined the inch to be 2.54 cm. |
| 1963 | The UK redefined the pound to be 0.453 592 37 kilograms. |
| 1985 | The UK redefined the gallon to be 4.546 09 litres. |
| Now  | The metric system has been adopted by virtually every country, with the only notable exception being the USA. |

It is vital that you understand and can use the metric system, but you should also have some understanding of the older imperial units. This will help you to understand what your grandparents sometimes say and the signs that are still in imperial units in the UK today.

# Measures: Units

1. Systems of measurement

2. Metric units

3. Imperial units

4. Conversion factors

**This chapter will show you ...**

**G** which units to use when measuring length, weight and capacity

**F** how to convert from one metric unit to another

**F** how to convert from imperial units to metric units

**E** how to convert from one imperial unit to another

**Visual overview**

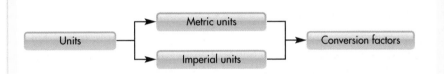

**What you should already know**

- The basic units used for measuring length, weight and capacity (KS3 level 4, GCSE grade F)

- The approximate size of these units (KS3 level 4, GCSE grade F)

- How to multiply or divide numbers by 10, 100 or 1000 (KS3 level 4, GCSE grade F)

**Quick check**

1 How many centimetres are there in one metre?

2 How many metres are there in one kilometre?

3 How many grams are there in one kilogram?

4 How many kilograms are there in one tonne?

This section will show you how to:
● decide which units to use when measuring length, weight and capacity

Key words
capacity
imperial
length
metric
volume
weight

There are two systems of measurement currently in use in Britain: the **imperial** system and the **metric** system.

The imperial system is based on traditional units of measurement, many of which were first introduced several hundred years ago. It is gradually being replaced by the metric system, which is used throughout Europe and in many other parts of the world.

The main disadvantage of the imperial system is that it has a lot of awkward conversions, such as 12 inches = 1 foot. The metric system has the advantage that it is based on powers of 10, namely 10, 100, 1000 and so on, so it is much easier to use when you do calculations.

It will be many years before all the units of the imperial system disappear, so you have to know units in both systems.

| System | Unit | How to estimate it |
|---|---|---|
| | **Length** | |
| Metric system | 1 metre | A long stride for an average person |
| | 1 kilometre | Two and a half times round a school running track |
| | 1 centimetre | The distance across a fingernail |
| Imperial system | 1 foot | The length of an A4 sheet of paper |
| | 1 yard | From your nose to your fingertips when you stretch out your arm |
| | 1 inch | The length of the top joint of an adult's thumb |
| | **Weight** | |
| Metric system | 1 gram | A 1p coin weighs about 4 grams |
| | 1 kilogram | A bag of sugar |
| | 1 tonne | A saloon car |
| Imperial system | 1 pound | A jar full of jam |
| | 1 stone | A bucket three-quarters full of water |
| | 1 ton | A saloon car |
| | **Volume/Capacity** | |
| Metric system | 1 litre | A full carton of orange juice |
| | 1 centilitre | A small wine glass is about 10 centilitres |
| | 1 millilitre | A full teaspoon is about 5 millilitres |
| Imperial system | 1 pint | A full bottle of milk |
| | 1 gallon | A half-full bucket of water |

# Volume and capacity

The term 'capacity' is normally used to refer to the volume of a liquid or a gas.

For example, when referring to the volume of petrol that a car's fuel tank will hold, people may say its capacity is 60 litres or 13 gallons.

In the metric system, there is an equivalence between the units of capacity and volume, as you can see on page 58.

---

**EXAMPLE 1**

Choose an appropriate metric unit for each of the following.

a your own height
b the thickness of this book
c the distance from home to school

d your own weight
e the weight of a coin
f the weight of a bus

g a large bottle of lemonade
h a dose of medicine
i a bottle of wine

a metres or centimetres
b millimetres
c kilometres

d kilograms
e grams
f tonnes

g litres
h millilitres
i centilitres

---

## EXERCISE 3A

**1** Decide the metric unit you would be most likely to use to measure each of the following.

a The height of your classroom
b The distance from London to Barnsley

c The thickness of your little finger
d The weight of this book

e The amount of water in a fish tank
f The weight of water in a fish tank

g The weight of an aircraft
h A spoonful of medicine

i The amount of wine in a standard bottle
j The length of a football pitch

k The weight of your head teacher
l The amount of water in a bath

m The weight of a mouse
n The amount of tea in a teapot

o The thickness of a piece of wire

**F**

**2** Estimate the approximate metric length, weight or capacity of each of the following.

a This book (both length and weight)

b The length of your school hall

c The capacity of a milk bottle

d A brick (length, width and weight)

e The diameter of a 10p coin, and its weight

f The distance from your school to Manchester

g The weight of a cat

h The amount of water in one raindrop

i The dimensions of the room you are in

j Your own height and weight

**FM 3** Bob was asked to put up some decorative bunting from the top of each lamp post in his street. He had three sets of ladders he could use, a two metre, a 3.5 metre and a five metre ladder.

He looked at the lamp posts and estimated that they were about three times his height. He is slightly below average height for an adult male.

Which of the ladders should he use? Give a reason for your choice.

**AU 4** The distance from Bournemouth to Basingstoke is shown on a website as 55 miles.

Explain why this unit is used instead of inches, feet or yards.

## 3.2 Metric units

**This section will show you how to:**
- convert from one metric unit to another

**Key words**

centilitre (cl)
centimetre (cm)
gram (g)
kilogram (kg)
kilometre (km)
litre (l)
metre (m)
millilitre (ml)
millimetre (mm)
tonne (t)

You should already know the relationships between these metric units.

| Length | Weight |
|---|---|
| 10 **millimetres** = 1 **centimetre** | 1000 **grams** = 1 **kilogram** |
| 1000 millimetres = 100 centimetres = 1 **metre** | 1000 kilograms = 1 **tonne** |
| 1000 metres = 1 **kilometre** | |

| Capacity | Volume |
|---|---|
| 10 **millilitres** = 1 **centilitre** | 1000 litres = 1 metre$^3$ |
| 1000 millilitres = 100 centilitres = 1 **litre** | 1 millilitre = 1 centimetre$^3$ |

Note the equivalence between the units of capacity and volume:

1 litre = 1000 cm$^3$   which means   1 ml = 1 cm$^3$

You need to be able to convert from one metric unit to another.

Since the metric system is based on powers of 10, you should be able easily to multiply or divide to change units. Work through the following examples.

---

**EXAMPLE 2**

To change *small* units to *larger* units, always *divide*.

Change:

**a** 732 cm to metres

732 ÷ 100 = 7.32 m

**b** 410 mm to centimetres

410 ÷ 10 = 41 cm

**c** 840 mm to metres

840 ÷ 1000 = 0.84 m

**d** 450 cl to litres

450 ÷ 100 = 4.5 l

---

**EXAMPLE 3**

To change *large* units to *smaller* units, always *multiply*.

Change:

**a** 1.2 m to centimetres

1.2 × 100 = 120 cm

**b** 0.62 cm to millimetres

0.62 × 10 = 6.2 mm

**c** 3 m to millimetres

3 × 1000 = 3000 mm

**d** 75 cl to millilitres

75 × 10 = 750 ml

## EXERCISE 3B

**1** Fill in the gaps, using the information in this section.

**a** 125 cm = ... m      **b** 82 mm = ... cm      **c** 550 mm = ... m

**d** 2100 m = ... km      **e** 208 cm = ... m      **f** 1240 mm = ... m

**g** 4200 g = ... kg      **h** 5750 kg = ... t      **i** 85 ml = ... cl

**j** 2580 ml = ... l      **k** 340 cl = ... l      **l** 600 kg = ... t

**m** 755 g = ... kg      **n** 800 ml = ... l      **o** 200 cl = ... l

**p** 630 ml = ... cl      **q** 8400 l = ... $m^3$      **r** 35 ml = ... $cm^3$

**s** 1035 l = ... $m^3$      **t** 530 l = ... $m^3$      **u** 34 km = ... m

**2** Fill in the gaps, using the information in this section.

**a** 3.4 m = ... mm      **b** 13.5 cm = ... mm      **c** 0.67 m = ... cm

**d** 7.03 km = ... m      **e** 0.72 cm = ... mm      **f** 0.25 m = ... cm

**g** 0.64 km = ... m      **h** 2.4 l = ... ml      **i** 5.9 l = ... cl

**j** 8.4 cl = ... ml      **k** 5.2 $m^3$ = ... l      **l** 0.58 kg = ... g

**m** 3.75 t = ... kg      **n** 0.94 $cm^3$ = ... l      **o** 21.6 l = ... cl

**p** 15.2 kg = ... g      **q** 14 $m^3$ = ... l      **r** 0.19 $cm^3$ = ... ml

**FM 3** Sarif was planning to do some DIY. He wanted to buy two lengths of wood, each 2 m long, and 1.5 cm by 2 cm. He went to the local store where the types of wood were described as:

2000 mm × 15 mm × 20 mm

200 mm × 15 mm × 20 mm

200 mm × 150 mm × 2000 mm

1500 mm × 2000 mm × 20 000 mm

Should he choose any of these? If so, which one?

**AU 4** 1 litre is equivalent to 1000 millilitres.

Referring to centimetres, explain how you know this.

**PS 5** How many square millimetres are there in a square kilometre?

---

**HINTS AND TIPS**

The answer is not 1 000 000.

# Imperial units

This section will show you how to:

- convert from one imperial unit to another

**Key words**

foot (ft)
gallon (gal)
inch (in)
mile (m)
ounce (oz)
pint (pt)
pound (lb)
stone (st)
ton (T)
yard (yd)

You need to be familiar with imperial units that are still in daily use. The main ones are:

| | | |
|---|---|---|
| **Length** | 12 **inches** | = 1 **foot** |
| | 3 feet | = 1 **yard** |
| | 1760 yards | = 1 **mile** |
| **Weight** | 16 **ounces** | = 1 **pound** |
| | 14 pounds | = 1 **stone** |
| | 2240 pounds | = 1 **ton** |
| **Capacity** | 8 **pints** | = 1 **gallon** |

Examples of the everyday use of imperial measures are:

miles for distances by road

pints for milk

gallons for petrol (in conversation)

pounds for the weight of babies (in conversation)

feet and inches for people's heights

ounces for the weight of food ingredients in a food recipe

## EXAMPLE 4

- To change *large* units to *smaller* units, always *multiply*.
- To change *small* units to *larger* units, always *divide*.

Change:

**a** 4 feet to inches

  $4 \times 12 = 48$ inches

**b** 5 gallons to pints

  $5 \times 8 = 40$ pints

**c** 36 feet to yards

  $36 \div 3 = 12$ yards

**d** 48 ounces to pounds

  $48 \div 16 = 3$ pounds

## EXERCISE 3C

**1** Fill in the gaps, using the information in this section.

**a** 2 feet = … inches

**b** 4 yards = … feet

**c** 2 miles = … yards

**d** 5 pounds = … ounces

**e** 4 stone = … pounds

**f** 3 tons = … pounds

**g** 5 gallons = … pints

**h** 4 feet = … inches

**i** 1 yard = … inches

**j** 10 yards = … feet

**k** 4 pounds = … ounces

**l** 60 inches = … feet

**m** 5 stone = … pounds

**n** 36 feet = … yards

**o** 1 stone = … ounces

**2** Fill in the gaps, using the information in this section.

**a** 8800 yards = … miles

**b** 15 gallons = … pints

**c** 1 mile = … feet

**d** 96 inches = … feet

**e** 98 pounds = … stones

**f** 56 pints = … gallons

**g** 32 ounces = … pounds

**h** 15 feet = … yards

**i** 11 200 pounds = … tons

**j** 1 mile = … inches

**k** 128 ounces = … pounds

**l** 72 pints = … gallons

**m** 140 pounds = … stones

**n** 15 840 feet = … miles

**o** 1 ton = … ounces

**FM 3** Andrew was asked to do some shopping for his grandmother. She sent him out to get a two-pound bag of sugar from the market. When Andrew got to the market, the only bags of sugar that he saw were:

8-ounce bags, 16-ounce bags, 32-ounce bags and 40-ounce bags

Which bag should he take back for his grandmother?

**PS 4** How many square inches are there in a square mile?

**AU 5** 1 kilogram is approximately 2.2 pounds.

Explain how you know that 1 ton is heavier than 1 tonne.

# Conversion factors

**This section will show you how to:**
- use the approximate conversion factors to change between imperial units and metric units

**Key words**

conversion factor

imperial

metric

You need to know the approximate conversions between certain **imperial** units and **metric** units.

The **conversion factors** you should be familiar with are given below.

The symbol '≈' means 'is approximately equal to'.

Those you do need to know for your examination are in **bold** type.

| **Length** | 1 inch | ≈ 2.5 centimetres | **Weight** | 1 pound | ≈ 450 grams |
|---|---|---|---|---|---|
| | 1 foot | ≈ 30 centimetres | | **2.2 pounds** | **≈ 1 kilogram** |
| | 1 mile | ≈ 1.6 kilometres | | | |
| | **5 miles** | **≈ 8 kilometres** | | | |
| **Capacity** | 1 pint | ≈ 570 millilitres | | | |
| | **1 gallon** | **≈ 4.5 litres** | | | |
| | $1\frac{3}{4}$ pints | ≈ 1 litre | | | |

---

**EXAMPLE 5**

Use the conversion factors above to find the following approximations.

a Change 5 gallons into litres.

$5 \times 4.5 \approx 22.5$ litres

b Change 45 miles into kilometres.

$45 \times 1.6$ kilometres ≈ 72 kilometres

c Change 5 pounds into kilograms.

$5 \div 2.2 \approx 2.3$ kilograms (rounded to 1 decimal place)

**Note:** An answer should be rounded when it has several decimal places, since it is only an approximation.

**EXERCISE 3D**

**1** Fill in the gaps to find the approximate conversions for the following. Use the conversion factors on page 65.

**a** 8 inches = … cm

**b** 6 kg = … pounds

**c** 30 miles = … km

**d** 15 gallons = … litres

**e** 5 pints = … ml

**f** 45 litres = … gallons

**g** 30 cm = … inches

**h** 80 km = … miles

**i** 11 pounds = … kg

**j** 1710 ml = … pints

**k** 100 miles = … km

**l** 56 kg = … pounds

**m** 40 gallons = … litres

**n** 200 pounds = … kg

**o** 1 km = … yards

**p** 1 foot = … cm

**q** 1 stone = … kg

**r** 1 yard = … cm

**FM 2** Which is heavier, a tonne or a ton? Show your working clearly.

**FM 3** Which is longer, a metre or a yard? Show your working clearly.

**FM 4** The weight of 1 cm$^3$ of water is about 1 gram.

**a** What is the weight of 1 litre of water:

**i** in grams     **ii** in kilograms?

**b** What is the approximate weight of 1 gallon of water:

**i** in grams     **ii** in kilograms?

**FM 5** While on holiday in France, I saw a sign that said: 'Paris 216 km'. I was travelling on a road that had a speed limit of 80 km/h.

**a** Approximately how many miles was I from Paris?

**b** What was the approximate speed limit in miles per hour?

**c** If I travelled at the top speed all the way, how long would it take me to get to Paris? Give your answer in hours and minutes.

**PS 6** While cycling on holiday in France, Tom had to cover a 200-km stretch in one day. He knew that, at home, he averaged 30 mph on the roads.

How long would he expect the journey to take, with no stops?

**AU 7** A cowboy's 'ten-gallon' hat could actually hold only 1 gallon of water.

How many cubic inches could a 'ten-gallon' hat hold?

## GRADE BOOSTER

**F** You can convert from one metric unit to another

**E** You can convert from one imperial unit to another

**E** You can use the approximate conversion factors to change from imperial units to metric units

**D** You can solve problems, using conversion factors

### What you should know now

- How to convert from one metric unit to another
- How to convert from one imperial unit to another
- How to use conversion factors to change imperial units into metric units
- How to solve problems, using metric units and imperial units

**1** Write down the metric units that are used to measure

    **a** the length of a basketball court    (1)

    **b** the thickness of a coin    (1)

    **c** the capacity of a kettle.    (1)

                      (Total 3 marks)

*AQA, June 2007, Module 5 Foundation, Question 2*

**2** Which metric unit would you use to measure the following?

    **a** The length of a pencil    (1)

    **b** The amount of petrol in a car's tank    (1)

    **c** The area of a football pitch    (1)

    **d** The weight of a bus    (1)

                      (Total 4 marks)

*AQA, June 2007, Paper 1 Foundation, Question 6*

**3** Magazines are stored in piles of 100.

Each magazine is 4 mm thick.

Calculate the height of one pile of magazines.

Give your answer in centimetres.

                      (Total 2 marks)

**4**  **a** Convert 8 gallons to litres.    (2)

    **b** Convert 40 litres to gallons.    (2)

                      (Total 4 marks)

*AQA, November 2006, Paper 2 Intermediate, Question 2*

**5** This measuring jug is marked in pints and litres.

    **a** Use the scale to estimate how many pints there are in 1 litre.    (2)

    **b** Estimate the number of litres in 8 pints.    (2)

                      (Total 4 marks)

**6** When he was on holiday in Spain, Gianni noticed that the speed limit was 90 kilometres per hour.

He was travelling at 65 mph.

Was he breaking the speed limit?

You **must** show all your working.

                      (Total 2 marks)

**7** 1 ounce ≈ 28.33 grams.

Nikki says that 16 ounces is less than half a kilogram.

Is she correct?

You **must** show your working.    (3)

                      (Total 3 marks)

*AQA, June 2007, Module 5 Foundation, Question 13*

**8** Jenny has a storage unit with shelves 32 cm apart.

She has some files which she wants to store vertically on the shelves.

Her files are 13 inches high.

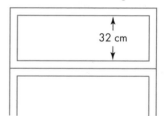

Not drawn accurately

You are given that 12 inches = 1 foot.

Can Jenny fit these files onto the shelves?

You **must** show your working.    (3)

                      (Total 3 marks)

*AQA, November 2007, Module 5 Intermediate, Question 6*

# Worked Examination Questions

**PS** **1** Two towns are 60 km apart.

Driving at 30 mph, how long will it take, in hours and minutes, to drive from one town to the other?

30 mph = 30 × 8 ÷ 5 kph
　　　= 48 kph

> You receive 1 method mark for the calculation 30 × 8 ÷ 5 which converts mph into kph 1 accuracy mark for 48 kph.

Time to drive = 60 ÷ 48
　　　　　　= 1.25 hours

> You get 1 method mark for 60 (minutes) ÷ 48 (kph) (or the figure you had).
> You then get 1 accuracy mark for the figure 1.25.

The 0.25 means one quarter of an hour, which is 15 minutes.

Hence time taken is 1 hour 15 minutes.

> You get 1 mark for interpreting 1.25 as 1 hour 15 minutes. If you had left your answer as 1.25 hours you would not get this mark.

**Total:** 5 marks

**AU** **2** A café ordered 94 pints of milk, but the milkman delivered 49 litres.

Is the amount delivered more or less than what was ordered?
Show your working.

1 gallon = 4.5 litres = 8 pints

So 1 litre = 8 ÷ 4.5
　　　　　= 1.78 pints

> You get 1 method mark for the calculation to convert litres into pints (8 ÷ 4.5) and 1 mark for working out that 1.78 pints is equal to 4.5 litres.
> The 1.78 is rounded. Any correct rounding from the accurate 1.77777, using 1 or more decimal places, will get the mark.
> An alternative approximation is 1 litre = 1.75 pints. If this has been used as the starting point here, then 2 marks would be awarded.

49 litres = 1.78 × 49
　　　　　= 87.22 pints

So, less has been delivered than was ordered.

> You get 1 method mark for 1.78 (or the figure you have) × 49.
> 1 accuracy mark for any figure between 87 and 89.

**Total:** 4 marks out of a possible 5

> This final statement receives 1 mark for independent workings.

The first Olympic Games were held in Greece in 776 BC, but they were very different to the Games that we know today. In 1896 the first Olympic Games of modern times were held in Athens. Since then, the Games have gradually evolved, giving us our current system of international Olympic Games.

The Olympic Games show us that the way we measure things, from distance to weight, have changed over time. For example, over the centuries many countries have moved from using the imperial system of measurements to the metric system. This has meant that in order to maintain world records and make comparisons, measurements must be converted.

### Your task

On the right are results from Olympic Games in two different years.

Write a report for team Great Britain, comparing the two sets of data. In your report you should:

- Show who was the best athlete overall in each category
- State any assumptions that you have made when completing your calculations, comparing the data and making statements.

### Getting started

Use these questions to remind yourself of the key metric and imperial conversions.

1 Name three metric units of length.
2 Name three imperial units of length.
3 State the metric-to-metric conversions for length and use these in three conversions.
4 State the imperial-to-imperial conversion for length and use these in three conversions.
5 State the conversion facts that you know for metric-to-imperial measurements of length.

### Extension

Design a stadium for the next Olympic Games.

- Plan the dimensions of your stadium using imperial and metric units, and draw it to scale.
- You will need to research past Olympic stadiums in order to find out the approximate sizes and requirements of an Olympic Stadium.

### Year 1

| Event | Winner (Women) | Result |
| --- | --- | --- |
| 100-yard sprint | Kathryn Ball | 10.6 s |
| 220-yard race | Kathryn Ball | 25.2 s |
| 880-yard race | Dianne Edwards | 2 min 10 s |
| 80-yards hurdle | Cho Ming | 15.8 s |
| 440-yards hurdle | Alejandra Lopez | 58.3 s |
| High jump | Janet Guggiani | 4 ft 5 in |
| Long jump | Barbara Charlton | 5 yd 1 ft 8 in |
| Discus | Ife Adebayor | 26 yd 2 ft 3 in |
| Javelin | Paula Ivan | 25 yd 2 ft 11 in |

### Year 2

| Event | Winner (Women) | Result |
| --- | --- | --- |
| 100-metre sprint | Aneta Jarzebska | 13.1 s |
| 200-metre race | Karim Djebli | 28.3 s |
| 800-metre race | Marie Auvergne | 2 min 25 s |
| 80-metre hurdle | Li Du | 14.3 s |
| 300-metre hurdle | Gabriela Lopez | 56.7 s |
| High jump | Rachel Evans | 1.45 m |
| Long jump | Brittany Banks | 5.03 m |
| Discus | Ola Kubot | 24.31 m |
| Javelin | Naveen Challa | 23.72 m |

# Why this chapter matters

Civil and mechanical engineers, decorators, plumbers, industrial and structural engineers, town planners, landscape architects, surveyors, interior designers, builders and computer designers all need to work with great precision. Some projects involve measures in units that seem too big to work with; some require accuracy to within infinitesimally small margins. So how do they manage to work with these difficult measures?

The answer is that they all work with drawings drawn to scale. This allows them to represent the lengths they cannot easily measure with standard equipment. Most products and structures in everyday life were probably designed originally by someone who used a scale drawing.

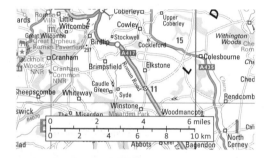

In a scale drawing, one length is used to represent another. For example, a map cannot be drawn to the same size as the area it represents. The measurements are scaled down, to make a map of a size that can be conveniently used by motorists, tourists and walkers.

Satellite navigation can now bring maps to life when you are driving.

Architects use scale drawings to show views of a planned house from different directions.

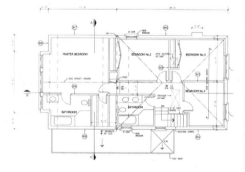

Computers can be programmed to design nets to produce boxes and cartons that use the minimum possible amount of material.

In computer design, people who design microchips need to scale up their drawings, as the dimensions they work with are so small. Use the Internet to research more about how scale drawings are used.

# Geometry and measures: Scale and drawing

1. Reading scales

2. Sensible estimates

3. Scale drawings

4. Nets

5. Using an isometric grid

## This chapter will show you ...

- **G** how to read scales
- **F** how to make estimations
- **E** how to read map scales
- **E** how to draw nets of 3D shapes
- **D** how to draw plans and elevations

## Visual overview

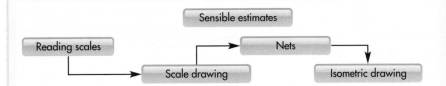

## What you should already know

- The names of common 3D shapes **(KS3 level 3, GCSE grade G)**
- How to measure lengths of lines **(KS3 level 4, GCSE grade G)**
- The metric units for length **(KS3 level 4, GCSE grade G)**

## Quick check

Name these 3D shapes.

**1**

**2**

**3**

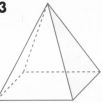

**4**

**5**

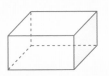

**6**

This section will show you how to:
● read and interpret scales

Key words
divisions
scales
units

You will come across **scales** in a lot of different places.

For example, there are scales on thermometers, car speedometers and weighing scales. It is important that you can read scales accurately.

There are two things to do when reading a scale. First, make sure that you know what each **division** on the scale represents. Second, make sure you read the scale in the right direction, for example some scales read from right to left.

Also, make sure you note the **units**, if given, and include them in your answer.

**EXAMPLE 1**

Read the values from the following scales.

a

b
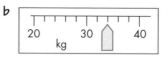

c
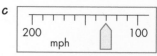

a The scale shows 7. This is a very straightforward scale. It reads from left to right and each division is worth 1 unit.

b The scale shows 34 kg. The scale reads from left to right and each division is worth 2 units.

c The scale shows 130 mph. The scale reads from right to left and each division is worth 10 units. You should know that mph stands for miles per hour. This is a unit of speed found on most British car speedometers.

**FM** Functional Maths   **AU** (AO2) Assessing Understanding   **PS** (AO3) Problem Solving

## EXERCISE 4A

**1** Read the values from the following scales.
Remember to state the units if they are shown.

**a** **i**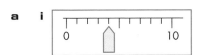

**ii**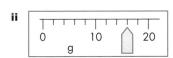

**iii**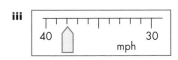

**b** **i** 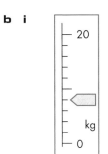  **ii** 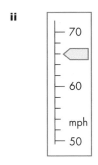  **iii**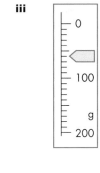

**c** **i** 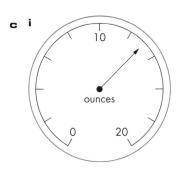  **ii** 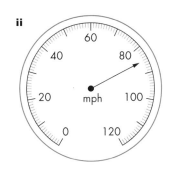  **iii**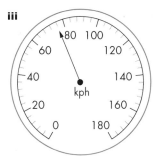

**d** **i** 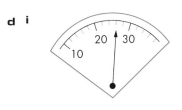  **ii** 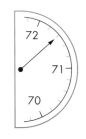  **iii**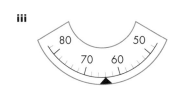

**2** Copy (or trace) the following dials and mark on the values shown.

**a**

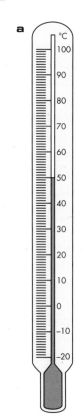

7 kg

**b**

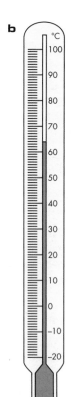

34 mph

**c**

37 mph

**d**

470 kg

**e**

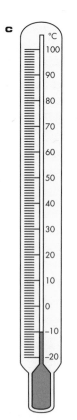

92 kph

**f**

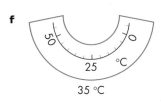

35 °C

**3** Read the temperatures shown by each of these thermometers.

**a**  **b**  **c**  **d**  **e**

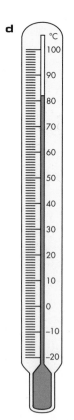

**4** Read the values shown on these scales.

a

b

c

d

**5** Susie is using kitchen scales to weigh out flour.

a   What is the weight of the flour shown on the scales?

b   These scales can weigh items up to 400 g. Susie needs to weigh 700 g of currants using these scales. Explain how she could do this.

**6** A pineapple was weighed.

A pineapple and an orange were weighed together.

a   How much does the pineapple weigh?
Give your answer in kilograms.

b   How much does the orange weigh?
Give your answer in grams.

**PS** **7** **a** What speed is shown on the scale?

**b** Copy this scale and show the same speed as in part **a**.

0                                                                                200

km/h

**AU** **8** Dean says that the arrow on this scale is pointing to 7.49 m.

Dean is not correct. Explain the mistake that he has made.

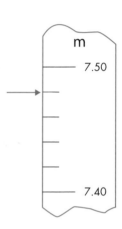

## 4.2 Sensible estimates

| This section will show you how to: | Key word |
|---|---|
| • make sensible estimates using standard measures | estimate |

The average height of a man is 1.78 m. For a sensible **estimate**, we would usually say that the height of a man is about 1.8 m. From this information, you can estimate the lengths or heights of other objects.

**EXAMPLE 2**

Look at the picture.

Estimate, in metres, the height of the lamppost and the length of the bus.

Assume the man is about 1.8 m tall. The lamppost is about three times as high as he is. **Note:** One way to check this is to use tracing paper to mark off the height of the man and then measure the other lengths against this. This makes the lamppost about 5.4 m high, or close to 5 m high. As it is an estimate, there is no need for an exact value.

The bus is about four times as long as the man so the bus is about 7.2 m long, or close to 7 m long.

**EXAMPLE 3**

Look at the picture.

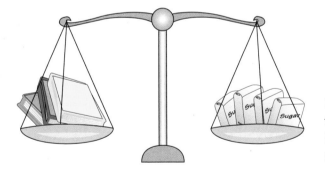

It shows three maths textbooks balanced by four bags of sugar. Estimate the mass of one textbook.

You should know that a bag of sugar weighs 1 kilogram, so the three maths books weigh 4000 grams. This means that each one weighs about 1333 grams or about 1.3 kg.

**F**

**EXERCISE 4B**

**1** The car in the picture is 4 metres long. Use this to estimate the length of the bicycle, bus and the train.

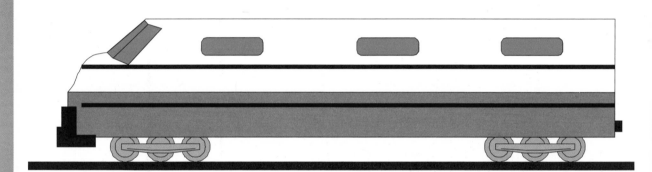

**2** Estimate the greatest height and length of the whale.

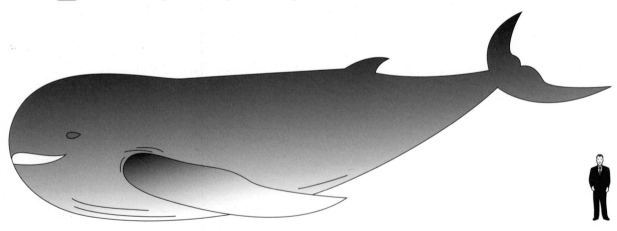

**3** Estimate the weight of one apple.

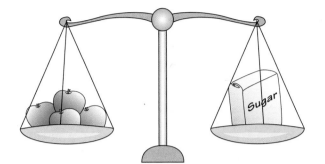

**4**

Estimate the following.

**a** the height of the traffic lights

**b** the width of the road

**c** the height of the flagpole

**5**

A charity collection balances pound coins against a bag of sugar. It take £105 to balance the bag of sugar. Estimate the weight of one pound coin.

**6** This is an illustration of Joel standing next to a statue.

Joel's height is 1.5 m. Explain how he could use this information to estimate the height of the statue.

**AU** **7** Estimate the height of Tyrannosaurus Rex.

**HINTS AND TIPS**

Remember, a man is about 1.8 m tall.

# Scale drawings

**This section will show you how to:**
- read scales and draw scale drawings

**Key words**
measurement
ratio
scale drawing
scale factor

A **scale drawing** is an accurate representation of a real object.

Scale drawings are usually smaller in size than the original objects. However, in certain cases, they have to be enlargements, typical examples of which are drawings of miniature electronic circuits and very small watch movements.

In a scale drawing:

- all the measurements must be in proportion to the corresponding measurements on the original object

- all the angles must be equal to the corresponding angles on the original object.

To obtain the measurements for a scale drawing, all the actual measurements are multiplied by a common **scale factor**, usually referred to as a scale. (See the section on enlargements in Chapter 10.)

Scales are often given as **ratios**, for example, 1 cm : 1 m.

When the units in a ratio are the *same*, they are normally not given. For example, a scale of 1 cm : 1000 cm is written as 1 : 1000.

**Note** When making a scale drawing, take care to express *all* **measurements** in the *same* unit.

**EXAMPLE 4**

The diagram shows the front of a kennel.
It is drawn to a scale of 1 : 30. Find:

**a** the actual width of the front

**b** the actual height of the doorway.

The scale of 1 : 30 means that a measurement of 1 cm on the diagram represents a measurement of 30 cm on the actual kennel.

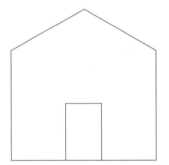

**a** So, the actual width of the front is
4 cm × 30 = 120 cm

**b** The actual height of the doorway is
1.5 cm × 30 = 45 cm

Map scales are usually expressed as ratios, such as 1 : 50 000 or 1 : 200 000.

The first ratio means that 1 cm on the map represents 50 000 cm or 500 m on the land.
The second ratio means that 1 cm represents 200 000 cm or 2 km.

**EXAMPLE 5**

Find the actual distances between the following towns.

**a** Bran and Kelv      **b** Bran and Daid      **c** Daid and Malm

This map is drawn to a scale of
1 : 2 000 000.

2 000 000 cm = 20 000 m = 20 km
so the scale means that a distance of
1 cm on the map represents a distance of
20 km on the land.

So, the actual distances are:

**a** Bran and Kelv: 4 × 20 km = 80 km

**b** Bran and Daid: 3 × 20 km = 60 km

**c** Daid and Malm: 2.5 × 20 km = 50 km

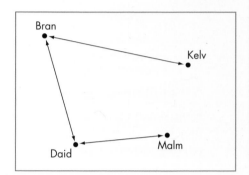

**EXERCISE 4C**

**1** Look at this plan of a garden.

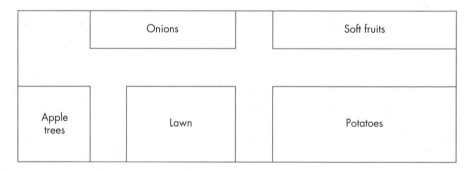

Scale: 1 cm represents 10 m

**a** State the actual dimensions of each plot of the garden.

**b** Calculate the actual area of each plot.

**2** Below is a plan for a mouse mat.

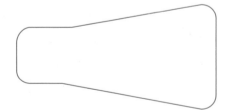

Scale: 1 cm represents 6 cm

**HINTS AND TIPS**

Remember to check the scale.

**a** How long is the actual mouse mat?

**b** How wide is the narrowest part of the mouse mat?

**3** Below is a scale plan of the top of Derek's desk, where the scale is 1 : 10.

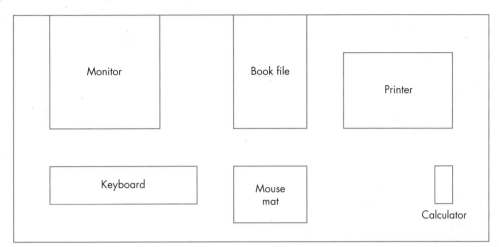

What are the actual dimensions of each of these objects?

**a** monitor            **b** keyboard            **c** mouse mat

**d** book file            **e** printer            **f** calculator

**FM 4** The diagram shows a sketch of a garden.

   **a** Make an accurate scale drawing of the garden.

      Use a scale of 1 cm to represent 2 m.

   **b** Marie wants to plant flowers along the side
      marked $x$ on the diagram. The flowers need to
      be planted 0.5 m apart. Use your scale drawing
      to work out how many plants she needs.

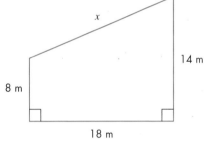

**5** Look at the map below, drawn to a scale of 1 : 200 000.

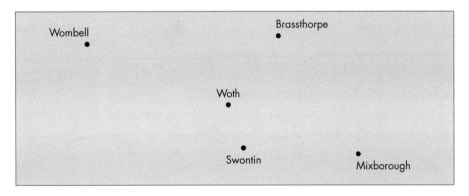

State the following actual distances to the nearest tenth of a kilometre.

**a** Wombell to Woth            **b** Woth to Brassthorpe

**c** Brassthorpe to Swontin         **d** Swontin to Mixborough

**e** Mixborough to Woth           **f** Woth to Swontin

**6** This map is drawn to a scale of 1 : 4 000 000.

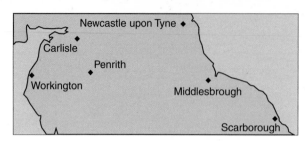

Give the approximate direct distances for each of the following.

**a** Penrith to:

   **i** Workington                         **ii** Scarborough

   **iii** Newcastle upon Tyne          **iv** Carlisle

**b** Middlesbrough to:

   **i** Scarborough                     **ii** Workington

   **iii** Carlisle                          **iv** Penrith

**7** This map is drawn to a scale of 1 : 2 000 000.

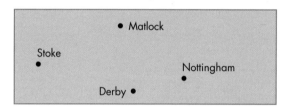

State the direct distance, to the nearest 5 kilometres, from Matlock to the following.

**a** Stoke               **b** Derby              **c** Nottingham

**AU 8** Here is a scale drawing of the Great Beijing Wheel in China.

The height of the wheel is 210 m.

Which of the following is the correct scale?

**a** 1 : 30

**b** 1 : 700

**c** 1 : 3000

**d** 1 : 30 000

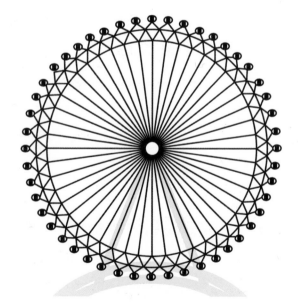

PS **9** Maps for walkers often give a scale of 1 inch represents 1 mile. Use these measurements to write this scale as a ratio.

12 inches = 1 foot

3 feet = 1 yard

1760 yards = 1 mile

## ACTIVITY

### Little and large!

Ask your teacher for a map of Britain.

- Use the scale that is given in miles.
- Use the scale on the map to find the direct distance between:
    - Sheffield and London
    - Birmingham and Oxford
    - Glasgow and Bristol.
- Give your answers to the nearest 10 miles.

## 4.4 Nets

This section will show you how to:

- draw and recognise shapes from their nets

Key words

net

3D shape

Many of the **3D shapes** that you come across can be made from **nets**.

A net is a flat shape that can be folded into a 3D shape.

**EXAMPLE 6**

Sketch the net for each of these shapes.

**a** cube

**b** square-based pyramid

**a** This is a sketch of a net for a cube.

**b** This is a sketch of a net for a square-based pyramid.

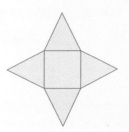

**EXERCISE 4D**

**1** Draw, on squared paper, an accurate net for each of these cuboids.

**a**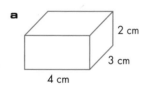

**b**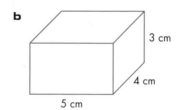

**c**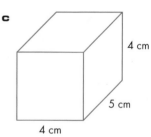

**FM 2** Jenny is making an open box from card.

This is a sketch of the box.

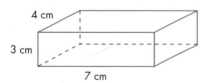

Jenny has a piece of card that measures 15 cm by 21 cm. Can she make the box using this card?

**3** The shape on the right is a triangular prism. Its ends are isosceles triangles and its other faces are rectangles. Draw an accurate net for this prism on squared paper.

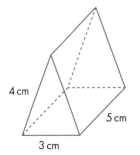

4 cm

5 cm

3 cm

**4** Sketch the nets of these shapes.

**a**

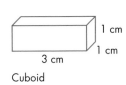

1 cm

1 cm

3 cm

Cuboid

**b**

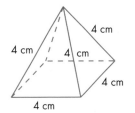

4 cm

4 cm

4 cm

4 cm

4 cm

Square-based pyramid

**c**

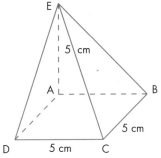

E

5 cm

A

B

5 cm

D    5 cm    C

Square-based pyramid, with point E directly above point A

**d**

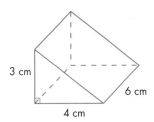

3 cm

6 cm

4 cm

Right-angled triangular prism

**PS 5** Here is a net for a cube.

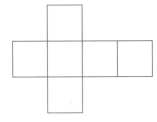

How many different nets can you draw for a cube?

**AU 6** Which of the following are nets for a square-based pyramid?

**a**

**b**

**c**

# Using an isometric grid

This section will show you how to:
- read from and draw on isometric grids
- interpret diagrams to find plans and elevations

Key words

elevation

front elevation

isometric grid

plan

side elevation

## Isometric grids

The problem with drawing a 3D shape is that you have to draw it on a flat (2D) surface so that it looks like the original 3D shape. The drawing is given the appearance of depth by slanting the view.

One easy way to draw a 3D shape is to use an **isometric grid** (a grid of equilateral triangles).

**EXAMPLE 7**

Below are two drawings of the same cuboid, one on squared paper, the other on isometric paper. The cuboid measures 5 × 4 × 2 units.

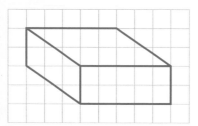
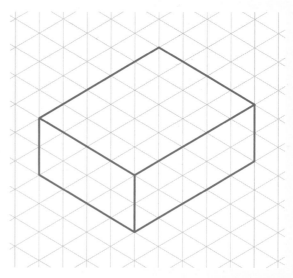

**Note:** The dimensions of the cuboid can be taken straight from the isometric drawing, whereas they cannot be taken from the drawing on squared paper.

You can use a triangular dot grid instead of an isometric grid but you *must* make sure that it is the correct way round – as shown here.

## Plans and elevations

A **plan** is the view of a 3D shape when it is seen from above.

An **elevation** is the view of a 3D shape when it is seen from the front or from another side.

---

**EXAMPLE 8**

The 3D shape below is drawn on an triangular dot grid.

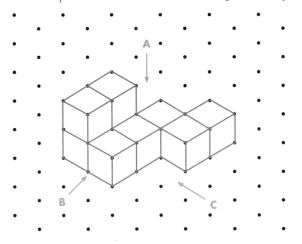

Its plan, front elevation and side elevation can be drawn on squared paper.

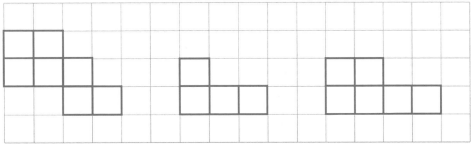

**Plan** from **A**          **Front elevation** from **B**          **Side elevation** from **C**

---

**EXERCISE 4E**

**1** Draw each of these cuboids on an isometric grid.

a
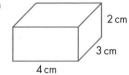
2 cm
3 cm
4 cm

b
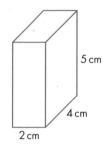
5 cm
4 cm
2 cm

c
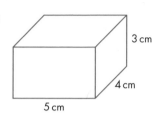
3 cm
4 cm
5 cm

**AU** **2** The diagram shows an L-shaped prism.

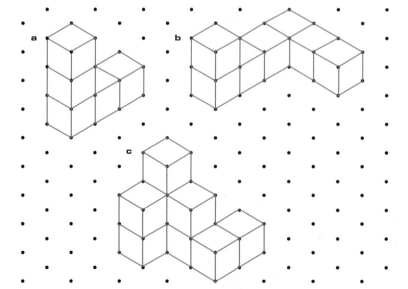

On squared paper, draw a front elevation and a side elevation.

**3** For each of the following 3D shapes, draw the following on squared paper.

i   the plan          ii   the front elevation          iii   the side elevation

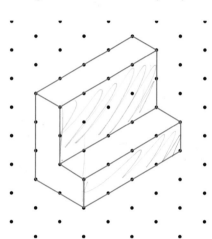

**4** This drawing shows the plan view of a solid made from five cubes.

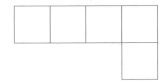

Draw the solid on an isometric grid.

**PS 5** Here are three views of a 3D shape.

 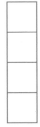 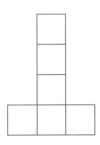

Plan                    Front elevation                    Side elevation

Draw the 3D shape on an isometric dotted grid.

**6**

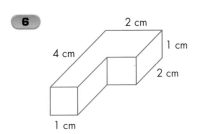

2 cm

4 cm

1 cm

2 cm

1 cm

The diagram shows a toy brick.

**a** Draw an accurate diagram of the brick on an isometric grid.

**b** How many of the bricks can be packed into a box measuring 12 cm by 9 cm by 5 cm?

## GRADE BOOSTER

**G** You can read and interpret different scales

**F** You can make sensible estimates

**F** You can draw nets for cuboids

**F** You can draw simple scale drawings, using a given scale

**E** You can use ratios when drawing scale drawings

**E** You can draw nets for other 3D shapes

**E** You can draw cuboids on an isometric grid

**D** You can draw plans and elevations of 3D shapes

### What you should know now

- How to read a variety of scales
- How to draw scale diagrams and construct accurate diagrams, using mathematical instruments
- How to interpret and draw 3D representations on an isometric grid

**1** Give the values shown by the arrows on these scales.

**a** (1)

60 70 80 90

cm

**b** (1)

500

400

300

kg

200

**c** (1)

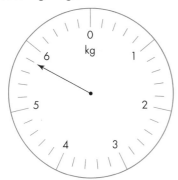

60 70 80
50 90
40 100
30 110
20 Wind speed 120
10 **mph** 130
0 140

(Total 3 marks)

*AQA, June 2005, Module 5 Foundation, Question 2*

**2** The diagram shows a weighing scale for measuring kilograms.

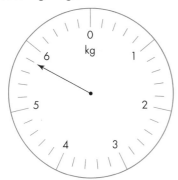

0
kg
6 1
5 2
4 3

**a** What is the reading on the scale? (1)

**b** Draw a line on the diagram to indicate a reading of 3.1 kg. (1)

**c** Convert 3 kg to pounds. (2)

(Total 4 marks)

*AQA, November 2008, Paper 2 Foundation, Question 10*

**3** The diagram shows a cuboid 4 cm by 2 cm by 1 cm.

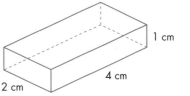

Not to scale

1 cm

4 cm

2 cm

On a centimetre grid, complete the net of the cuboid started below.

Not to scale

(Total 3 marks)

*AQA, June 2005, Paper 2 Foundation, Question 11*

**4 a** Put a circle around the ratio which is equivalent to 1 cm represents 2 km.

1 : 2000        1 : 200 000
1 : 200          1 : 2 000 000        (1)

**b** The scale on a map is 1 cm represents 2 km.

**i** The distance between two towns on the map is 10.5 cm.

What is the actual distance between the towns? (2)

**ii** The actual distance between two cities is 60 km.

Work out the distance between the two cities on the map. (2)

(Total 5 marks)

*AQA, May 2008, Module 5, Paper 1 Foundation, Question 10(a), (b)*

**5** This 3-D shape is made from seven cubes.
It is drawn on an isometric grid.

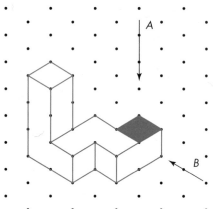

**a** Tim looks down on the shape from *A*.

One of the faces of a cube that he sees is shaded.

Shade all the other faces that he sees. (1)

**b** On this grid draw the plan from *A*. (1)

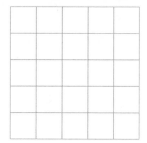

**c** On this grid draw the front elevation from *B*. (1)

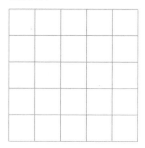

(Total 3 marks)

*AQA, November 2005, Paper 1 Intermediate, Question 11*

## Worked Examination Questions

1   Draw a net of an open box that has measurements 2 cm by 3 cm by 6 cm.

**Step 1:** Start with the base. Draw a 3 cm by 6 cm rectangle.

Your measurements must be accurate, so make sure you use a ruler. This step is worth 1 method mark.

**Step 2:** Now draw the two long sides as 2 cm by 6 cm rectangles on the long sides of the base.

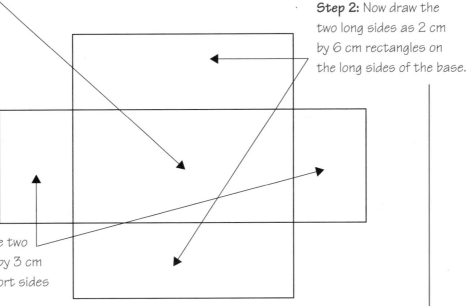

**Step 3:** Now draw the two short sides as 2 cm by 3 cm rectangles on the short sides of the base.

Drawing these two rectangles accurately is worth 1 mark for accuracy.

Drawing these two rectangles accurately is worth 1 mark for accuracy.

**Total:** 3 marks

# Worked Examination Questions

**AU** **2** The diagram shows seven **cubes** arranged to make a **3D shape**

Study the diagrams below.

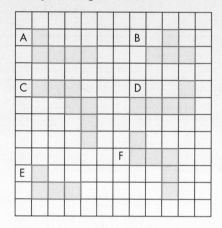

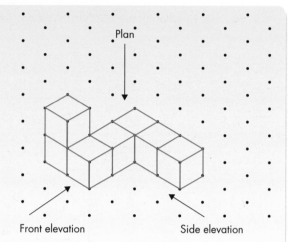

Plan

Front elevation    Side elevation

**a** Which is the **plan** view?

**b** Which is the **front elevation** view?

**c** Which is the **side elevation view**?

*a* F

1 mark

> You get 1 mark for accuracy for the correct answer.

*b* A

1 mark

> You get 1 mark for accuracy for the correct answer.

*c* E

1 mark

> You get 1 mark for accuracy for the correct answer.

**Total:** 3 marks

# Worked Examination Questions

**FM** **3** Aleks is planning a holiday in Madrid.

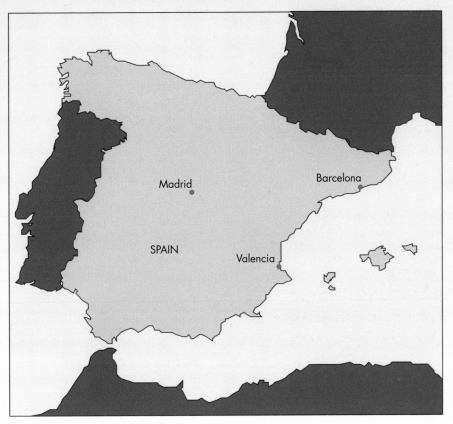

He looks at a map of Spain. The scale of the map is 1 : 10 000 000

Work out the direct distance from Madrid to

   **a**  Valencia

   **b**  Barcelona

1 cm = 10 000 000 cm = 100 000 m = 100 km ——— Convert the scale into a suitable format.

According to this, 1 cm represents 100 km

You earn 1 method mark for identifying the key fact that 1 cm = 100 km.

  1 mark

   **a**  The direct distance from Madrid to Valencia is 310 km

On the map, Madrid to Valencia measures 3.1 cm. So, as 1 cm = 100 km, 3.1 cm must be multiplied by 100 to give the direct distance in kilometres.
You earn 1 mark for accuracy for the correct answer.

  1 mark

   **b**  The direct distance from Madrid to Barcelona is 460 km

On the map, Madrid to Barcelona measures 4.6 cm. As above, multiply 4.6 cm by 100 to give the direct distance in kilometres.
You earn 1 mark for accuracy for the correct answer.

  1 mark

  **Total: 3 marks**

Many people buy houses abroad with the idea of renting them out to holidaymakers. They must consider many factors, such as the location, size and nearby attractions, before making their purchase so they can be sure that they have picked a property that will be popular and turn a profit.

**Villa Hinojos**
Cost: €264 000
Floor space: 110 m$^2$
Rent per week: £500
Weeks rented per year: 24

**Villa Rosa**
Cost: €180 000
Floor space: 80 m$^2$
Rent per week: £350
Weeks rented per year: 25

**Villa Cartref**
Cost: €189 000
Floor space: 90 m$^2$
Rent per week: £300
Weeks rented per year: 20

**Villa Amapola**
Cost: €252 000
Floor space: 105 m$^2$
Rent per week: £400
Weeks rented per year: 25

**Villa Azul**
Cost: €237 000
Floor space: 100 m$^2$
Rent per week: £450
Weeks rented per year: 26

**Villa Blanca**
Cost: €198 000
Floor space: 72 m$^2$
Rent per week: £350
Weeks rented per year: 30

£1 = €1.50

Map scale 1 : 300 000
Map not drawn accurately

## Your task

Jenny is going to buy a villa in Spain to rent to holidaymakers. She is looking at six properties and must now decide which would make her the most profit.

Investigate which villa would be the best buy and write up your findings as a report to advise Jenny on which property she should buy.

Remember to fully justify your advice using suitable mathematics.

## Getting started

Use the scale 1 : 300 000 when working out the real-life distances.

When writing your report you should consider:

- What holidaymakers would look for in their ideal property, including:
  - distance from the airport by road (in kilometres)
  - distance to the coast by road (in kilometres).
- How much each property will cost, including:
  - the cost per square metre (in euros)
  - the cost of the villa (in British pounds)
  - the potential rental income per year (in British pounds).
- Is there anything else that you think Jenny should take into account when choosing her property?
- Think about how to use scales and conversions. For example:
  - What does the scale 2 cm : 100 km, mean?
  - What does the scale 1 : 20, mean?
  - What is £100 in euros, if the conversion rate is £1.00 = €1.50?
  - What is $30 in British pounds, if the conversion rate is $2 = £1?
  - How far is 3500 m in kilometres?

# Why this chapter matters

We use proportion and speed in our everyday lives to help us to deal with facts, or to compare two or more pieces of information.

Proportions are often used to compare sizes; speed is used to compare distances with the time taken to travel them.

A 100-m sprinter

## Speed

When is a speed fast?

On 16 August 2009 Usain Bolt set a new world record for the 100-m sprint of 9.58 seconds. This is an average speed of 23.3 mph.

The sailfish is the fastest fish and can swim at 68 mph.

Sailfish

The cheetah is the fastest land animal and can travel at 75 mph.

The fastest bird is the swift which can travel at 106 mph.

Swift

Cheetah

## Proportion facts

Russia is the largest country. Vatican City is the smallest country. The area of Russia is nearly 39 million times the area of Vatican City.

Monaco has the most people per square mile. Mongolia has the least people per square mile. The number of people per square mile in Monaco to the number of people in Mongolia is in the ratio 10 800 : 1.

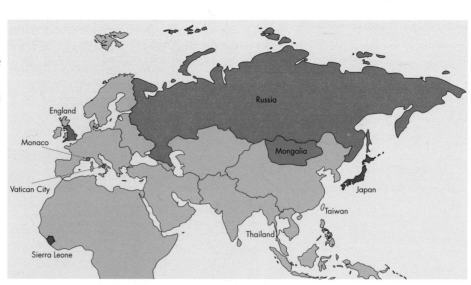

Japan has the highest life expectancy. Sierra Leone has the lowest life expectancy. On average people in Japan live over twice as long as people in Sierra Leone.

Taiwan has the most mobile phones per 100 people (106.5). This is approximately four times that of Thailand (26.04).

About one-seventh of England is green-belt land.

This chapter is about comparing pieces of information. You can compare the speeds of Usain Bolt, the sailfish, the cheetah and the swift by answering questions such as: How much faster is a sailfish than Usain Bolt? Who is fastest on land?

Now, consider what questions you would ask to compare countries, using the information given on the left.

# 5

# Number: Speed and proportion

1 Speed, time and distance

2 Direct proportion problems

3 Best buys

## This chapter will show you …

- **D** how to solve problems involving direct proportion
- **D** how to compare prices of products
- **D** how to calculate speed

## Visual overview

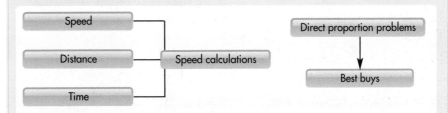

## What you should already know

- Multiplication tables up to $10 \times 10$ **(KS3 level 4, GCSE grade G)**
- How to simplify fractions **(KS3 level 5, GCSE grade G)**
- How to find a fraction of a quantity **(KS3 level 5, GCSE grade F)**
- How to multiply and divide, with and without a calculator **(KS3 level 4, GCSE grade G)**

## Quick check

1 Cancel the following fractions.

a $\dfrac{6}{10}$   b $\dfrac{4}{20}$   c $\dfrac{4}{12}$   d $\dfrac{32}{50}$   e $\dfrac{36}{90}$   f $\dfrac{18}{24}$   g $\dfrac{16}{48}$

2 Find the following quantities.

a $\dfrac{2}{5}$ of £30   b $\dfrac{3}{4}$ of £88   c $\dfrac{7}{10}$ of 250 litres   d $\dfrac{5}{8}$ of 24 kg

e $\dfrac{2}{3}$ of 60 m   f $\dfrac{5}{6}$ of £42   g $\dfrac{9}{20}$ of 300 g   h $\dfrac{3}{10}$ of 3.5 litres

**This section will show you how to:**
- recognise the relationship between speed, distance and time
- calculate average speed from distance and time
- calculate distance travelled from the speed and the time taken
- calculate the time taken on a journey from the speed and the distance

**Key words**
average
distance
speed
time

The relationship between **speed**, **time** and **distance** can be expressed in three ways:

$$\text{speed} = \frac{\text{distance}}{\text{time}} \qquad \text{distance} = \text{speed} \times \text{time} \qquad \text{time} = \frac{\text{distance}}{\text{speed}}$$

In problems relating to speed, you usually mean **average** speed, as it would be unusual to maintain one exact speed for the whole of a journey.

This diagram will help you remember the relationships between distance ($D$), time ($T$) and speed ($S$).

$$D = S \times T \qquad S = \frac{D}{T} \qquad T = \frac{D}{S}$$

**EXAMPLE 1**

Paula drove a distance of 270 miles in 5 hours. What was her average speed?

$$\text{Paula's average speed} = \frac{\text{distance she drove}}{\text{time she took}} = \frac{270}{5} = 54 \text{ miles per hour (mph)}$$

**EXAMPLE 2**

Sarah drove from Sheffield to Peebles in $3\frac{1}{2}$ hours at an average speed of 60 mph. How far is it from Sheffield to Peebles?

Since:

distance = speed × time

the distance from Sheffield to Peebles is given by:

60 × 3.5 = 210 miles

**Note:** You need to change the time to a decimal number and use 3.5 (*not* 3.30).

**EXAMPLE 3**

Sean is going to drive from Newcastle upon Tyne to Nottingham, a distance of 190 miles. He estimates that he will drive at an average speed of 50 mph. How long will it take him?

$$\text{Sean's time} = \frac{\text{distance he covers}}{\text{his average speed}} = \frac{190}{50} = 3.8 \text{ hours}$$

Change the 0.8 hour to minutes by multiplying by 60, to give 48 minutes.

So, the time for Sean's journey will be 3 hours 48 minutes.

**Remember:** When you calculate a time and get a decimal answer, as in Example 3, *do not mistake* the decimal part for minutes. You must either:

- leave the time as a decimal number and give the unit as hours, or

- change the decimal part to minutes by multiplying it by 60 (1 hour = 60 minutes) and give the answer in hours and minutes.

**EXERCISE 5A**

**1** A cyclist travels a distance of 90 miles in 5 hours. What was her average speed?

**2** How far along a motorway would you travel if you drove at 70 mph for 4 hours?

**3** I drive to Bude in Cornwall from Sheffield in about 6 hours. The distance from Sheffield to Bude is 315 miles. What is my average speed?

**4** The distance from Leeds to London is 210 miles. The train travels at an average speed of 90 mph. If I catch the 9.30 am train in London, at what time should I expect to arrive in Leeds?

**5** How long will an athlete take to run 2000 m at an average speed of 4 metres per second?

> **HINTS AND TIPS**
>
> **Remember** to convert time to a decimal if you are using a calculator, for example, 8 hours 30 minutes is 8.5 hours.

> **HINTS AND TIPS**
>
> km/h means kilometres per hour.
> m/s means metres per second.

**D**

**D**

**6** Copy and complete the following table.

|   | Distance travelled | Time taken | Average speed |
|---|---|---|---|
| a | 150 miles | 2 hours | |
| b | 260 miles | | 40 mph |
| c | | 5 hours | 35 mph |
| d | | 3 hours | 80 km/h |
| e | 544 km | 8 hours 30 minutes | |
| f | | 3 hours 15 minutes | 100 km/h |
| g | 215 km | | 50 km/h |

**7** Eliot drove from Sheffield to Inverness, a distance of 410 miles, in 7 hours 45 minutes.

 **a** Change the time 7 hours 45 minutes to a decimal.

 **b** What was the average speed of the journey? Round your answer to 1 decimal place.

**8** Colin drives home from his son's house in 2 hours 15 minutes. He says that he drives at an average speed of 44 mph.

 **a** Change the 2 hours 15 minutes to a decimal.

 **b** How far is it from Colin's home to his son's house?

**9** The distance between Paris and Le Mans is 200 km. The express train between Paris and Le Mans travels at an average speed of 160 km/h.

 **a** Calculate the time taken for the journey from Paris to Le Mans, giving your answer as a decimal number of hours.

 **b** Change your answer to part **a** to hours and minutes.

**C**

**FM 10** The distance between Sheffield and Land's End is 420 miles.

 **a** What is the average speed of a journey from Sheffield to Land's End that takes 8 hours 45 minutes?

 **b** If Sam covered the distance at an average speed of 63 mph, how long would it take him?

**FM 11** A train travels at 50 km/h for 2 hours, then slows down to do the last 30 minutes of its journey at 40 km/h.

 **a** What is the total distance of this journey?

 **b** What is the average speed of the train over the whole journey?

**FM 12** Jade runs and walks the 3 miles from home to work each day. She runs the first 2 miles at a speed of 8 mph, then walks the next mile at a steady 4 mph.

    **a** How long does it take Jade to get to work?

    **b** What is her average speed?

**13** Change the following speeds to metres per second.

    **a** 36 km/h    **b** 12 km/h    **c** 60 km/h

    **d** 150 km/h    **e** 75 km/h

**14** Change the following speeds to kilometres per hour.

    **a** 25 m/s    **b** 12 m/s    **c** 4 m/s

    **d** 30 m/s    **e** 0.5 m/s

**PS 15** A train travels at an average speed of 18 m/s.

    **a** Express its average speed in km/h.

    **b** Find the approximate time the train would take to travel 500 m.

    **c** The train set off at 7.30 on a 40 km journey. At approximately what time will it reach its destination?

**16** A cyclist is travelling at an average speed of 24 km/h.

    **a** What is this speed in metres per second?

    **b** What distance does he travel in 2 hours 45 minutes?

    **c** How long does it take him to travel 2 km?

    **d** How far does he travel in 20 seconds?

**AU 17** How much longer does it take to travel 100 miles at 65 mph than at 70 mph?

---

**HINTS AND TIPS**

**Remember** that there are 3600 seconds in an hour and 1000 metres in a kilometre. So to change from km/h to m/s multiply by 1000 and divide by 3600.

**HINTS AND TIPS**

To change from m/s to km/h multiply by 3600 and divide by 1000.

**HINTS AND TIPS**

To convert a decimal fraction of an hour to minutes, just multiply by 60.

**This section will show you how to:**
- recognise and solve problems using direct proportion

**Key words**

direct proportion

unit cost

unitary method

Suppose you buy 12 items which each cost the *same*. The total amount you spend is 12 times the cost of one item.

That is, the total cost is said to be in **direct proportion** to the number of items bought. The cost of a single item (the **unit cost**) is the constant factor that links the two quantities.

Direct proportion is not only concerned with costs. Any two related quantities can be in direct proportion to each other.

The best way to solve all problems involving direct proportion is to start by finding the single unit value. This method is called the **unitary method**, because it involves referring to a single unit value. Work through Examples 4 and 5 to see how it is done.

**Remember:** Before solving a direct proportion problem, think about it carefully to make sure that you know how to find the required single unit value.

---

**EXAMPLE 4**

If eight pens cost £2.64, what is the cost of five pens?

First, find the cost of one pen. This is £2.64 ÷ 8 = £0.33

So, the cost of five pens is £0.33 × 5 = £1.65

---

**EXAMPLE 5**

Eight loaves of bread will make packed lunches for 18 people. How many packed lunches can be made from 20 loaves?

First, find how many lunches *one* loaf will make.

One loaf will make 18 ÷ 8 = 2.25 lunches.

So, 20 loaves will make 2.25 × 20 = 45 lunches.

**EXERCISE 5B**

**1** If 30 matches weigh 45 g, what would 40 matches weigh?

**2** Five bars of chocolate cost £2.90. Find the cost of nine bars.

**3** Eight men can chop down 18 trees in a day. How many trees can 20 men chop down in a day?

**4** Find the cost of 48 eggs when 15 eggs can be bought for £2.10.

**5** Seventy maths textbooks cost £875.

   **a** How much will 25 maths textbooks cost?

   **b** How many maths textbooks can you buy for £100?

> **HINTS AND TIPS**
>
> **Remember** to work out the value of one unit each time. Always check that answers are sensible.

**FM 6** A lorry uses 80 litres of diesel fuel on a trip of 280 miles.

   **a** How much diesel would the same lorry use on a trip of 196 miles?

   **b** How far would the lorry get on a full tank of 100 litres of diesel?

**FM 7** During the winter, I find that 200 kg of coal keeps my open fire burning for 12 weeks.

   **a** If I want an open fire all through the winter (18 weeks), how much coal will I need to buy?

   **b** Last year I bought 150 kg of coal. For how many weeks did I have an open fire?

**8** It takes a photocopier 16 seconds to produce 12 copies. How long will it take to produce 30 copies?

**9** A recipe for 12 biscuits uses:

   200 g margarine         400 g sugar

   500 g flour             300 g ground rice

   **a** What quantities are needed for:

      **i** 6 biscuits    **ii** 9 biscuits    **iii** 15 biscuits?

**PS**  **b** What is the maximum number of biscuits I could make if I had just 1 kg of each ingredient?

**AU 10** Peter the butcher sells sausages in pack of 6 for £2.30.
Paul the butcher sells sausages in packs of 10 for £3.50.

I have £10 to spend on sausages.

If I want to buy as many sausages as possible from one shop, which shop should I use? Show your working.

**This section will show you how to:**
- find the cost per unit weight
- find the weight per unit cost
- use the above to find which product is the cheaper

**Key words**
best buy
better value
value for money

When you wander around a supermarket and see all the different prices for the many different-sized packets, it is rarely obvious which are the '**best buys**'. However, with a calculator you can easily compare **value for money** by finding either:

the cost per unit weight **or** the weight per unit cost

To find:

- *cost per unit weight*, divide *cost by weight*

- *weight per unit cost*, divide *weight by cost*.

The next two examples show you how to do this.

---

**EXAMPLE 6**

A 300 g tin of cocoa costs £1.20. Find the cost per unit weight and the weight per unit cost.

First change £1.20 to 120p. Then divide, using a calculator, to get:

Cost per unit weight  120 ÷ 300 = 0.4p per gram

Weight per unit cost  300 ÷ 120 = 2.5 g per penny

---

**EXAMPLE 7**

A supermarket sells two different-sized packets of Whito soap powder. The medium size contains 800 g and costs £1.60 and the large size contains 2.5 kg and costs £4.75. Which is the better buy?

Find the weight per unit cost for both packets.

Medium:    800 ÷ 160 = 5 g per penny

Large:    2500 ÷ 475 = 5.26 g per penny

From these it is clear that there is more weight per penny with the large size, which means that the large size is the better buy.

Sometimes it is easier to use a scaling method to compare prices and find **better value**.

## EXAMPLE 8

Which of these boxes of fish fingers is better value?

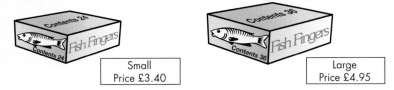

12 is a common factor of 24 and 36 so work out the cost of 12 fish fingers.

For the small box, 12 fish fingers cost £3.40 ÷ 2 = £1.70
For the large box, 12 fish fingers cost £4.95 ÷ 3 = £1.65

So the large box is better value.

## EXAMPLE 9

Which of these packs of yoghurt is better value?

30 is the least common multiple of 5 and 6 so work out the cost of 30 yoghurts.

For the six-pack the cost of 30 yoghurts is £1.45 × 5 = £7.25
For the five-pack the cost of 30 yoghurts is £1.20 × 6 = £7.20

So the five-pack is better value.

**EXERCISE 5C**

**1** Compare the prices of the following pairs of products and state which, if any, is the better buy.

   **a** Chocolate bars: £2.50 for a 5-pack, £4.50 for a 10-pack

   **b** Eggs: £1.08 for 6, £2.25 for 12

   **c** Car shampoo: £4.99 for 2 litres, £2.45 for 1 litre

   **d** Dishwasher tablets: £7.80 for 24, £3.90 for 12

   **e** Carrots: 29p for 250 grams, 95p for 750 grams

   **f** Bread rolls: £1.39 for a pack of 6, £5.60 for a pack of 24

   **g** Juice: £1.49 for 1 carton, £4 for 3 cartons

**FM 2**
**AU** Compare the following pairs of products and state which is the better buy. Explain why.

   **a** Coffee: a medium jar which contains 140 g for £1.10 or a large jar which contains 300 g for £2.18

   **b** Beans: a 125 g tin at 16p or a 600 g tin at 59p

   **c** Flour: a 3 kg bag at 75p or a 5 kg bag at £1.20

   **d** Toothpaste: a large tube containing 110 ml for £1.79 or a medium tube containing 75 ml for £1.15

   **e** Frosted Flakes: a large box which contains 750 g for £1.64 or a medium box which contains 500 g for £1.10

   **f** Rice Crisp: a medium box which contains 440 g for £1.64 or a large box which contains 600 g for £2.13

   **g** Hair shampoo: a bottle containing 400 ml for £1.15 or a bottle containing 550 ml for £1.60

**FM 3** Julie wants to respray her car with yellow paint. In the local automart, she sees the following tins:

   Small tin          350 ml at a cost of £1.79
   Medium tin         500 ml at a cost of £2.40
   Large tin          1.5 litres at a cost of £6.70

   **a** What is the cost per litre of paint in the small tin?

   **b** Which tin is offered at the lowest price per litre?

FM **4** Tisco's sells bottled water in three sizes.

Handy size 40 cl  Family size 2 litres  Giant size 5 litres
£0.38  £0.98  £2.50

**a** Work out the cost per litre of the 'handy' size.

**b** Which bottle is the best value for money?

PS **5** Two drivers are comparing the petrol consumption of their cars.

Ahmed says, 'I get 320 miles on a tank of 45 litres.'
Bashir says, 'I get 230 miles on a tank of 32 litres.'

Whose car is the more economical?

PS **6** Mary and Jane are arguing about which of them is better at mathematics.

Mary scored 49 out of 80 on a test.
Jane scored 60 out of 100 on a test of the same standard.

Who is better at mathematics?

PS **7**
AU  Paula and Kelly are comparing their running times.

Paula completed a 10-mile run in 65 minutes.
Kelly completed a 10-kilometre run in 40 minutes.

Given that 8 kilometres are equal to 5 miles, which girl has the greater average speed?

## GRADE BOOSTER

**D** You can calculate average speeds from data

**D** You can calculate distance from speed and time

**D** You can calculate time from speed and distance

**D** You can compare prices of products to find the 'best buy'

**D** You can solve direct proportion problems

### What you should know now

- The relationships between speed, time and distance
- How to solve problems involving direct proportion
- How to compare the prices of products

**1** Jim's class and Rosie's class go on a trip to the zoo.

Each pupil pays the same amount.

There are 30 pupils from my class on the trip. The total cost for my class is £90

There are 25 pupils from my class on the trip.

Jim

Rosie

What is the total cost for Rosie's class?

(Total 3 marks)

*AQA, June 2005, Paper 1, Question 17*

**2** The ingredients needed to make 500 millilitres (ml) of a fruit drink are

orange juice 300 ml
mango juice 60 ml
lemonade 140 ml

**a** What percentage of the fruit drink is orange juice? (2)

**b** Robert wants to make 750 ml of the fruit drink.

How much lemonade will he need? (2)

(Total 4 marks)

*AQA, November 2006, Module 3 Foundation, Question 18*

**3** The same type of crystal glasses is sold in two different packs.

| Small pack | Large pack |
|---|---|
| Contents | Contents |
| **4 glasses** | **12 glasses** |
| **£3.20** | **£10.20** |

Which size is the better value for money?
You **must** show your working.

(Total 2 marks)

*AQA, November 2005, Module 3 Foundation, Question 17*

**4** **a** Sue took a holiday in Scotland.
She arrived on 26 April 2007.
She departed on 9 May 2007.
How many days did the holiday last?
Include the arrival and departure days. (2)

**b** Sue travelled to Scotland by car.
Her average speed was 36 miles per hour.
Her journey time was 4 hours 15 minutes.
How many miles did she travel? (3)

(Total 5 marks)

*AQA, March 2008, Module 3 Foundation, Question 5*

**5** Here is part of a railway timetable.

| | Departure Times | | | |
|---|---|---|---|---|
| Newcastle | 0840 | 0935 | 1040 | 1122 |
| York | 0943 | 1034 | 1144 | 1225 |
| Leeds | 1010 | – | 1210 | – |
| Derby | 1124 | 1157 | 1324 | 1355 |
| Birmingham | 1215 | 1315 | 1415 | 1515 |

**a** A train leaves Newcastle at 1040.
How long is the journey to Birmingham for this train?
Give your answer in hours and minutes. (3)

**b** The 1225 train from York takes 1 hour 30 minutes to reach Derby.
The distance from York to Derby is 96 miles. (3)
Calculate the average speed of the train in miles per hour.

(Total 6 marks)

*AQA, June 2007, Paper 2 Foundation, Question 18*

**6** Two advertisements for the same type of sun oil are shown.

The sun oil is usually sold in 100 ml bottles which cost £4 each.

Which offer gives the better value for money?

You **must** show all your working.

(Total 5 marks)

*AQA, March 2005, Module 3 Foundation, Question 9*

**7** Gudrun boards a train at 10.15 in the morning and arrives at her destination at 12.45 the same day.

**a** How long did the journey take? (2)

She had travelled 225 miles.

**b** What was the average speed of the train? (2)

**c** She picked up her car from her father's home, 15 miles from the station, and then drove herself home, at total distance of 240 miles, at an average speed of 60 miles per hour. How long did the journey home take her? (2)

(Total 6 marks)

**8** Tom saw a leaflet that advertised forest walks and cycle rides.

He went for a cycle ride that was 24 miles long. The leaflet said it should take 2 hours.

**a** Calculate the speed he needed to maintain, to do the ride in the stated time. (2)

**b** Tom cycled at 8 mph for the first quarter of the journey. How fast did he need to travel, to finish in the stated time? (2)

(Total 4 marks)

# Worked Examination Questions

**PS** **1** Jonathan is comparing two ways to travel from his flat in London to his parents' house.

**Tube, train and taxi**

It takes 35 minutes to get to the train station by tube in London.

A train journey from London to Doncaster takes 1 hour 40 minutes.

From Doncaster it is 15 miles by taxi at an average speed of 20 mph.

**Car**

The car journey is 160 miles at an average speed of 50 mph.

Which is the slower journey: tube, train and taxi or car?

Time = Distance ÷ Speed = $\frac{15}{20}$

= 0.75 hour (or 45 minutes)

> Work out the time taken by taxi. You get 1 method mark for using the correct formula.

> You get 1 mark for accuracy for arriving at the correct time taken.

Total time = 35 minutes + 1 hour 40 minutes + 45 minutes

= 3 hours

Time = Distance ÷ Speed = 160 ÷ 50

= 3.2 hours (or 3 hours 12 minutes)

> Work out the **total time** for tube, train and taxi.

> This is required to compare with the car. This is worth 1 mark.

Car is 12 minutes slower.

**Total:** 6 marks

> Work out the time taken by car. You get 1 method mark for using the correct formula.
> You get 1 mark for accuracy for arriving at the correct time taken.

> State the conclusion following from your results to get 1 mark.

You are planning a dinner party but have not finalised your guest list or menu.

You have decided to make your dessert from scratch because it will be cheaper than buying it from the local shop. Your Aunt Mildred has helped you by giving you four recipes for desserts that all your friends will like: crème caramel, blueberry and lime cheesecake, mango sorbet and chocolate brownies. You have already researched the prices of the ingredients required to make these desserts and are now ready to plan which ones to make!

### Getting started

Consider the questions below to get you started.

- How many 150-g portions can I get from 1 kg?
- How many 75-g chocolate bars would I need to buy if I wanted 0.5 kg?
- Which is cheaper, three 330-ml cans of lemonade at 59p per can or a litre bottle of lemonade at £1.80?
- In a school meeting, one packet of biscuits was provided for every three people attending. How many packets would be needed if 20 students attend the meeting?

### Your task

You can work on your own or in pairs for this activity.

1 Imagine that 8 people confirm that they can come to your dinner party.

   Work out the ingredients you would need for 8 people for each recipe.

   Work out the total cost for each recipe for 8; then work out the cost of one portion.

2 Now suppose three more people have accepted. Repeat the task, this time catering for 11 people, and yourself.

3 Work out the cost if all invited arrived. (There would be 20 altogether, including yourself.)

### Ingredient costs

| Item | Amount | Cost |
|---|---|---|
| Butter | 500 g | £2.40 |
| Eggs | 6 | £1.10 |
| Lime | 1 | 20p |
| Mango | 1 | £1.50 |
| Milk | 2.272 litres | £1.53 |
| Plain chocolate | 200 g | £1.09 |
| Plain flour | 1.5 kg | 75p |
| Caster sugar | 1 kg | £1.25 |
| Granulated sugar | 2 kg | £1.90 |
| Walnuts | 200 g | £2.50 |
| Vanilla extract | 30 ml | £1.55 |
| Baking powder | 50 g | £1.25 |
| Biscuits | 275 g | 89p |
| Blueberries | 500 g | £3.99 |
| Quark | 10 oz | £2.49 |
| Double cream | 284 ml | £1.89 |
| Sour cream | 284 ml | £1.39 |
| Gelatine sachet | 25 g | 99p |

(Ingredients can only be bought in these amounts or multiples of these amounts.)

## Recipes

### Crème Caramel – serves 6

500 ml milk
2 eggs
4 egg yolks
225 g caster sugar
1 teaspoon of vanilla extract

### Mango Sorbet – serves 8

4 large ripe mangos
Juice of 2 large limes
450 ml sugar syrup
(150 g granulated sugar and
300 ml water)

### Blueberry and Lime Cheesecake – serves 8

10 oz sweet oaty biscuits
4 oz butter
1 lb 2 oz blueberries
$8\frac{1}{2}$ oz caster sugar
Grated zest and juice of two limes
20 oz of quark
$\frac{1}{2}$ pint of double cream
4 tsp powdered gelatine
$\frac{1}{2}$ pint sour cream

### Chocolate Brownies – serves 15

50 g plain flour
110 g butter
2 eggs
225 g granulated sugar
175 g walnuts
1 level teaspoon of baking powder

### Extension

1 You have a maximum of £50 to spend.

Assume that everyone will come to the party, so you are catering for 20 people, including yourself.

Work out what combinations of dessert you could provide.

Try to provide a variety of desserts to offer everyone a choice.

2 After the party, you decide to take Aunt Mildred a box of chocolates.

She lives 15 miles away but you know she will provide an excellent lunch when you get there.

You can cycle at 12 miles per hour. How long should you allow for the journey?

Perimeter and area both require an understanding of basic measurements. It is useful to go back in history and find out about the different measurements that have been used over time. Look back to the beginning of Chapter 1 in Book 1 to remind yourself of some of the ways that ancient people recorded numbers using simple symbols.

## Measures of length and area in ancient times

When humans first recognised the need to measure length they used what was available. Most commonly, they used parts of the human body, such as the width of a man's thumb, which became known as an *inch*. Other measures included the *palm*, the width of a man's hand, and the *span*, the width of a man's spread fingers. Similarly, measures of area were based upon everyday units, such as the area of a strip of ground farmed by a peasant.

Over the centuries, recognising the need for standard units, people adopted common measures. In the UK, the imperial system was used. More recently, the metric system has been accepted, almost worldwide.

### Ancient Greek units of length and area

Greek measures of length were also based on the relative lengths of body parts, such as the foot (*pous*) and the finger (*dactylos*). An area called a *plethron* was the amount of land a yoke (a pair) of oxen could plough in one day.

|  | Greek unit | Metric equivalent |
|---|---|---|
| Length | *dactylos* *pous* | 1.8 cm 29.6 cm |
| Area | *plethron* | 12 140 m² |

### Ancient Roman units of length and area

The Romans used a system based on the Greek units, with some influence from the Egyptian, Hebrew and Mesopotamian systems. They would have used these units when they built the Colosseum in Rome in the first century, although they used their own words. For finger (*dactylos*) they used *uncia*, for foot (*pous*) they used *pes*. Other measures they used included pace (*passus*), the length of a stadium (*stadium*) and what is now known as a mile (*milliarium*).

For area, the Romans used the square foot (*pes quadratus*), the acre (*acnua*) and the *clima*, which was a quarter of an *acnua*.

Even today, Olympic stadiums are a similar size to some of the ancient Roman buildings.

|  | Roman unit | Metric equivalent |
|---|---|---|
| Length | *uncia* *pes* *passum* *stadium* *milliarium* | 2.46 cm 29.6 cm 1.48 m 185 m 1.48 km |
| Area | *pes quadratus* *clima* *acnua* | 876 cm² 315 m² 1260 m² |

The Greeks would have used the units given in the table above when they built the Parthenon in Athens in the fifth century BC.

The Colosseum has a perimeter of approximately 1835 Roman *pes*. The perimeter was important to the building's designers as they wanted to created equally sized entrance arches – a perimeter of 1835 *pes* allowed them to create 80 grand entrance arches.

# Geometry: Perimeter and area

**This chapter will show you ...**

**G** how to find the perimeters and areas of shapes by counting squares

**F** how to work out the perimeters and areas of rectangles

**D** how to work out the areas of triangles, parallelograms, trapeziums and compound shapes

**Visual overview**

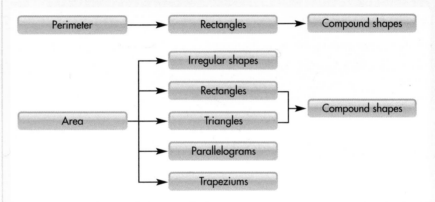

**What you should already know**

● The common units of length **(KS3 level 3, GCSE grade G)**
● What is meant by 'area'.
  The common units of area **(KS3 level 3, GCSE grade G)**

**Quick check**

This rectangle has sides of length 8 cm and 2 cm.

**a** What is the total length of all four sides?

**b** How many centimetre squares are there in the rectangle?

8 cm

2 cm

This section will show you how to:
- find the perimeter of a rectangle and compound shapes

**Key words**

compound shape
perimeter
rectangle

The **perimeter** of a rectangle is the sum of the lengths of all its sides.

## ACTIVITY

### Round about

Using centimetre-squared paper, draw this **rectangle**.

Measure its perimeter. You should get:

3 cm + 2 cm + 3 cm + 2 cm = 10 cm

Draw a different rectangle that also has a perimeter of 10 cm.

There are only three different rectangles that each have a perimeter of 14 cm and whole numbers of centimetres for their length and width. Can you draw all three?

Can you draw a rectangle that has a perimeter of 7 cm?

Can you do it using only whole squares?

If not, why not? If you can, what is different about it?

Try drawing a rectangle that has a perimeter of 13 cm.

### EXAMPLE 1

Find the perimeter of this rectangle.

7 cm

3 cm

Perimeter = 7 + 3 + 7 + 3 = 20 cm

**FM** Functional Maths   **AU** (AO2) Assessing Understanding   **PS** (AO3) Problem Solving

A **compound shape** is any 2D shape that is made up of other simple shapes such as rectangles and triangles.

**EXAMPLE 2**

Find the perimeter of this compound shape.

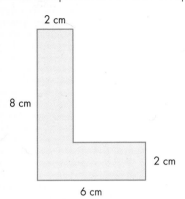

The lengths of the two missing sides are 6 cm and 4 cm.

So, the perimeter = 2 + 6 + 4 + 2 + 6 + 8 = 28 cm

**EXERCISE 6A**

**1** Find the perimeter of each of the following shapes. Draw them first on squared paper if it helps you.

**a**

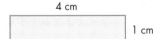

**b**

**c**

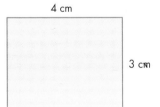

**d**

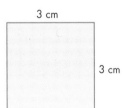

**e**

**f**

**F**

**2** Find the perimeter of each of the following shapes.

**a**

3 cm
1 cm
2 cm
1 cm

**b**

4 cm
1 cm
2 cm
1 cm
1 cm

**c**

4 cm
1 cm
2 cm
3 cm

**d**

2 cm
1 cm
3 cm
1 cm
1 cm
4 cm

**e**

2 cm
1 cm
1 cm
3 cm
1 cm

**f**

1 cm
1 cm
1 cm
1 cm

**FM 3** Joe is putting new skirting board in a room.
This is the plan of the room.
The width of each door is 1 m.

What is the minimum length of skirting board
he needs to buy?

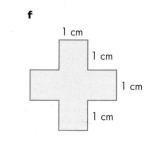

6 m

door

3 m

4 m

door

4 m

**PS 4** The sides of this square are 5 cm.

Katie puts two of these squares together to make a rectangle.
She says that the perimeter of the rectangle is 40 cm.
Is she correct?

Give a reason for your answer.

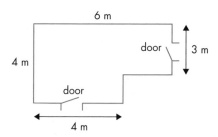

5 cm

5 cm

**AU 5** Is this statement true or false?

Explain your decision ...

The perimeter of this
shape is 24 cm.

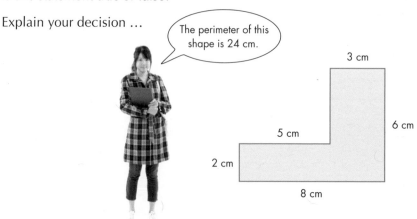

3 cm

5 cm

6 cm

2 cm

8 cm

# Area of an irregular shape

**This section will show you how to:**
● estimate the area of an irregular 2D shape by counting squares

**Key words**
area
estimate

## ACTIVITY

### A different area

Using centimetre-squared paper, draw a rectangle 2 cm by 6 cm.

Check that it has a perimeter of 16 cm.

Count the number of squares inside the rectangle. This should come to 12.

This means that the **area** of this shape is 12 square centimetres.

Draw a different rectangle that has an area of 12 square centimetres but a perimeter that is smaller than 16 cm.

Draw another different rectangle that also has an area of 12 square centimetres, but a perimeter that is larger than 16 cm.

Using whole squares only, how many rectangles can you draw that have *different* perimeters but the *same* area of 16 square centimetres?

To find the area of an irregular shape, you can put a square grid over the shape and **estimate** the number of complete squares that are covered.

The most efficient way to do this is:

● First, count all the whole squares.

● Second, put together parts of squares to make whole and almost whole squares.

● Finally, add together the two results.

**EXAMPLE 3**

Below is a map of a lake. Each square represents 1 km². Estimate the area of the lake.

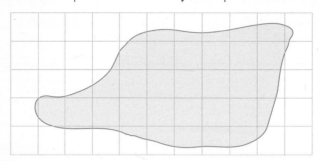

First, count all the whole squares. You should count 16.

Next, put together the parts of squares around the edge of the lake.

This should make up about 10 squares.

Finally, add together the 16 and the 10 to get an area of 26 km².

**Note:** This is only an *estimate*. Someone else may get a slightly different answer. However, provided the answer is close to 26, it is acceptable.

## EXERCISE 6B

**1** These shapes were drawn on centimetre-squared paper. By counting squares, estimate the area of each of them, giving your answers in square centimetres.

a

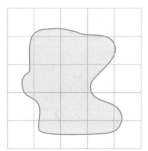

b

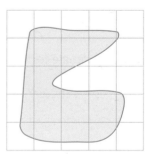

c

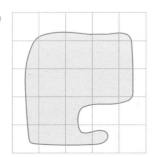

d

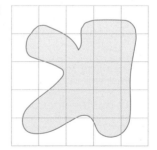

**2** On a piece of 1-centimetre squared paper, draw round each of your hands to find its area. Do both hands have the same area?

**3** Draw an irregular shape of your own, on centimetre-squared paper. First, guess the area of the shape. Then by counting squares, estimate the area of the shape. How close was your guess to your estimate?

**AU 4** Estimate the area of this oval shape.

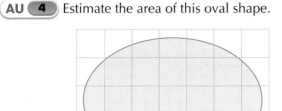

**FM 5** Mr Ahmed needs to estimate the area of his lawn.

He draws a sketch of the lawn on squared paper, so that the length of each square on his sketch represents 1 m.

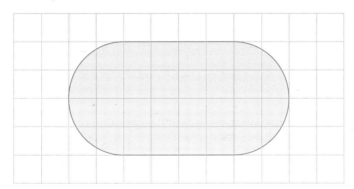

Find an estimate for the area of the lawn.

**PS 6** This shape is drawn on centimetre-squared paper.

The area of the shape must be less than 24 cm². Explain how you know this.

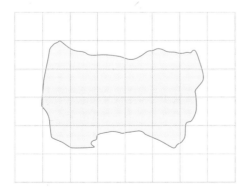

# Area of a rectangle

**This section will show you how to:**
- find the area of a rectangle
- use the formula for the area of a rectangle

**Key words**
area
length
width

Look at these rectangles and their areas.

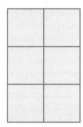

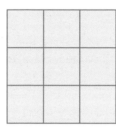

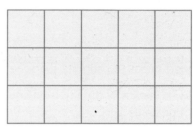

Area 6 cm²          Area 9 cm²              Area 15 cm²

Notice that the area of each rectangle is given by its length multiplied by its width.

So, the formula to find the area of a rectangle is:

**area = length × width**

As an algebraic formula, this is written as:

$A = lw$

---

**EXAMPLE 4**

Calculate the area of this rectangle.

Area of rectangle = length × width
= 11 cm × 4 cm
= 44 cm²

11 cm

4 cm

---

## EXERCISE 6C

**1** Calculate the area and the perimeter for each of the rectangles.

**a**
7 cm
5 cm

**b**
11 cm
3 cm

**c**
15 cm
3 cm

**d**
10 cm
7 cm

**e**
8 cm
7 cm

**f**
5 cm
2 cm

**2** Calculate the area and the perimeter for each of the rectangles.

**a**
8.2 cm
6.5 cm

**b**
11.8 cm
7.2 cm

**3** Copy and complete the table on the right for rectangles **a** to **h**.

| | Length | Width | Perimeter | Area |
|---|---|---|---|---|
| **a** | 7 cm | 3 cm | | |
| **b** | 5 cm | 4 cm | | |
| **c** | 4 cm | | 12 cm | |
| **d** | 5 cm | | 16 cm | |
| **e** | 6 mm | | | 18 mm² |
| **f** | 7 mm | | | 28 mm² |
| **g** | | 2 m | 14 m | |
| **h** | | 5 m | | 35 m² |

**FM 4** A rectangular field is 150 m long and 45 m wide.

Fencing is needed to go all the way around the field.

The fencing is sold in 10-metre long pieces.

How many pieces will Kevin need to buy?

**FM 5** A rugby pitch is 160 m long and 70 m wide.

**a** Before a game, the players have to run about 1500 m to help them loosen up. How many times will they need to run round the perimeter of the pitch to do this?

**b** The groundsman waters the pitch at the rate of 100 m² per minute. How long will it take him to water the whole pitch?

**FM 6** How much will it cost to buy enough carpet for a rectangular room 12 m by 5 m, if the carpet costs £13.99 per square metre?

**7** What is the perimeter of a square with an area of 100 cm²?

**AU 8** Jim is tiling this wall.

3 m

2 m

> **HINTS AND TIPS**
>
> Find how many tiles fit across the length and the height of the wall.

Each tile measures 25 cm by 25 cm. How many tiles does he need?

**AU 9** Which rectangle has the largest area?

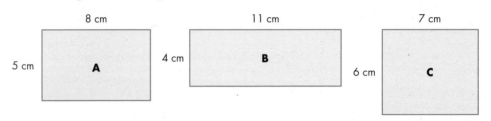

8 cm

5 cm  **A**

11 cm

4 cm  **B**

7 cm

6 cm  **C**

Explain your answer.

**PS 10** Doubling the length and width of a rectangle doubles the area of the rectangle.
Is this statement:

- always true

- sometimes true

- never true?

> **HINTS AND TIPS**
>
> Draw some diagrams with different lengths and widths.

Explain your answer.

**11 a** The two squares on the right have the same area.
Calculate the areas of square A and square B.
Copy and complete: 1 cm² = …… mm²

**b** Change the following into square millimetres.

   **i** 3 cm²   **ii** 5 cm²   **iii** 6.3 cm²

1 cm

**A**   1 cm

10 mm

**B**   10 mm

**12 a** The two squares on the right have the same area.
Calculate the areas of square A and square B.
Copy and complete: 1 m² = …… cm²

**b** Change the following into square centimetres.

   **i** 2 m²   **ii** 4 m²   **iii** 5.6 m²

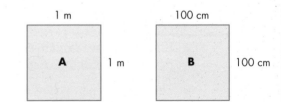

1 m

**A**   1 m

100 cm

**B**   100 cm

# Area of a compound shape

**This section will show you how to:**
- find the area of a compound shape by splitting it into rectangles

**Key words**

area

compound shape

Some 2D shapes are made up of two or more rectangles or triangles.

These **compound shapes** can be split into simpler shapes, which makes it easy to calculate the **areas** of these shapes.

**EXAMPLE 5**

Find the area of the shape below.

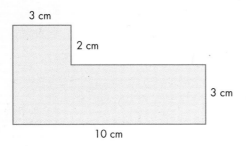

First, split the shape into two rectangles, A and B.

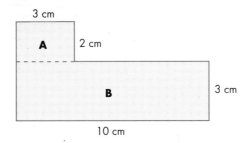

Then, calculate the area of each one.

area of A = $2 \times 3 = 6$ cm$^2$

area of B = $10 \times 3 = 30$ cm$^2$

The area of the shape is given by:

area of A + area of B = $6 + 30 = 36$ cm$^2$

**EXERCISE 6D**

**1** Calculate the area of each of the compound shapes below.

**a**
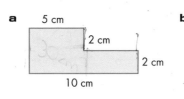
5 cm
2 cm
2 cm
10 cm

**b**
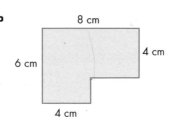
8 cm
4 cm
6 cm
4 cm

**c**
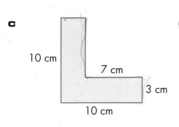
10 cm
7 cm
3 cm
10 cm

**d**
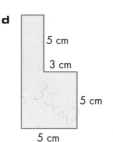
5 cm
3 cm
5 cm
5 cm

**e**
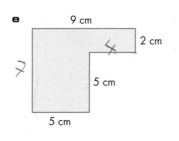
9 cm
2 cm
5 cm
5 cm

**f**
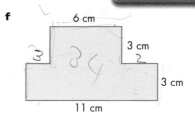
6 cm
3 cm
3 cm
11 cm

**g**
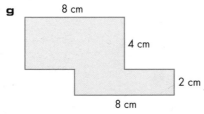
8 cm
4 cm
2 cm
8 cm

**h**
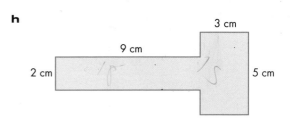
3 cm
9 cm
2 cm
5 cm

**FM 2** A square lawn of side 5 m has a rectangular path, 1 m wide, running all the way round the outside of it. Carlos is laying paving stones on the path. The area of each one is 1m². How many paving stones does he need?

**AU 3** Tom is working out the area of this shape.

This is what Tom wrote down.

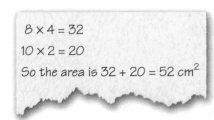

$8 \times 4 = 32$
$10 \times 2 = 20$
So the area is $32 + 20 = 52$ cm²

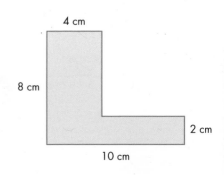
4 cm
8 cm
2 cm
10 cm

Explain why Tom is wrong.

**D**

**PS 4** This compound shape is made from four rectangles that are all the same size.

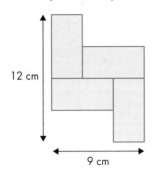

12 cm

9 cm

Work out the area of the compound shape.

**PS 5** This shape is made from five squares that are all the same size.

It has an area of 80 cm².

Work out the perimeter of the shape.

**FM 6** Dave is painting a wall.

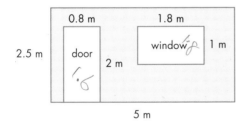

0.8 m          1.8 m

2.5 m      door   window   1 m

2 m

12.5

5 m

He buys a tin of paint that will cover 10 m².

Will he have enough paint?

> **HINTS AND TIPS**
>
> Find the total area of the door and window, then subtract this from the area of the large rectangle.

$2.5 \times 5 = 12.5 \text{ cm}^2$

$0.8 \times 2 = 1.6$

$1.8 \times 1 = 1.8$   Yes

$\overline{\phantom{00}3.4}$

# Area of a triangle

**This section will show you how to:**
- find the area of a triangle
- use the formula for the area of a triangle

**Key words**
area
base
height
perpendicular height
triangle

## Area of a right-angled triangle

It is easy to see that the **area** of a right-angled **triangle** is half the area of the rectangle with the same **base** and **height**. Hence:

area = $\frac{1}{2}$ × base × height

As an algebraic formula, this is written as:

$A = \frac{1}{2}bh$

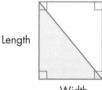

Length    Width

Height    Base

---

**EXAMPLE 6**

Find the area of this right-angled triangle.

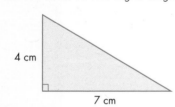

4 cm

7 cm

$$\text{Area} = \frac{1}{2} \times 7\text{ cm} \times 4\text{ cm}$$
$$= \frac{1}{2} \times 28\text{ cm}^2$$
$$= 14\text{ cm}^2$$

---

**EXERCISE 6E**

**D**

**1** Write down the area and the perimeter of each triangle.

**a**

4 cm    5 cm

3 cm

**b**

10 cm    26 cm

24 cm

**c**

5 cm

13 cm    12 cm

**2** Find the area of the shaded triangle RST.

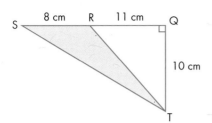

**HINTS AND TIPS**

Find the area of triangle QST and subtract the area of triangle QRT.

**FM 3** A tree is in the middle of a garden.
Around the tree there is a square region where nothing will be planted. The dimensions of the garden are shown in the diagram.

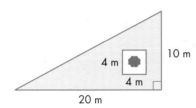

**HINTS AND TIPS**

Find the area of the triangle and subtract the area of square.

How much area can be planted?

**4** Find the area of the shaded part of each triangle.

**a**

**b**

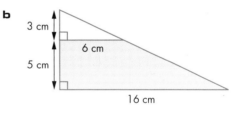

**c**

**5** Which of these three triangles has the largest area?

**a**

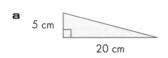
5 cm
20 cm

**b**

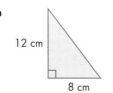
12 cm
8 cm

**c**

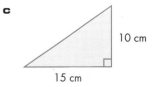
10 cm
15 cm

D

**AU** **6** This shape is made from two right-angled triangles.

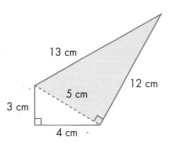

Work out the perimeter and the area of the shape.

**PS** **7** This compound shape is made from a rectangle and two right-angled triangles that are the same size.

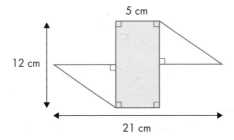

Work out the area of the shape.

**FM** **8** Chris is working out the area of one of the walls of his garden shed.

The diagram shows the dimensions.

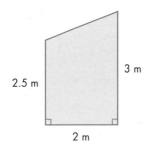

> **HINTS AND TIPS**
>
> Find the area of the rectangle and the right-angled triangle.

**a** Calculate the area of the wall.

**b** Chris wants to repaint the shed.

The length of the shed is 4 m and Chris knows that a tin of paint covers 10 m$^2$.

How many tins of paint does he need?

# Area of any triangle

The area of any triangle is given by the formula:

area = $\frac{1}{2}$ × base × **perpendicular height**

As an algebraic formula, this is written as:

$A = \frac{1}{2}bh$

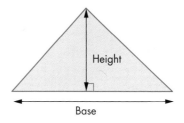

---

**EXAMPLE 7**

Calculate the area of this triangle.

Area = $\frac{1}{2}$ × 9 cm × 4 cm

= $\frac{1}{2}$ × 36 cm$^2$

= 18 cm$^2$

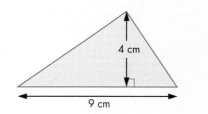

---

**EXAMPLE 8**

Calculate the area of the shape shown below.

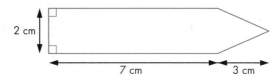

This is a compound shape that can be split into a rectangle (R) and a triangle (T).

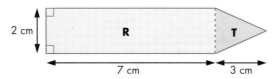

Area of the shape = area of R + area of T
= 7 × 2 + $\frac{1}{2}$ × 2 × 3
= 14 + 3
= 17 cm$^2$

**D**

**1** Calculate the area of each of these triangles.

**a**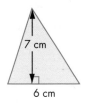
7 cm
6 cm

**b**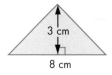
3 cm
8 cm

**c**
7 cm
4 cm

**d**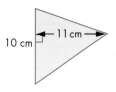
11 cm
10 cm

**e**
12 cm
15 cm

**f**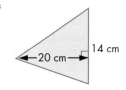
14 cm
20 cm

**2** Copy and complete the following table for triangles **a** to **f**.

|   | Base | Perpendicular height | Area |
|---|------|----------------------|------|
| **a** | 8 cm | 7 cm | |
| **b** | | 9 cm | 36 cm$^2$ |
| **c** | | 5 cm | 10 cm$^2$ |
| **d** | 4 cm | | 6 cm$^2$ |
| **e** | 6 cm | | 21 cm$^2$ |
| **f** | 8 cm | 11 cm | |

**PS 3** This regular hexagon has an area of 48 cm$^2$.

What is the area of the square that surrounds the hexagon?

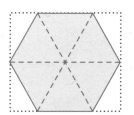

**4** Find the area of each of these shapes.

**a**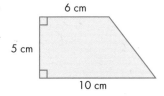
6 cm
5 cm
10 cm

**b**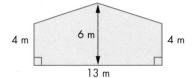
4 m
6 m
4 m
13 m

**c**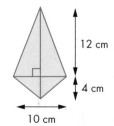
12 cm
4 cm
10 cm

**5** Find the area of each shaded shape.

**a**

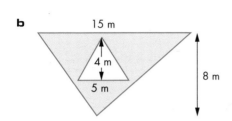

**b**

15 m

4 m

5 m

8 m

**AU 6** Write down the dimensions of two different-sized triangles that have the same area of 50 cm².

**FM 7** Lee is making a kite. He cuts the kite from a rectangular piece of material measuring 60 cm by 40 cm.

**a** What is the area of the material that is left?

**b** Work out the area of the material he will need, to cover both sides of the kite.

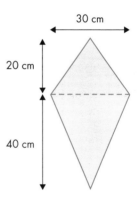

30 cm

20 cm

40 cm

**AU 8** Which triangle is the odd one out?
Give a reason for your answer.

**a**

5 cm

6 cm

**b**

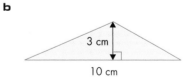

3 cm

10 cm

**c**

4 cm

8 cm

# Area of a parallelogram

This section will show you how to:
- find the area of a parallelogram
- use the formula for the area of a parallelogram

**Key words**

area
base
height
parallelogram

A **parallelogram** can be changed into a rectangle by moving a triangle.

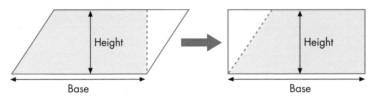

This shows that the **area** of the parallelogram is the area of a rectangle with the same **base** and **height**. The formula is:

area of a parallelogram = base × height

As an algebraic formula, this is written as:

$A = bh$

---

**EXAMPLE 9**

Find the area of this parallelogram.

Area = 8 cm × 6 cm
= 48 cm$^2$

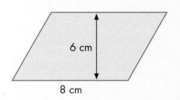

---

**EXERCISE 6G**

**D**

**1** Calculate the area of each parallelogram below.

a
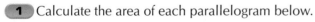
8 cm
12 cm

b
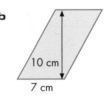
10 cm
7 cm

c
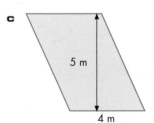
5 m
4 m

**D**

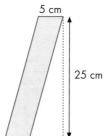 d 5 cm · 25 cm

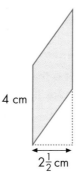 e 4 cm · $2\frac{1}{2}$ cm

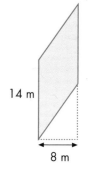 f 14 m · 8 m

**AU 2** Sandeep says that the area of this parallelogram is 30 cm².

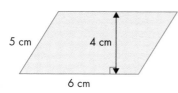
5 cm · 4 cm · 6 cm

Is she correct? Give a reason for your answer.

**PS 3** This shape is made from four parallelograms that are all the same size.
The area of the shape is 120 cm².

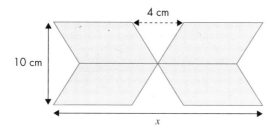
4 cm · 10 cm · $x$

Work out the length marked $x$ on the diagram.

**FM 4** This logo, made from two identical parallelograms, is cut from a sheet of card.

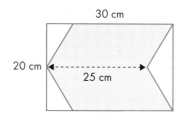
30 cm · 20 cm · 25 cm

**a** Calculate the area of the logo.

**b** How many logos can be cut from a sheet of card that measures 1 m by 1 m?

# Area of a trapezium

**This section will show you how to:**
- find the area of a trapezium
- use the formula for the area of a trapezium

**Key words**

area

height

trapezium

The **area** of a **trapezium** is calculated by finding the average of the lengths of its parallel sides and multiplying this by the perpendicular **height** between them.

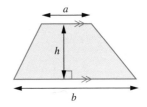

The area of a trapezium is given by this formula:

$A = \frac{1}{2}(a + b)h$

## EXAMPLE 10

Find the area of the trapezium ABCD.

$$\text{Area} = \frac{1}{2}(4 + 7) \times 3$$
$$= \frac{1}{2} \times 11 \times 3$$
$$= 16.5 \text{ cm}^2$$

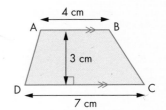

## EXERCISE 6H

**1** Copy and complete the following table for each trapezium.

| | Parallel side 1 | Parallel side 2 | Perpendicular height | Area |
|---|---|---|---|---|
| **a** | 8 cm | 4 cm | 5 cm | |
| **b** | 10 cm | 12 cm | 7 cm | |
| **c** | 7 cm | 5 cm | 4 cm | |
| **d** | 5 cm | 9 cm | 6 cm | |
| **e** | 3 cm | 13 cm | 5 cm | |
| **f** | 4 cm | 10 cm | | 42 cm$^2$ |
| **g** | 7 cm | 8 cm | | 22.5 cm$^2$ |

D

**2** Calculate the perimeter and the area of each trapezium.

**a**

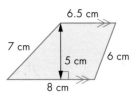

6.5 cm

7 cm

5 cm

6 cm

8 cm

**b**

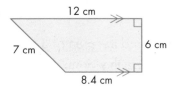

12 cm

7 cm

6 cm

8.4 cm

**c**

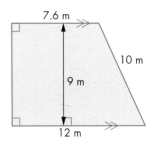

7.6 m

10 m

9 m

12 m

**AU** **3** A trapezium has an area of 25 cm². Its vertical height is 5 cm. Work out a possible pair of lengths for the two parallel sides.

**4** Which of the following shapes has the largest area?

**a**

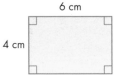

6 cm

4 cm

**b**

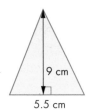

9 cm

5.5 cm

**c**

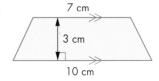

7 cm

3 cm

10 cm

**5** Which of the following shapes has the smallest area?

**a**

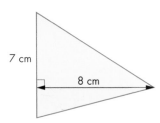

7 cm

8 cm

**b**

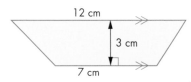

12 cm

3 cm

7 cm

**c**

11.5 cm

2.5 cm

**AU 6** Which of the following is the area of this trapezium?

**a** 45 cm$^2$  **b** 65 cm$^2$  **c** 70 cm$^2$

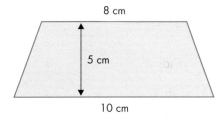

You must show your workings.

**PS 7** Work out the value of *a* so that the square and the trapezium have the same area.

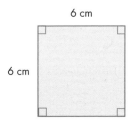 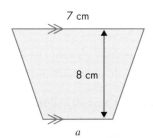

**8** The side of a ramp is a trapezium, as shown in the diagram. Calculate its area, giving your answer in square metres.

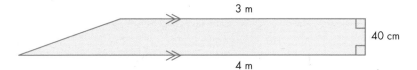

**HINTS AND TIPS**

Change the height into metres first.

## GRADE BOOSTER

**G** You can find the perimeter of a 2D shape

**G** You can find the area of a 2D shape by counting squares

**F** You can find the area of a rectangle using the formula $A = lw$

**D** You can find the area of a triangle using the formula $A = \frac{1}{2}bh$

**D** You can find the area of a parallelogram using the formula $A = bh$

**D** You can find the area of a trapezium using the formula $A = \frac{1}{2}(a + b)h$

**D** You can find the area of a compound shape

### What you should know now

- How to find the perimeter and area of 2D shapes by counting squares
- How to find the area of a rectangle
- How to find the area of a triangle
- How to find the area of a parallelogram and a trapezium
- How to find the area of a compound shape

**1** The grids for this question are made of squares of side 1 cm.

**a** Find the area of this shape. (1)

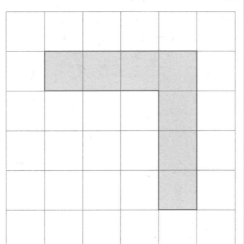

**b** On an centimetre-squared grid, draw a rectangle with area 8 cm². (2)

**c** Estimate the area of this shape. (2)

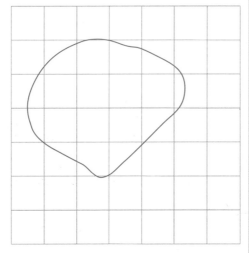

(Total 5 marks)

*AQA, June 2008, Module 5, Paper 2 Foundation, Question 2*

**2** The diagram shows the measurements of a rectangle.

2 cm | Not drawn accurately

4 cm

Four of the rectangles are arranged to form a larger rectangle.

Not drawn accurately

**a** Work out the perimeter of the larger rectangle. (2)

**b** Work out the area of the larger rectangle. (2)

(Total 4 marks)

*AQA, November 2008, Paper 1 Foundation, Question 11*

**3** A shop sells square carpet tiles in two different sizes.

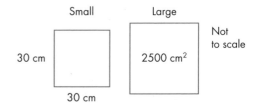

Small    Large    Not to scale

30 cm    2500 cm²

30 cm

**a** What is the area of a small carpet tile? (2)

**b** What is the length of a side of a large carpet tile? (1)

**c** The floor of a rectangular room is 300 cm long and 180 cm wide.

How many **small** tiles are needed to carpet the floor? (3)

(Total 6 marks)

*AQA, June 2005, Paper 1 Foundation, Question 15*

**4** Find the area of each of these shapes.

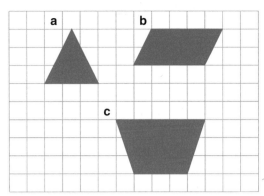

(Total 6 marks)

**5** Find the area of each shape.

**a** (2)

4 cm

5 cm

**b** (2)

7 cm

9 cm

(Total 4 marks)

**6** Calculate the area of this shape.

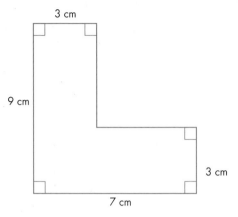

3 cm

9 cm

3 cm

7 cm

(3 marks)

*AQA, Question 22, Paper 1 Foundation, June 2003*

**7** The diagram shows a trapezium ABCD.
AB = 7 cm, AD = 7 cm, DC = 10 cm

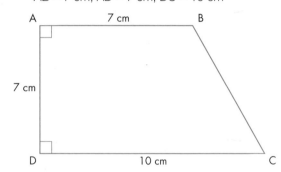

A          7 cm          B

7 cm

D          10 cm          C

Find the area of the trapezium ABCD.
Remember to state the units of your answer.

(2 marks)

*AQA, Question 14b, Paper 2 Intermediate, November 2000*

# Worked Examination Questions

**FM** **1** Sam is using these square tiles to tile a wall.

25 cm

25 cm ☐

4 m

2.5 m

The tiles come in boxes of 30.

How many boxes does Sam need?

4 m = 400 cm and 2.5 m = 250 cm ———— First change the length and height of the wall into centimetres.

400 ÷ 25 = 16 ————

250 ÷ 25 = 10 ———— This shows how many tiles fit across the wall and gains 1 method mark.

16 × 10 = 160 ————

160 ÷ 30 = 5.33 ———— This shows how many tiles fit up the wall and gains 1 method mark.

Number of full boxes = 6 ————

**Total:** 4 marks

This is the number of tiles needed and is worth 1 mark.

This is an important part of the real-life problem. We need to find the number of **full** boxes needed.

The correct answer is worth 1 mark.

**2** Work out the area of this trapezium. State the units of your answer.

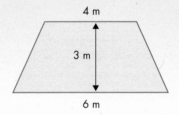

4 m

3 m

6 m

The formula is $A = \frac{1}{2}(a + b)h$ ———— This is on the formula sheet at the front of the examination paper.

$A = \frac{1}{2}(4 + 6) \times 3$ ————

$A = \frac{1}{2} \times 10 \times 3$ ———— Substitute the numbers into the formula. This is worth 1 mark.

$A = 15$ ————

$A = 15 \text{ m}^2$ ———— Make sure you work out the brackets first.

**Total:** 3 marks

The correct answer is worth 1 mark.

1 mark for accuracy is given for the unit $m^2$, even if you did not get 15.

## Worked Examination Questions

**PS** **3** A shape is made up of two squares and an equilateral triangle as shown.

Rebecca says,

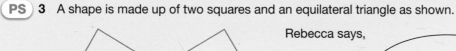

The **area** of the shape is greater than 50 cm$^2$ and less than 75 cm$^2$.

← 5 cm →

Is Rebecca correct?

Area of one square = 5 × 5 = 25 cm$^2$

The area of two squares = 50 cm$^2$

So, the area of the shape must be greater than 50 cm$^2$. The area of the triangle must be less than the area of a square.

The area of the shape must be less than the area of three squares, which is 75 cm$^2$.

So, Rebecca is correct.

The side of each square is 5 cm, since the triangle is equilateral.

Remember that there are two squares. Doubling your previous answer gains you 1 mark.

You do not need to find the area of the triangle.

You gain 1 mark for showing how you found 75 cm$^2$.

You gain 1 mark for making this statement and showing how you got the values 50 and 75.

**Total:** 3 marks

Steve is building an extension in his house to accommodate an extra family room. He will want to lay a carpet in the new room.

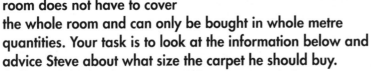

The carpet for the sitting room does not have to cover the whole room and can only be bought in whole metre quantities. Your task is to look at the information below and advice Steve about what size the carpet he should buy.

# Geometry: Symmetry

**1** Lines of symmetry

**2** Rotational symmetry

## This chapter will show you ...

**G** how to draw the lines of symmetry on a 2D shape

**F** how to find the order of rotational symmetry for a 2D shape

## Visual overview

## What you should already know

- A triangle is a 2D shape with three straight sides.
  **(KS3 level 3, GCSE grade G)**

- A quadrilateral is a 2D shape with four straight sides.
  **(KS3 level 3, GCSE grade G)**

## Quick check

Write down the names of these 2D shapes.

**a**  **b**  **c**  **d**

**e**  **f**

**g** 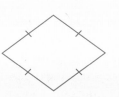 **h**  **i**

This section will show you how to:
- draw the lines of symmetry on a 2D shape
- recognise shapes with reflective symmetry

**Key words**
line of symmetry
mirror line
symmetry

ACTIVITY

## Mirror writing

You need a plane mirror and some plain or squared paper.

You probably know that certain styles of some upright capital letters have one or more lines of symmetry. For example, the upright A given below has one line of symmetry (shown here as a dashed line).

Draw a large A on your paper and put the mirror along the line of symmetry.

What do you notice when you look in the mirror?

Upright capital letters such as **A**, **O** and **M** have a vertical line of symmetry. Can you find any others?

Other upright capital letters (**E**, for example) have a horizontal line of symmetry. Can you find any others?

Now try to form words that have a vertical or a horizontal line of symmetry.

Here are two examples:

Make a display of all the different words you have found.

**FM** Functional Maths  **AU** (AO2) Assessing Understanding  **PS** (AO3) Problem Solving

Many 2D shapes have one or more lines of **symmetry**.

A **line of symmetry** is a line that can be drawn through a shape so that what can be seen on one side of the line is the mirror image of what is on the other side. This is why a line of symmetry is sometimes called a **mirror line**.

It is also the line along which a shape can be folded exactly onto itself.

## Finding lines of symmetry

In an examination, you cannot use a mirror to find lines of symmetry but it is just as easy to use tracing paper, which is always available in any mathematics examination.

For example, to find the lines of symmetry for a rectangle, follow these steps.

**1**    Trace the rectangle.

**2**  Draw a line on the tracing paper where you think there is a line of symmetry.

**3**  Fold the tracing paper along this line. If the parts match, you have found a line of symmetry. If they do not match, try a line in another position.

**4** 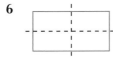 Next, find out whether this is also a line of symmetry. You will find that it is.

**5**    Now see whether this is a line of symmetry. You will find that it is *not* a line of symmetry.

**6**    Your completed diagram should look like this. It shows that a rectangle has *two* lines of symmetry.

---

**EXAMPLE 1**

Find the number of lines of symmetry for this cross.

First, follow steps 1 to 4, which give the vertical and horizontal lines of symmetry.

Then, search for any other lines of symmetry in the same way.

There are two more, as the diagram shows.

So, this cross has a total of four lines of symmetry.

## EXERCISE 7A

**1** Copy these shapes and draw on the lines of symmetry for each one. If it will help you, use tracing paper or a mirror to check your results.

a

Isosceles
triangle

b

Equilateral
triangle

c

Square

d

Parallelogram

e

Rhombus

f

Kite

g

Trapezium

**2** How many shapes with lines of symmetry can you find in this drawing of a temple?

Copy each one you find and draw on the lines of symmetry.

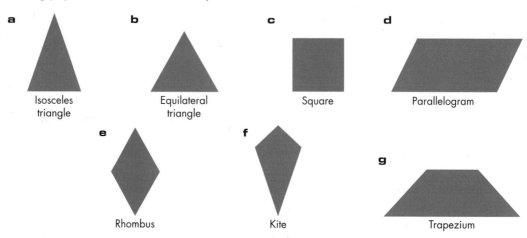

**3** **a** Find the number of lines of symmetry for each of these regular polygons.

i

Regular pentagon

ii

Regular hexagon

iii

Regular octagon

**b** How many lines of symmetry do you think a regular decagon has? (A decagon is a ten-sided polygon.)

**4** Copy these star shapes and draw in all the lines of symmetry for each one.

a

b

c

**5** Copy these patterns and draw in all the lines of symmetry for each one.

a

b

c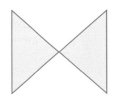

d

e

f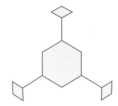

**6** Write down the number of lines of symmetry for each of these flags.

Austria  Canada  Iceland  Switzerland  Greece

**7** **a** These road signs all have lines of symmetry. Copy them and draw on the lines of symmetry for each one.

  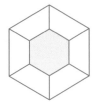

**b** Draw sketches of other common signs that also have lines of symmetry. State the number of lines of symmetry in each case.

**8** The animal and plant kingdoms are full of symmetry. Four examples are given below. State the number of lines of symmetry for each one.

a

b

c

d

Can you find other examples? Find suitable pictures, copy them and state the number of lines of symmetry each one has.

**9**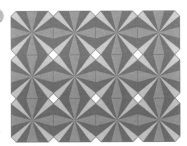

This decorative wallpaper pattern is made by repeating shapes that have lines of symmetry. By using squared or isometric paper, try to make a similar pattern of your own.

**F**

**PS** **10** Copy this diagram. On your copy, shade in four more squares so that the diagram has four lines of symmetry.

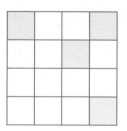

**AU** **11** Billy says that all triangles have none or one or two or three lines of symmetry. Is Billy correct? Explain your answer.

## 7.2 Rotational symmetry

**This section will show you how to:**
- find the order of rotational symmetry for a 2D shape
- recognise shapes with rotational symmetry

**Key words**
order of rotational symmetry
rotational symmetry

A 2D shape has **rotational symmetry** if it can be rotated about a point to look exactly the same in a new position.

The **order of rotational symmetry** is the number of different positions in which the shape looks the same when it is rotated about the point.

The easiest way to find the order of rotational symmetry for any shape is to trace it and count the number of times that the shape stays the same as you turn the tracing paper through one complete turn.

**EXAMPLE 2**

Find the order of rotational symmetry for this shape.

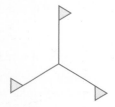

First, hold the tracing paper on top of the shape and trace the shape. Then rotate the tracing paper and count the number of times the tracing matches the original shape in one complete turn.

You will find three different positions.

So, the order of rotational symmetry for the shape is 3.

## EXERCISE 7B

**1** Copy these shapes and write below each one the order of rotational symmetry. If it will help you, use tracing paper.

a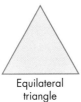
Square

b
Rectangle

c
Parallelogram

d
Equilateral triangle

e
Regular hexagon

**2** Find the order of rotational symmetry for each of these shapes.

a    b    c    d    e

**3** The following are Greek capital letters. Write down the order of rotational symmetry for each one.

a Φ   b H   c Z   d Θ   e Ξ

**4** Copy these shapes on tracing paper and find the order of rotational symmetry for each one.

a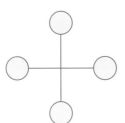

b

c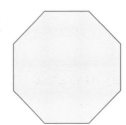

d

e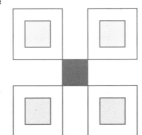

f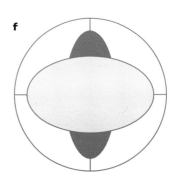

**5** The upright capital letter A fits exactly onto itself only *once*. So, its order of rotational symmetry is 1. This means that it has *no* rotational symmetry. Write down all the upright capital letters of the alphabet that have rotational symmetry of order 1.

**6** Obtain a pack of playing cards or a set of dominoes. Which cards or dominoes have rotational symmetry? Can you find any patterns? Write down everything you discover about the symmetry of the cards or dominoes.

**7** Here is an Islamic star pattern.

Inside the star there are two patterns that have rotational symmetry.

**a** What is the order of rotational symmetry of the whole star?

**b** What is the order of rotational symmetry of the two patterns inside the star?

**FM 8** Design a logo that has rotational symmetry of order 2 to advertise a new brand of soap.

**PS 9** Copy the grid on the right. On your copy, shade in four squares so that the shape has rotational symmetry of order 2.

**AU 10** Copy the table below. On your copy, write the letter for each shape in the correct box. The first one has been done for you.

| | | Number of lines of symmetry | | | |
| --- | --- | --- | --- | --- | --- |
| | | **0** | **1** | **2** | **3** |
| **Order of rotational symmetry** | 1 | | A | | |
| | 2 | | | | |
| | 3 | | | | |

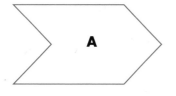

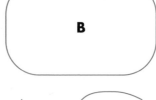

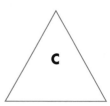

## ACTIVITY

### Pentomino patterns

Pentominoes are shapes made with five squares that touch edge-to-edge.

There are 12 possible pentomino shapes.

Two of them are shown here.

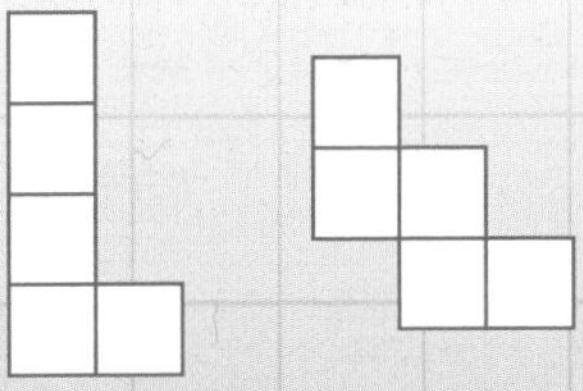

Find the other 10.

When you have found them all, investigate the line symmetry and rotational symmetry for each pentomino.

## GRADE BOOSTER

**G** You can draw lines of symmetry on basic 2D shapes

**F** You can draw lines of symmetry on more complex 2D shapes

**F** You can find the order of rotational symmetry for any 2D shape

### What you should know now

- How to recognise lines of symmetry and draw them on 2D shapes
- How to recognise whether a 2D shape has rotational symmetry and find its order of rotational symmetry

**1**   **A  E  F  H  M  N**

Write down **one** letter from this list which has

**a** no lines of symmetry (1)

**b** only one line of symmetry (1)

**c** two lines of symmetry (1)

**d** rotational symmetry of order 2. (1)

(Total 4 marks)

*AQA, June 2007, Module 5, Paper 2 Foundation, Question 9*

**2 a** Draw the lines of symmetry on these shapes. (3)

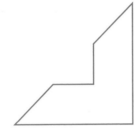

**b** The shape below is made from squares.

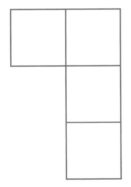

Add one more square to form a shape with rotational symmetry of order 2. (1)

(Total 4 marks)

*AQA, June 2008, Paper 2 Foundation, Question 8*

**3** This shape is made from three equilateral triangles and a regular hexagon.

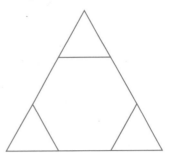

**a** Write down the order of rotational symmetry of the shape. (1)

**b** Copy the shape and draw all the lines of symmetry. (2)

(Total 3 marks)

**4 a** This is a diagram of a wall tile. Copy the diagram and draw in all the lines of symmetry. (1)

**b** Four of these tiles are used to make a pattern.

**i** Copy and complete this diagram to show the final pattern. (2)

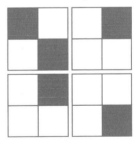

**ii** How many lines of symmetry does your final pattern have? (1)

(Total 4 marks)

**a** Reflect the shaded shape in the mirror line.

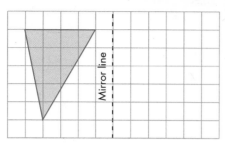

**b** Draw all the lines of symmetry on this shape. (1)

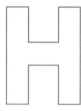

(Total 2 marks)

*AQA, June 2006, Module 5, Paper 2 Foundation, Question 5(b)*

## Worked Examination Questions

# M A T H S

**1** Which of the letters above has
  **a** line symmetry
  **b** rotational symmetry of order 2?

**a**  ——————

2 marks

> These letters have line symmetry as shown. 2 marks are available for finding all five lines of symmetry. You would lose a mark if you left one out.

**b** **H S** ——————

> You need to get both letters for this mark.

1 mark    **Total:** 3 marks

---

**2** A pattern has rotational symmetry of order 4 and no line symmetry. Part of the pattern is shown on the right. Complete the pattern.

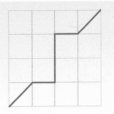

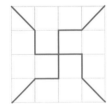 ——————

> Trace the part of the pattern and rotate it about the centre of the grid three times through 90° to form the pattern.
> You get 2 marks for completing the pattern correctly.
> You would lose a mark if you made an error in the pattern.

**Total:** 2 marks

---

**3** Add two squares to the diagram below so that it has rotational symmetry of order 2.

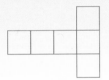

> You can use tracing paper to check your answer. You get 1 mark for the correct pattern.

**Total:** 1 mark

---

**PS** **4** Copy the diagram. Shade in more squares so that the pattern has rotational symmetry of order 4.

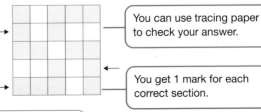

> You can use tracing paper to check your answer.

> You get 1 mark for each correct section.

**Total:** 3 marks

Symmetrical objects are all around us: in our homes, at school and work, and in the 'great outdoors'.
In this task you are going to investigate two types of symmetry: line symmetry and rotational symmetry.

### Getting started

To start with, think about the following questions.

● Think of five objects in your room at home that have line symmetry.
  How many **lines** of symmetry does each object have?

● Look around your classroom and find two objects that have rotational symmetry.
  What is their **order of rotational** symmetry?

● Where does symmetry naturally occur? Name some plants and animals that have symmetry and give the number of **lines** of symmetry and/or the **order of rotational** symmetry found on each.

## Your task

Here are some examples of symmetry in modern art and ornate metal railings. With a partner, discuss the symmetry that you can see in each picture.

Now, design your own modern art piece or metal railings that have line symmetry, rotational symmetry, or both. You must explain the symmetry in your design to your partner.

### Symmetry in art

Stephen Pitts – Triangular Colour Wheel

Shana McCormick – Symmetrical Unison

### Symmetry in railings

It is essential that we understand angles. They help us to construct everything, from a building to a table. So, angles literally shape our world.

## Ancient measurement of angles

Ancient civilisations used **right angles** in surveying and in constructing buildings, however, not everything can be measured in right angles. There is a need for a smaller, more useful unit. The ancient Babylonians chose a unit angle that led to the development of the **degree**, which is what we still use now.

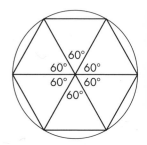

Most historians think that the ancient Babylonians believed that the 'circle' of the year consisted of 360 days. Mathematics historians also generally believe that the ancient Babylonians knew that the side of a **regular hexagon** inscribed in a circle is equal to the **radius** of the circle. This may have led to the division of the full circle (360 'days') into six equal parts, each part consisting of 60 'days', as shown opposite. They divided one angle of an **equilateral triangle** into 60 equal parts, now called degrees, then further subdivided a degree into 60 equal parts, called **minutes**, and a minute into 60 equal parts, called **seconds**.

The divisions 'minutes' and 'second' are also used in time-keeping.

Modern theodolite.

## Modern measurement of angles

Modern surveyors use a **theodolite** for measuring angles. A modern theodolite comprises a movable telescope mounted within horizontal and a vertical axis. When the telescope is pointed at a desired object, the angle of each of these axes can be measured with great precision, typically on the scale of **arcseconds**. (There are 3600 arcseconds in 1°.)

This can be used for measuring both horizontal and vertical angles. It is a key tool in surveying and engineering work, particularly on inaccessible ground, but theodolites have been adapted for other specialised purposes in fields such as meteorology and rocket-launch technology.

# Chapter

# Geometry and measures: Angles

**1** Measuring and drawing angles

**2** Angle facts

**3** Angles in a triangle

**4** Angles in a polygon

**5** Regular polygons

**6** Parallel lines

**7** Special quadrilaterals

**8** Bearings

## This chapter will show you ...

- **F** how to measure and draw angles
- **F** how to find angles on a line and at a point
- to **E** **D** how to find angles in a triangle and in any polygon
- **D** how to use bearings
- **D** how to calculate angles in parallel lines
- **C** how to calculate interior and exterior angles in polygons

## Visual overview

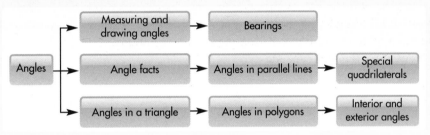

## What you should already know

- How to use a protractor to measure an acute angle **(KS3 level 5, GCSE grade F)**
- The meaning of the terms 'acute', 'obtuse', 'reflex', 'right' and how to use these terms to describe angles **(KS3 level 5, GCSE grade G)**
- That a polygon is a 2D shape with any number of straight sides **(KS3 level 5, GCSE grade G)**
- That a diagonal is a line joining two vertices of a polygon **(KS3 level 5, GCSE grade G)**
- The meaning of the terms 'parallel lines' and 'perpendicular lines' **(KS3 level 5, GCSE grade G)**

## Quick check

State whether these angles are acute, obtuse or reflex.

**1** 135°    **2** 68°    **3** 202°    **4** 98°    **5** 315°

This section will show you how to:

● measure and draw an angle of any size

**Key words**

acute angle
obtuse angle
protractor
reflex angle

When you are using a **protractor**, it is important that you:

● place the centre of the protractor *exactly* on the corner (vertex) of the angle

● lay the base-line of the protractor *exactly* along one side of the angle.

You must follow these two steps to obtain an accurate value for the angle you are measuring.

You should already have discovered how easy it is to measure **acute angles** and **obtuse angles**, using the common semicircular protractor.

**EXAMPLE 1**

Measure the angles ABC, DEF and GHI in the diagrams below.

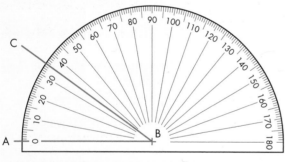
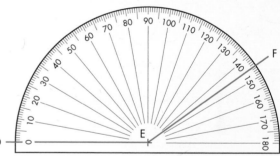

Acute angle ABC is 35° and obtuse angle DEF is 145°.

To measure **reflex angles**, such as angle GHI, it is easier to use a circular protractor if you have one.

Note the notation for angles.

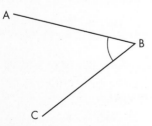

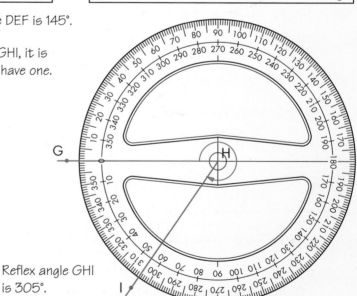

Angle ABC, or ∠ABC, means the angle at B between the lines AB and BC.

Reflex angle GHI is 305°.

**FM** Functional Maths  **AU** (AO2) Assessing Understanding  **PS** (AO3) Problem Solving

## EXERCISE 8A

**1** Use a protractor to measure the size of each marked angle.

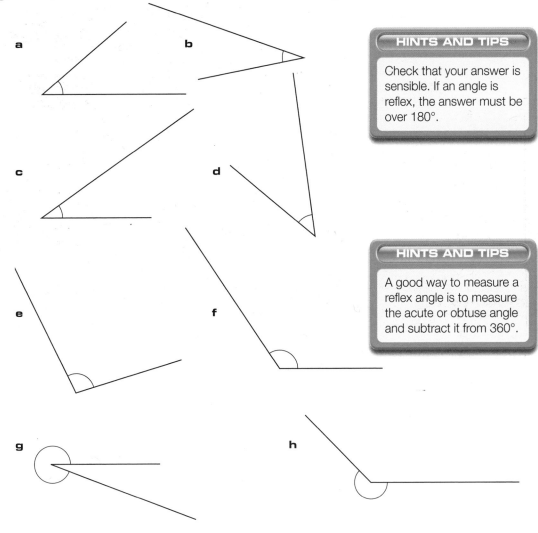

> **HINTS AND TIPS**
>
> Check that your answer is sensible. If an angle is reflex, the answer must be over 180°.

> **HINTS AND TIPS**
>
> A good way to measure a reflex angle is to measure the acute or obtuse angle and subtract it from 360°.

**2** Use a protractor to draw angles of the following sizes.

   **a** 30°    **b** 60°    **c** 90°    **d** 10°    **e** 20°    **f** 45°    **g** 75°

**3** **a** **i** Draw any three acute angles.

    **ii** Estimate their sizes. Record your results.

    **iii** Measure the angles. Record your results.

    **iv** Work out the difference between your estimate and your measurement for each angle. Add all the differences together. This is your total error.

  **b** Repeat parts **i** to **iv** of part **a** for three obtuse angles.

  **c** Repeat parts **i** to **iv** of part **a** for three reflex angles.

  **d** Which type of angle are you most accurate with, and which type are you least accurate with?

**FM 4** It is only safe to climb this ladder if the angle between the ground and the ladder is between 72° and 78°.

Is it safe for Oliver to climb the ladder?

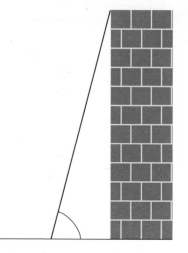

**PS 5** An obtuse angle is 10° more than an acute angle.
Write down a possible value for the size of the obtuse angle.

**AU 6** Which angle is the odd one out?

Give a reason for your answer.

a

b
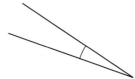

c

d
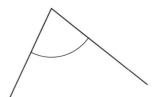

**7** Use a ruler and a protractor to draw these triangles accurately. Then measure the unmarked angle in each one.

a
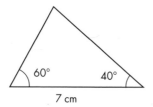
60°    40°
7 cm

b
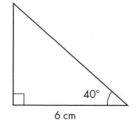
40°
6 cm

c
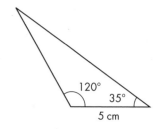
120°
35°
5 cm

# Angle facts

This section will show you how to:

- calculate angles on a straight line and angles around a point and use opposite angles

**Key words**

angles around a point

angles on a straight line

opposite angles

## Angles on a line

The **angles on a straight line** add up to 180°.

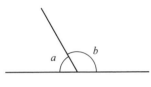

$a + b = 180°$

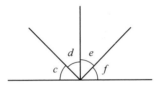

$c + d + e + f = 180°$

Draw an example for yourself (and measure $a$ and $b$) to show that the statement is true.

## Angles around a point

The sum of the **angles around a point** is 360°. For example:

$a + b + c + d + e = 360°$

Again, check this for yourself by drawing an example and measuring the angles.

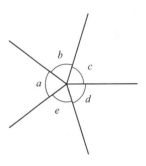

**EXAMPLE 2**

Find the size of angle $x$ in the diagram.

Angles on a straight line add up to 180°.

$$x + 72° = 180°$$

$$\text{So, } x = 180° - 72°$$

$$x = 108°$$

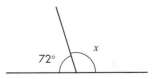

Sometimes equations can be used to solve angle problems.

**EXAMPLE 3**

Find the value of $x$ in the diagram.

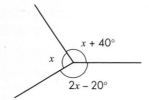

These angles are around a point, so they must add up to 360°.

Therefore, $x + x + 40° + 2x - 20° = 360°$

$$4x + 20° = 360°$$
$$4x = 340°$$
$$x = 85°$$

## Opposite angles

**Opposite angles** are equal.

So $a = c$ and $b = d$.

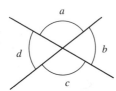

Sometimes opposite angles are called **vertically opposite angles**.

**EXAMPLE 4**

Find the value of $x$ in the diagram.

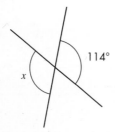

The two angles are opposite, so $x = 114°$.

**EXERCISE 8B**

Calculate the size of the angle marked $x$ in each of these examples.

**1**  **a**

132°  $x$

**b**

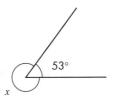
53°
$x$

**c**

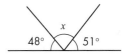
$x$   72°

**d**

38°  $x$

**e**

78°
$x$   43°

**f**

$x$
48°   51°

**g**

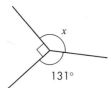
$x$
131°

**h**

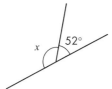
129°
$x$

**i**

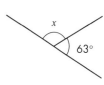
$x$
42°

**j**

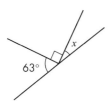
$x$   52°

**k**

313°
$x$

**l**

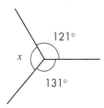
$x$
63°

**m**

$x$
63°

**n**

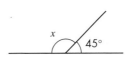
85°
$x$   50°

**o**

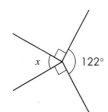
121°
$x$
131°

**p**

$x$   111°

**q**

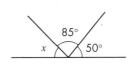
$x$
45°

**r**

$x$   122°

**F**

**s**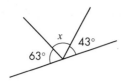

**t**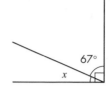

**u**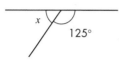

**v**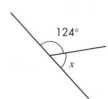

**2** Write down the value of *x* in each of these diagrams.

**a**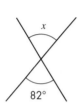

**b**

**c**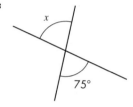

**AU 3** In the diagram, angle ABD is 45° and angle CBD is 125°.

Decide whether ABC is a straight line. Write down how you decided.

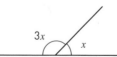

**E**

**4** Calculate the value of *x* in each of these examples.

**a**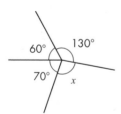

**b**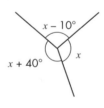

**c**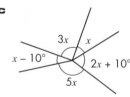

**5** Calculate the value of *x* in each of these examples.

**a**

**b**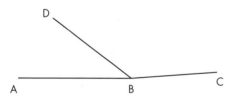

**c**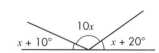

**6** Calculate the value of *x* first and then calculate the value of *y* in each of these examples.

**a**
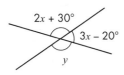
2*x* + 30°
3*x* − 20°
*y*

**b**
2*x* − 80°
*y*
*x* + 50°

**c**
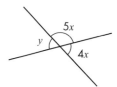
5*x*
*y*
4*x*

**AU 7** Ella has a collection of tiles. They are all equilateral triangles and are all the same size.

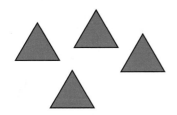

She says that six of the tiles will fit together and leave no gaps.

Explain why Ella is correct.

**PS 8** Work out the value of *y* in the diagram.

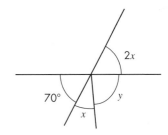
2*x*
70°
*y*
*x*

**8.3** # Angles in a triangle

**This section will show you how to:**
● calculate the size of angles in a triangle

**Key words**
angles in a triangle
equilateral triangle
exterior angle
interior angle
isosceles triangle
right-angled triangle

## ACTIVITY

### Angles in a triangle

You need a protractor.

Draw a triangle. Label the corners
(vertices) A, B and C.

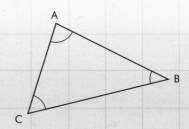

Use a ruler and make sure that the corners of your triangle form proper angles.

Like this.          Not like this ...          ... or  this.

Measure each angle, A, B and C.

Write them down and add them up:

Angle A  =  ......°

Angle B  =  ......°

Angle C  =  ......°

Total     =  ____

Repeat this for five more triangles, including at least one with an obtuse angle.

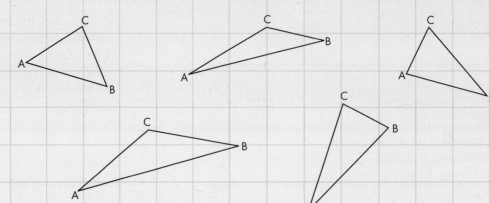

What conclusion can you draw about the sum of the angles in a triangle?

**Remember:**

You will not be able to measure with total accuracy.

You should have discovered that the three **angles in a triangle** add up to 180°.

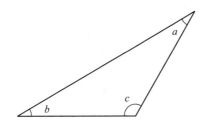

$a + b + c = 180°$

---

**EXAMPLE 5**

Calculate the size of angle *a* in the triangle below.

Angles in a triangle add up to 180°

Therefore, $a + 20° + 125° = 180°$

$$a + 145° = 180°$$

$$\text{So } a = 35°$$

---

## Special triangles

### Equilateral triangle

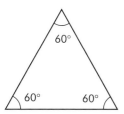

An **equilateral triangle** is a triangle with all its sides equal. Therefore, all three **interior angles** are 60°.

### Isosceles triangle

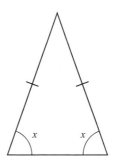

An **isosceles triangle** is a triangle with two equal sides and, therefore, with two equal interior angles (at the foot of the equal sides).

Notice how to mark the equal sides and equal angles.

### Right-angled triangle

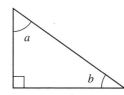

A **right-angled triangle** has an interior angle of 90°.
$a + b = 90°$

**EXERCISE 8C**

**1** Find the size of the angle marked with a letter in each of these triangles.

**a**

60°
50°
*a*

**b**

110°
*b*
20°

**c**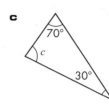

70°
*c*
30°

**d**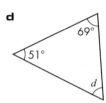

69°
51°
*d*

**e**

67°
*e*
38°

**f**

*f*
39°
32°

**g**

72°
70°
*g*

**h**

82°
*h*
35°

**2** Do any of these sets of angles form the three angles of a triangle? Explain your answer.

   **a** 35°, 75°, 80°                      **b** 50°, 60°, 70°

   **c** 55°, 55°, 60°                      **d** 60°, 60°, 60°

   **e** 35°, 35°, 110°                    **f** 102°, 38°, 30°

**3** Two interior angles of a triangle are given in each case. Find the third one indicated by a letter.

   **a** 20°, 80°, *a*                      **b** 52°, 61°, *b*

   **c** 80°, 80°, *c*                      **d** 25°, 112°, *d*

   **e** 120°, 50°, *e*                   **f** 122°, 57°, *f*

**4** In the triangle on the right, all the interior angles are the same.

   **a** What is the size of each angle?

   **b** What is the name of a special triangle like this?

   **c** What is special about the sides of this triangle?

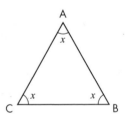

**5** In the triangle on the right, two of the angles are the same.

   **a** Work out the size of the lettered angles.

   **b** What is the name of a special triangle like this?

   **c** What is special about the sides AC and AB of this triangle?

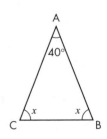

**AU** **6** In the triangle on the right, the angles at B and C are the same. Write down the size of the lettered angles.

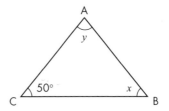

**7** Find the size of the **exterior angle** marked with a letter in each of these diagrams.

**a**

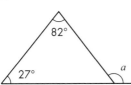

**b**

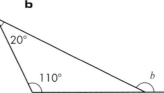

**c**

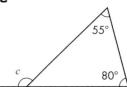

**FM** **8** A town planner has drawn this diagram to show three paths in a park but they have missed out the angle marked x.

Work out the value of x.

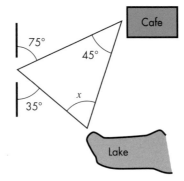

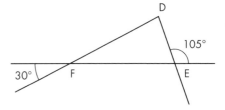

**PS** **9** What is the special name for triangle DEF?

Show all your working to explain your answer.

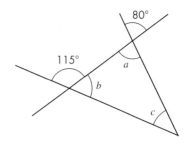

**AU** **10** The diagram shows three intersecting straight lines.

Work out the values of a, b and c.

Give reasons for your answers.

**11** By using algebra, show that x = a + b.

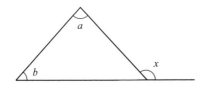

# Angles in a polygon

This section will show you how to:

- calculate the sum of the interior angles in a polygon

**Key words**

decagon
heptagon
hexagon
interior angle
nonagon
octagon
pentagon
polygon
quadrilateral

## ACTIVITY

### Angle sums from triangles

Draw a **quadrilateral** (a four-sided shape).
Draw in a diagonal to make it into two triangles.

You should be able to copy and complete this statement:

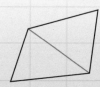

    The sum of the angles in a quadrilateral is equal to the sum of
    the angles in ...... triangles, which is ...... × 180° = ......°.

Now draw a **pentagon** (a five-sided shape).

Draw in the diagonals to make it into three triangles.

You should be able to copy and complete this statement:

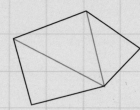

    The sum of the angles in a pentagon is equal to the
    sum of the angles in ...... triangles,
    which is ...... × 180° = ......°.

Next, draw a **hexagon** (a six-sided shape).

Draw in the diagonals to make it into four triangles.

You should be able to copy and complete this statement:

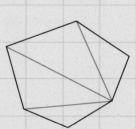

    The sum of the angles in a hexagon is equal to the sum of
    the angles in ...... triangles, which is ...... × 180° = ......°.

Now, complete the table below. Use the number pattern to carry on the angle sum up to a **decagon** (ten-sided shape).

| Shape | Number of sides | Triangles | Angle sum |
|---|---|---|---|
| triangle | 3 | 1 | 180° |
| quadrilateral | 4 | 2 | |
| pentagon | 5 | 3 | |
| hexagon | 6 | 4 | |
| heptagon | 7 | | |
| octagon | 8 | | |
| nonagon | 9 | | |
| decagon | 10 | | |

If you have spotted the number pattern, you should be able to copy and complete this statement:

The number of triangles in a 20-sided shape is ......, so the sum of the angles in a 20-sided shape is ...... × 180° = ......°.

So for an $n$-sided **polygon**, the sum of the **interior angles** is $180(n - 2)°$.

**EXAMPLE 6**

Calculate the size of angle $a$ in the quadrilateral below.

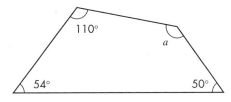

Angles in a quadrilateral add up to 360°.

Therefore, $a + 50° + 54° + 110° = 360°$

$a + 214° = 360°$

So, $a = 146°$

**EXERCISE 8D**

**1** Find the size of the angle marked with a letter in each of these quadrilaterals.

**a**

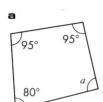

95° 95°
80° *a*

**b**

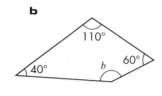

110°
40° *b* 60°

**c**

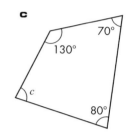

70°
130°
*c*
80°

**d**

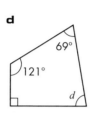

69°
121°
*d*

**e**

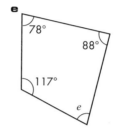

78°
88°
117°
*e*

**f**

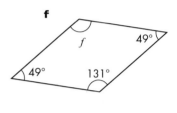

*f* 49°
49° 131°

**g**

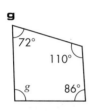

72°
110°
*g* 86°

**h**

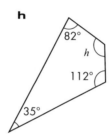

82°
*h*
112°
35°

> **HINTS AND TIPS**
>
> **Remember**, the sum of the interior angles of a quadrilateral is 360°.

**2** Do any of these sets of angles form the four interior angles of a quadrilateral? Explain your answer.

    **a** 135°, 75°, 60°, 80°             **b** 150°, 60°, 80°, 70°

    **c** 85°, 85°, 120°, 60°             **d** 80°, 90°, 90°, 110°

    **e** 95°, 95°, 60°, 110°             **f** 102°, 138°, 90°, 30°

**3** Three interior angles of a quadrilateral are given. Find the fourth one indicated by a letter.

    **a** 120°, 80°, 60°, *a*             **b** 102°, 101°, 90°, *b*

    **c** 80°, 80°, 80°, *c*               **d** 125°, 112°, 83°, *d*

    **e** 120°, 150°, 50°, *e*            **f** 122°, 157°, 80°, *f*

**4** In the quadrilateral on the right, all the angles are the same.

    **a** What is each angle?

    **b** What is the name of a special quadrilateral like this?

    **c** Is there another quadrilateral with all the angles the same? What is it called?

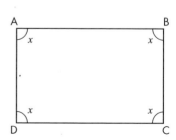

A                      B
*x*                     *x*
*x*                     *x*
D                      C

**5** Work out the size of the angle marked with a letter in each of the polygons below. You may find the table you completed on page 183 useful.

**a**

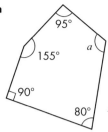

**b**

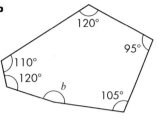

**c**

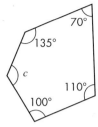

**d**

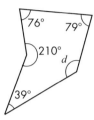

**e**

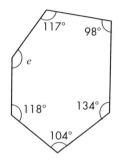

**f**

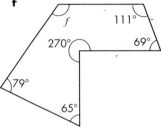

**g**

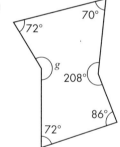

**h**

**HINTS AND TIPS**

**Remember**, the sum of the interior angles of an $n$-sided polygon is $180(n - 2)°$.

**FM 6** Anna is drawing this logo for a school magazine.

**HINTS AND TIPS**

First draw the four equilateral triangles on the diagram.

It is made up of four equilateral triangles that are all the same size.

She needs to know the sizes of the six angles so that she can draw it accurately.

What are the sizes of the six angles?

**D**

**PS** **7** This quadrilateral is made from two isosceles triangles.
They are both the same size.

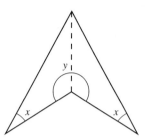

Find the value of $y$ in terms of $x$.

**AU** **8** The diagram shows the four angles in a quadrilateral.

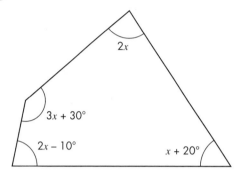

a Write down an equation in terms of $x$.

b Solve the equation and find the size of the smallest angle in the quadrilateral.

# Regular polygons

This section will show you how to:

- calculate the exterior angles and the interior angles of a regular polygon

Key words
exterior angle
interior angle
regular polygon

## ACTIVITY

### Regular polygons

To do this activity, you will need to have done the one on pages 182–183.

You will also need a calculator.

Below are five **regular polygons**.

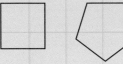   

| Square | Pentagon | Hexagon | Octagon | Decagon |
| 4 sides | 5 sides | 6 sides | 8 sides | 10 sides |

A polygon is regular if all its **interior angles** are equal and all its sides have the same length.

A square is a regular four-sided shape that has an angle sum of 360°.

So, each angle is 360° ÷ 4 = 90°.

A regular pentagon has an angle sum of 540°.

So, each angle is 540° ÷ 5 = 108°.

Copy and complete the table below.

| Shape | Number of sides | Angle sum | Each angle |
| --- | --- | --- | --- |
| square | 4 | 360° | 90° |
| pentagon | 5 | 540° | 108° |
| hexagon | 6 | 720° | |
| octagon | 8 | | |
| nonagon | 9 | | |
| decagon | 10 | | |

## Interior and exterior angles

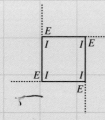 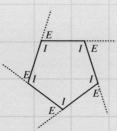 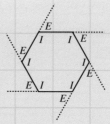

Look at these three regular polygons. At each vertex of each regular polygon, there is an interior angle, *I*, and an **exterior angle**, *E*. Notice that: $I + E = 180°$.

Clearly, the exterior angles of a square are each 90°. So, the sum of the exterior angles of a square is $4 \times 90° = 360°$.

You can calculate the exterior angle of a regular pentagon as follows. From the table on the previous page, you know that the interior angle of a regular pentagon is 108°.

108° \E     So, the exterior angle is $180° − 108° = 72°$.

Therefore, the sum of the exterior angles is $5 \times 72° = 360°$.

Now copy and complete the table below for regular polygons.

| Regular polygon | Number of sides | Interior angle | Exterior angle | Sum of exterior angles |
|---|---|---|---|---|
| square | 4 | 90° | 90° | $4 \times 90° = 360°$ |
| pentagon | 5 | 108° | 72° | $5 \times 72° =$ |
| hexagon | 6 | 120° | | |
| octagon | 8 | | | |
| nonagon | 9 | | | |
| decagon | 10 | | | |

From the table, you can see that the sum of the exterior angles is always 360°.

You can use this information to find the exterior angle and the interior angle for any regular polygon.

For an *n*-sided regular polygon, the exterior angle is given by $E = \dfrac{360°}{n}$

and the interior angle is given by $I = 180° − E$.

**EXAMPLE 7**

Calculate the size of the exterior and interior angle for a regular 12-sided polygon (a regular dodecagon).

$$E = \frac{360°}{12} = 30° \quad \text{and} \quad I = 180° - 30° = 150°$$

**EXERCISE 8E**

**1** Each diagram shows an interior angle of a regular polygon. For each polygon, answer the following.

**i** What is its exterior angle?

**ii** How many sides does it have?

**iii** What is the sum of its interior angles?

**a**  135°  **b** 160°  **c** 165°  **d** 144°

**2** Each diagram shows an exterior angle of a regular polygon. For each polygon, answer the following.

**i** What is its interior angle?

**ii** How many sides does it have?

**iii** What is the sum of its interior angles?

**HINTS AND TIPS**

**Remember** that the angle sum is calculated as (number of sides – 2) × 180°.

**a**  8°  **b** 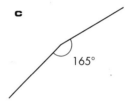 6°  **c** 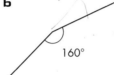 24°  **d** 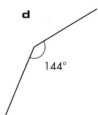 3°

**3** Each of these cannot be the interior angle of a regular polygon. Explain why.

**a**  173°  **b**  161°  **c**  169°  **d**  110°

**4** Each of these cannot be the exterior angle of a regular polygon. Explain why.

**a**
$7°$

**b**
$26°$

**c**
$44°$

**d**
$13°$

**5** Draw a sketch of a regular octagon and join each vertex to the centre.

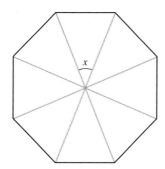

Calculate the value of the angle at the centre (marked $x$).

What connection does this have with the exterior angle?

Is this true for all regular polygons?

**FM** **6** A joiner is making tables so that the shape of each one is half a regular octagon, as shown in the diagram.

He needs to know the size of each angle on the table top.

What are the sizes of the angles?

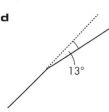

**PS** **7** This star shape has ten sides that are equal in length.

Each reflex interior angle is 200°.

Work out the size of each acute interior angle.

**AU** **8** The diagram shows part of a regular polygon.

Each interior angle is 144°.

**a** What is the size of each exterior angle of the polygon?

**b** How many sides does the polygon have?

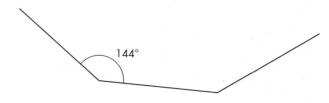

$144°$

# Parallel lines

This section will show you how to:
- find angles in parallel lines

**Key words**
allied angles
alternate angles
corresponding
    angles
interior angles

## ACTIVITY

### Angles in parallel lines

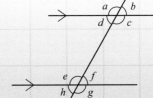

You need tracing paper or a protractor.

Draw two parallel lines about 5 cm apart and
a third line that crosses both of them.

The arrowheads indicate that the lines are parallel and
the line that crosses the parallel lines is called a *transversal.*

Notice that eight angles are formed. Label these *a*, *b*, *c*, *d*, *e*, *f*, *g* and *h*.

Measure or trace angle *a*. Find all the angles on the diagram that are the same size
as angle *a*.

Measure or trace angle *b*. Find all the angles on the diagram that are the same size
as angle *b*.

What is the sum of *a* + *b*?

Find all the pairs of angles on the diagram that add up to 180°.

Angles like these

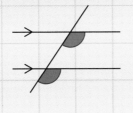

are called **corresponding angles**
(Look for the letter F).

Corresponding angles are equal.

Angles like these

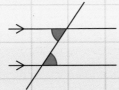

are called **alternate angles**
(Look for the letter Z).

Alternate angles are equal.

Angles like these are called **allied angles** or **interior angles** (Look for the letter C).

Allied angles add to 180°.

Copy and complete these statements to make them true.

1 Angles *h* and ...... are corresponding angles.

2 Angles *d* and ...... are alternate angles.

3 Angles *e* and ...... are allied angles.

4 Angles *b* and ...... are corresponding angles.

5 Angles *c* and ...... are allied angles.

6 Angles *c* and ...... are alternate angles.

Note that in examinations you should use the correct terms for types of angles. Do *not* call them F, Z or C angles as you will lose marks for quality of written communication.

**EXAMPLE 8**

State the size of each of the lettered angles in the diagram.

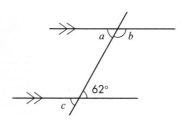

$a$ = 62° (alternate angle)

$b$ = 118° (allied angle or angles on a line)

$c$ = 62° (vertically opposite angle)

**EXERCISE 8F**

1. State the sizes of the lettered angles in each diagram.

**a**
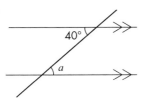

**b**
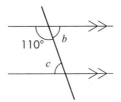

**c**
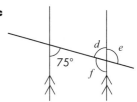

**d**
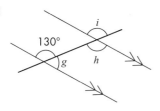

**e**
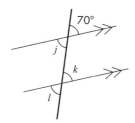

**f**
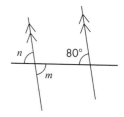

2. State the sizes of the lettered angles in each diagram.

**a**
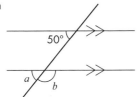

**b**
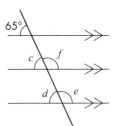

**c**
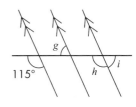

**d**
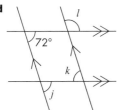

**e**
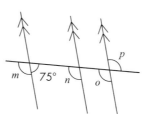

**f**
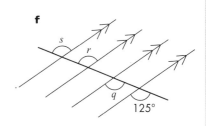

3. State the sizes of the lettered angles in these diagrams.

**a**
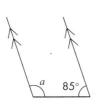

**b**
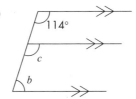

**D**

**4** Calculate the values of $x$ and $y$ in these diagrams.

**a**
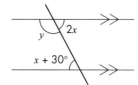

**b**
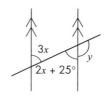

**c**
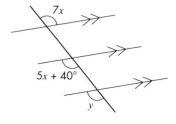

**5** Calculate the values of $x$ and $y$ in these diagrams.

**a**
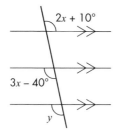

**b**
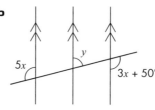

**c**
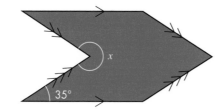

**FM 6** A company makes signs in the shape of a chevron.

This is one of their signs. It has one line of symmetry.

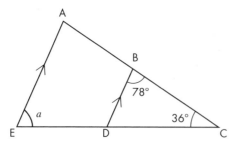

**HINTS AND TIPS**

Draw the line of symmetry on the shape first.

The designer for the company needs to know the size of the angle marked $x$ on the diagram.

Work out the size of angle $x$.

**PS 7** In the diagram, AE is parallel to BD.

Work out the size of angle $a$.

Give clear reasons as to how you obtained your answers.

**AU** **8** Lizzie is writing out a solution to this question.

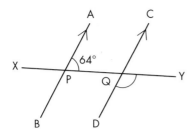

This is her solution.

> *Angle PQD = 64° (corresponding angles)*
>
> *So angle DQY = 124° (angles on a line = 190°)*

Lizzie has made a number of errors in her solution.

Write out a correct solution for the question.

**9** Use the diagram to prove that the three angles in a triangle add up to 180°.

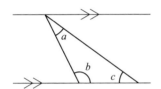

**10** Prove that $p + q + r = 180°$.

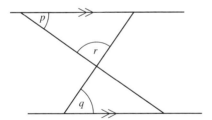

# Special quadrilaterals

**This section will show you how to:**
- use angle properties in quadrilaterals

**Key words**
kite
parallelogram
rhombus
trapezium

You should know the names of the following quadrilaterals, be familiar with their angle properties and know how to use the three-letter notation to describe any angle.

## Parallelogram

- A **parallelogram** has opposite sides parallel.

- Its opposite sides are equal.

- Its diagonals bisect each other.

- Its opposite angles are equal. That is:

    angle BAD = angle BCD
    angle ABC = angle ADC

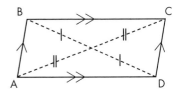

## Rhombus

- A **rhombus** is a parallelogram with all its sides equal.

- Its diagonals bisect each other at right angles.

- Its diagonals also bisect the angles.

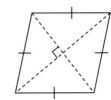

## Kite

- A **kite** is a quadrilateral with two pairs of equal adjacent sides.

- Its longer diagonal bisects its shorter diagonal at right angles.

- The opposite angles between the sides of different lengths are equal.

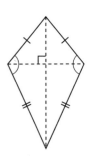

## Trapezium

- A **trapezium** has two parallel sides.

- The sum of the interior angles at the ends of each non-parallel side is 180°. That is:

    angle BAD + angle ADC = 180°
    angle ABC + angle BCD  = 180°

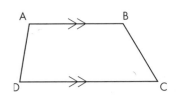

**EXERCISE 8G**

**D**

**1** For each of the trapeziums, calculate the sizes of the lettered angles.

**a**

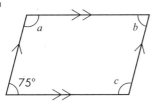

**b**

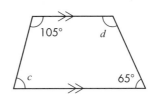

**c**

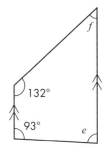

**2** For each of these parallelograms, calculate the sizes of the lettered angles.

**a**

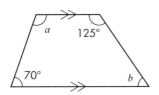

**b**

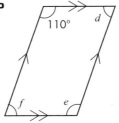

**c**

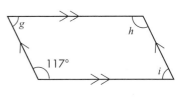

**3** For each of these kites, calculate the sizes of the lettered angles.

**a**

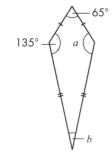

**b**

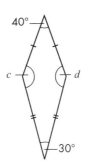

**c**

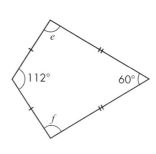

**4** For each of these rhombuses, calculate the sizes of the lettered angles.

**a**

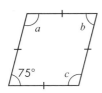

**b**

**c**

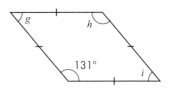

**5** For each of these shapes, calculate the sizes of the lettered angles.

**a**

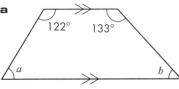

**b**

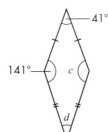

**c**

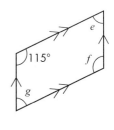

**D**

**6** Dani is making a kite.

She needs angle C to be half the size of angle A.

Work out the size of angles B and D.

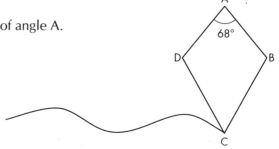

**AU 7**
**PS**
David says that a parallelogram is a special type of rectangle.

Marie says that he is wrong and that a rectangle is a special type of parallelogram.

Who is correct?

Give a reason for your answer.

**AU 8** The diagram shows a quadrilateral ABCD.

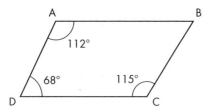

**a** Calculate the size of angle B.

**b** What special name is given to the quadrilateral ABCD? Explain your answer.

## 8.8 Bearings

| This section will show you how to: | Key words |
|---|---|
| • use a bearing to specify a direction | bearing |
| | three-figure bearing |

The **bearing** of a point B from a point A is the angle through which you turn *clockwise* as you change direction from *due north* to the direction of B.

For example, in this diagram the bearing of B from A is 060°.

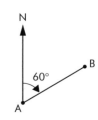

As a bearing can have any value from 0° to 360°, it is customary to give all bearings in three figures. This is known as a **three-figure bearing**. So, in the example on the previous page, the bearing is written as 060°, using three figures. Here are three more examples.

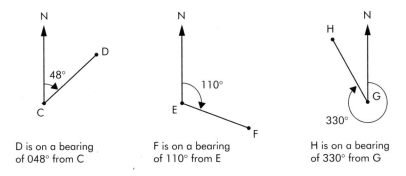

D is on a bearing
of 048° from C

F is on a bearing
of 110° from E

H is on a bearing
of 330° from G

There are eight bearings with which you should be familiar. They are shown in the diagram.

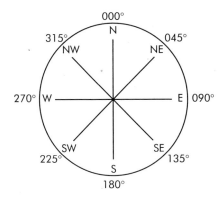

---

**EXAMPLE 9**

A, B and C are three towns.

a  Write down the bearing of B from A
and the bearing of C from A.

The bearing of B from A is 070°.

The bearing of C from A is
360° − 115° = 245°.

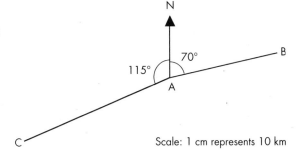

Scale: 1 cm represents 10 km

b  Use the scale to work out the
actual distances between
i  A and B      ii  A and C.

i   On the diagram AB is 3 cm, so the actual distance between A and B is 30 km.

ii  On the diagram AC is 4 cm, so the actual distance between A and C is 40 km.

## EXERCISE 8H

**D**

**1** Look at this map. By measuring angles, find the following bearings.

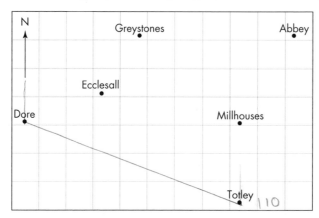

**a** Totley from Dore

**b** Dore from Ecclesall

**c** Millhouses from Dore

**d** Greystones from Abbey

**e** Millhouses from Greystones

**f** Totley from Millhouses

**2** Draw sketches to illustrate the following situations.

**a** Castleton is on a bearing of 170° from Hope.

**b** Bude is on a bearing of 310° from Wadebridge.

**3** A is due north from C. B is due east from A. B is on a bearing of 045° from C. Sketch the layout of the three points, A, B and C.

**4** Captain Bird decided to sail his ship around the four sides of a square kilometre.

**a** Assuming he started sailing due north, write down the further three bearings he would use in order to complete the square in a clockwise direction.

**b** Assuming he started sailing on a bearing of 090°, write down the further three bearings he would use in order to complete the square in an anticlockwise direction.

**5** The map shows a boat journey around an island, starting and finishing at S. On the map, 1 centimetre represents 10 kilometres. Measure the distance and bearing of each leg of the journey. Copy and complete the table below.

| Leg | Actual distance | Bearing |
|-----|-----------------|---------|
| 1   |                 |         |
| 2   |                 |         |
| 3   |                 |         |
| 4   |                 |         |
| 5   |                 |         |

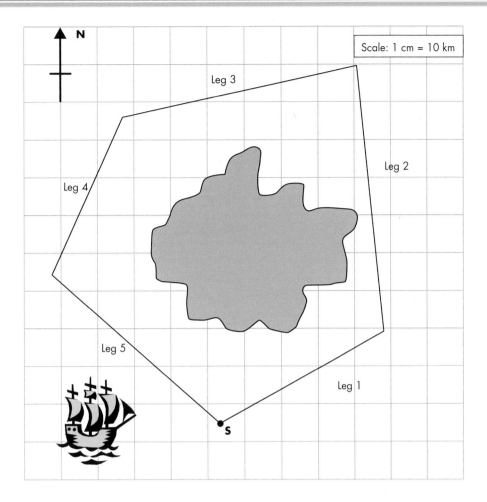

**6** The diagram shows a port *P* and two harbours *X* and *Y* on the coast.

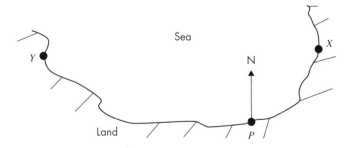

**a** A fishing boat sails to *X* from *P*.

What is the three-figure bearing of *X* from *P*?

**b** A yacht sails to *Y* from *P*.

What is the three-figure bearing of *Y* from *P*?

**D**

**7** Draw diagrams to solve the following problems.

    **a** The three-figure bearing of *A* from *B* is 070°. Work out the three-figure bearing of *B* from *A*.

    **b** The three-figure bearing of *P* from *Q* is 145°. Work out the three-figure bearing of *Q* from *P*.

    **c** The three-figure bearing of *X* from *Y* is 324°. Work out the three-figure bearing of *Y* from *X*.

**8** The diagram shows the position of Kim's house H and the college C.

Scale: 1 cm represents 200 m

    **a** Use the diagram to work out the actual distance from Kim's house to the college.

    **b** Measure and write down the three-figure bearing of the college from Kim's house.

    **c** The supermarket S is 600 m from Kim's house on a bearing of 150°.

       Mark the position of S on a copy of the diagram.

**FM 9** Trevor is flying a plane on a bearing of 072°.

He is instructed by a control tower to turn and fly due south towards an airport.

Through what angle does he need to turn?

**PS 10** Apple Bay (A), Broadside (B) and Caverly (C) are three villages in a bay.

The villages lie on the vertices of a square.

The bearing of B from A is 030°.

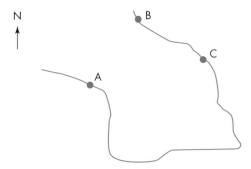

Work out the bearing of Apple Bay from Caverly.

## GRADE BOOSTER

**F** You can measure and draw angles

**F** You know that the sum of the angles on a line is 180°

**F** You know that the sum of the angles at a point is 360°

**E** You know that the sum of the angles in a triangle is 180°

**E** You know that the sum of the angles in a quadrilateral is 360°

**E** You can find the exterior angle of a triangle

**D** You can find angles in parallel lines

**D** You know all the properties of special quadrilaterals

**D** You can find interior and exterior angles in regular polygons

**D** You can use three-figure bearings

**C** You can use interior angles and exterior angles to find the number of sides in a regular polygon

### What you should know now

- How to measure and draw angles
- How to find angles on a line or at a point
- How to find angles in triangles, quadrilaterals and polygons
- How to find interior and exterior angles in polygons
- How to use bearings

**1** Here is a list of words connected with angles.

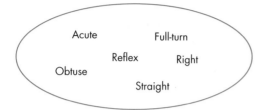

Acute      Full-turn

Reflex      Right

Obtuse

Straight

Choose the correct word to describe each
of these angles.                                    (4)

**a**

**b**

**c**

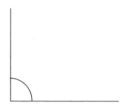

**d**

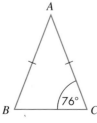

(Total 4 marks)

*AQA, June 2005, Paper 1 Foundation, Question 3*

**2** **a** Triangle $ABC$ is isosceles.

$AB = AC$

Angle $C = 76°$

*A*

Not drawn
accurately

*B*  76°  *C*

Calculate the size of angle $A$.        (2)

**b** Triangle ACD is also isosceles.

$AC = CD$

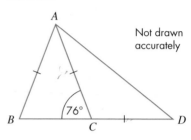

*A*

Not drawn
accurately

*B*  76°  *C*      *D*

Calculate the size of angle $D$.        (2)

(Total 4 marks)

*AQA, November 2007, Module 5, Paper 2 Intermediate,
Question 2(a), (b)*

**3** **a** Explain why the sum of the angles in
any quadrilateral is 360°.            (2)

**b** A quadrilateral has one right angle.
The other angles are $2x$, $3x - 12$ and $x - 6$

Not drawn
accurately

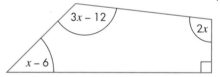

$3x - 12$

$2x$

$x - 6$

**i** Write down an equation in terms
of $x$.                            (1)

**ii** Solve your equation and find the size
of the largest angle in the
quadrilateral.                  (3)

(Total 6 marks)

*AQA, June 2007, Paper 1 Higher, Question 3*

**4** The standard quadrilaterals are

**Square**      **Rectangle**      **Parallelogram**

**Kite**         **Rhombus**        **Trapezium**

**a** Three different quadrilaterals have these two properties.

   Both pairs of opposite sides are equal.

   Rotational symmetry order 2

   Name the **three** quadrilaterals.          (2)

**b** Two of the quadrilaterals in part (a) also have this property.

   Diagonals do not cross at right angles.

   Name the **two** quadrilaterals.          (1)

**c** For one of the quadrilaterals in part (b), write down an extra property that will distinguish it from the other.          (1)

(Total 4 marks)

*AQA, November 2008, Paper 2 Foundation, Question 22*

**5** The diagram shows a scale drawing of one side, $AB$, of a triangular field, $ABC$.

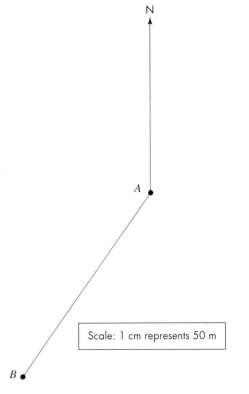

**a** Use the diagram to calculate the actual distance from $A$ to $B$.          (2)

**b** Measure and write down the three-figure bearing of $B$ from $A$.          (1)

**c** The bearing of $C$ from $A$ is 130°.

   The actual distance from $A$ to $C$ is 350 metres.

   Mark the point $C$ on the diagram.          (2)

(Total 5 marks)

*AQA, June 2005, Paper 1 Intermediate, Question 6(a), (b), (c)*

**6** **a** The diagram below shows a regular hexagon. One side has been extended and the **exterior** angle is $x$.

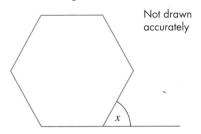

Not drawn accurately

Explain why angle $x$ is 60°.          (1)

**b** This diagram shows a regular octagon.

One of its **interior** angles is $y$.

Not drawn accurately

Calculate the value of $y$.          (3)

(Total 4 marks)

*AQA, November 2006, Paper 1 Higher, Question 1*

# Worked Examination Questions

**1** ABC is a triangle.
D is a point on AB such that BC = BD.

   **a** Work out the value of $x$.

   **b** Work out the value of $y$.

   **c** Is it true that AD = DC?
      Give a reason for your answer.

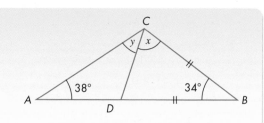

**a** Triangle BCD is isosceles, so angle BDC is also $x$.

   Angles in a triangle = 180°,

   so       $2x + 34° = 180°$

              $2x = 146°$

   So         $x = 73°$

> You get 1 mark for setting up an equation.

> $180 - 34 = 146$
> You get 1 mark for first step of solving the equation.

> You get 1 mark for the correct answer.

( 3 marks )

**b** Angle ADC = 180° − 73° = 107° (angles on a line)

      $y + 38° + 107° = 180°$ (angles in a triangle)

          $y + 145° = 180°$

   So           $y = 35°$

> You get 1 method mark for finding 107°.

> You get 1 mark for finding $y = 35°$.

( 2 marks )

**c** No, since triangle ACD is not an isosceles triangle.

> You get 1 mark for stating that triangle ACD is not an isosceles triangle.

( 1 mark )

( **Total:** 6 marks )

# Worked Examination Questions

**2** The lines AB and CD are parallel.

**a** Write down the value of $a$.
Give a reason for your answer.

**b** Write down the value of $b$.
Give a reason for your answer.

**c** Work out the value of $c$.
Give a reason for your answer.

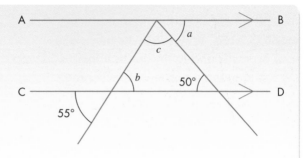

**a** $a = 50°$

It is an *alternate angle between* the parallel lines.

( 2 marks )

> Never measure the angles with a protractor as the diagrams in examinations are not drawn accurately.

> You get 1 accuracy mark for the correct answer.

**b** $b = 55°$

It is an *opposite angle* in two intersecting lines.

( 2 marks )

> You get 1 mark for a correct reason.
> Stating "It is a Z angle" is not acceptable in examinations. You must identify it as an alternate angle to get a mark for quality of written communication.

> You get 1 accuracy mark for the correct answer.

**c** $c = 75°$

The three angles in the triangle add up to 180°.

( 2 marks )

( **Total:** 6 marks )

> You get 1 mark for a correct reason.

> You get 1 accuracy mark for the correct answer.

> You get 1 mark for a correct reason.

Product designers will make a model of their product before the final product is manufactured. They use these models to trial products and to ensure that their design is suitable and fully-functioning.

In this task you are going to make a model of a chip holder, following instructions and using your knowledge of angles and properties of shapes to calculate unknown angles.

### Getting started

● What is an angle?
● If one of the angles in a triangle is 36°, what could the other two angles be?
● Name some quadrilaterals that have at least one pair of parallel sides.
   – How many can you name?
   – What other properties do they have?

### Your task

Alan owns a fish and chip shop. He uses plastic containers for his chips, but he wants to switch to paper holders. He has seen a design for a chip holder on the internet and thinks that it will work for him.

1 Follow the instructions to make the chip holder. Write a summary, giving the name of the shape, the effect of changing the size of the holder on the angles, and a description of how effective the holder would be.

2 Alan wants the chip holders to sit in a rack. To do this, he needs to work out the angles of his chip holder. However, he does not have a protractor.

   Use your knowledge of angles and properties of shape to calculate the angles for Alan. Then, design a rack to fit the chip holders. You must include the rack's dimensions, angles and at least two different elevations (views) of the final product design.

## Instructions for Alan's design

1 Fold a square piece of paper in half along its diagonal.

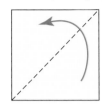 to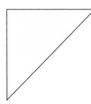

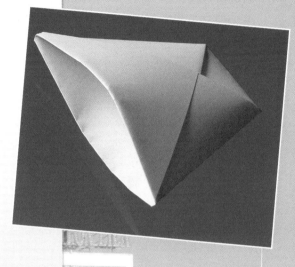

2 Turn the paper so that the longest side is along the bottom. Fold corner A to meet the opposite side, so that the top and bottom edges are parallel.

 to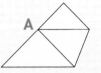

3 Fold corner B to meet point C.

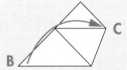 to

4 Fold the top layer down so that it lies over the folded sides.

5 Turn over and repeat step 4 for this side.

 to     to

**Extension**
- Find a way to check the angles that you have worked out.
- In step 2 of the instructions, you need to fold point A. There is a way to deduce the position to which you need to fold point A, without relying on estimating by eye. What is this and why does it work?

# Why this chapter matters

One of the most important numbers in mathematics is the ratio of the circumference of a circle to its diameter – also known as pi ($\pi$). Many formulae from mathematics, science and engineering involve this number. It has been found to be a constant, but its exact value has never been calculated.

Mathematicians (or philosophers, as they used to be known) since biblical times have attempted to accurately calculate the value of pi. This was difficult in the times before calculators! It was variously calculated to be 3 (which was almost certainly found by measurement), $4\frac{8}{9}^2$ (by the ancient Egyptians) and $\frac{22}{7}$ (by Archimedes).

However, the European Renaissance brought with it a whole new world of mathematics. By then, mathematicians had discovered formulae for calculating $\pi$. The only difficulty in computing $\pi$ was, and still is, the sheer tedium of continuing the calculation. Mathematicians devoted a vast amount of time and effort to this pursuit. In 1873 a mathematician called Shanks calculated $\pi$ to 707 places. Soon after this, another mathematician called De Morgan found that Shanks had made an error in the 528th place, after which all his digits were wrong!

In 1949, one of the first computers was used to calculate $\pi$ to 2000 places.

While the value of $\pi$ has been computed to more than a trillion digits, elementary applications, such as calculating the circumference of a circle, will rarely require more than a dozen decimal places. For example, the value of $\pi$ to 11 decimal places is accurate enough to calculate the circumference of a circle the size of the Earth with a precision of a millimetre. The value of $\pi$ to 39 decimal places is sufficient to calculate the circumference of any circle that fits in the observable universe to a precision comparable to the size of a hydrogen atom.

$\pi$ can help us calculate the circumference of the 'building blocks' of life, atoms (left) and Earth itself (above).

The value of $\pi$ to 200 decimal places is:

3.141 592 653 589 793 238 462 643 383 279 502 884 197 169 399 375 105 820 974 944 592 307 816 406 286 208 998 628 034 825 342 117 067 982 148 086 513 282 306 647 093 844 609 550 582 231 725 359 408 128 481 117 450 284 102 701 938 521 105 559 644 622 948 954 930 381 96

So far no one has spotted any patterns in the digits.

The current record for the highest number of decimals places for $\pi$ is 1 241 100 000 000, set by Yasumasa Kanada of Japan.

# Geometry: Circles

**1** Drawing circles

**2** The circumference of a circle

**3** The area of a circle

**4** Answers in terms of π

## This chapter will show you ...

to **G** **F** how to draw circles

**D** how to calculate the circumference of a circle

**D** how to calculate the area of a circle

**D** how to write answers in terms of π

### Visual overview

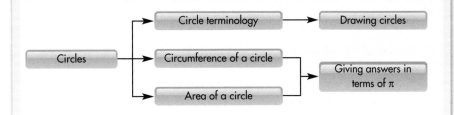

### What you should already know

- How to use a pair of compasses to draw a circle **(KS3 level 4, GCSE grade G)**
- The words 'radius' and 'diameter' **(KS3 level 4, GCSE grade G)**
- How to use a protractor to draw angles **(KS3 level 5, GCSE grade F)**
- How to round numbers to a given number of decimal places **(KS3 level 4, GCSE grade F)**
- How to find the square and square root of a number **(KS3 level 5, GCSE grade F)**

### Quick check

Write down the answer to each of the following, giving your answers to one decimal place.

**1** $5.21^2$      **2** $8.78^2$      **3** $15.5^2$

**4** $\sqrt{10}$      **5** $\sqrt{65}$      **6** $\sqrt{230}$

This section will show you how to:
- draw accurate circles
- draw diagrams made from circles

**Key words**

arc
centre
chord
circumference
diameter
radius
sector
segment
tangent

You need to know the following terms when dealing with circles.

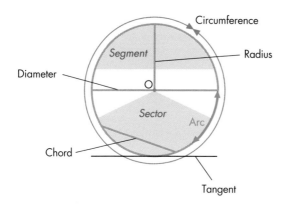

| | |
|---|---|
| **O** | The **centre** of a circle. |
| **Diameter** | The 'width' of a circle. Any diameter passes through O. |
| **Radius** | The distance from O to the edge of a circle. The length of the diameter is twice the length of the radius. |
| **Circumference** | The perimeter of a circle. |
| **Chord** | A line joining two points on the circumference. |
| **Tangent** | A line that touches the circumference at one point only. |
| **Arc** | A part of the circumference of a circle. |
| **Sector** | A part of the area of a circle, lying between two radii and an arc. |
| **Segment** | A part of the area of a circle, lying between a chord and an arc. |

**FM** Functional Maths   **AU** (AO2) Assessing Understanding   **PS** (AO3) Problem Solving

When drawing a circle, you first need to set your compasses to a given radius.

**EXAMPLE 1**

Draw a circle with a radius of 3 cm.

Set your compasses to a radius of 3 cm, as shown in the diagram.

Draw a circle and mark the centre O.

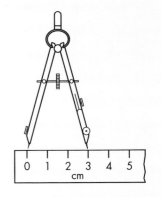

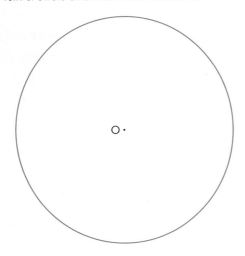

**EXERCISE 9A**

**1** Measure the radius of each of the following circles, giving your answers in centimetres. Write down the diameter of each circle.

a            b            c

**2** Draw circles with the following measurements.

    **a** radius = 2 cm                **b** radius = 3.5 cm

    **c** diameter = 8 cm            **d** diameter = 10.6 cm

**AU 3** The centre of this circle is O and the four points A, B, C and D are on the circumference.

Here are some words that are used with circles.

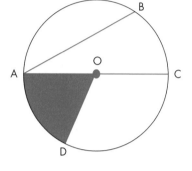

| chord | circumference | diameter |
|-------|---------------|----------|
| radius | sector | segment |
| tangent | | |

Use a different one of these words to complete each of these sentences.

    **a** The line AC is a …

    **b** The line AB is a  …

    **c** The line OD is a …

    **d** The shaded part is a …

**4** Draw the following shapes accurately.

**a**

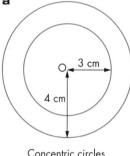

Concentric circles

**b**

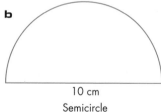

10 cm
Semicircle

**c**

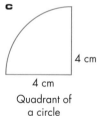

4 cm

4 cm
Quadrant of a circle

**5** Draw accurate copies of these diagrams.

**a**

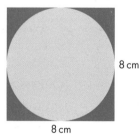

8 cm

8 cm

**b**

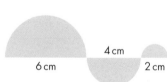

4 cm

6 cm

2 cm

**c**

5 cm

5 cm

**6** **a** Draw a circle of radius 4 cm.

   **b** Keeping your compasses set to a radius of 4 cm, step round the circle making marks on the circumference that are 4 cm apart.

   **c** Join the points with a pencil and ruler to make a polygon.

   **d** What name is given to the polygon you have drawn?

**PS 7** **a** Draw a circle of radius 4 cm.

   **b** Draw a tangent at any point on the circumference.

   **c** Draw a radius to meet the tangent.

   **d** Measure the angle between the tangent and the radius.

   **e** Repeat the exercise for circles with different radii.

   **f** Write down what you have found out about a radius touching a tangent at a point.

**PS 8** The shape in the diagram is made from three identical semicircles.

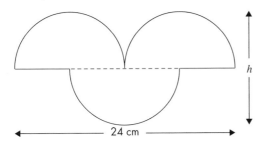

24 cm

$h$

   **a** Work out the radius of one of the semicircles.

   **b** Work out the height, $h$, marked on the diagram.

**9.2**

# The circumference of a circle

**This section will show you how to:**
- calculate the circumference of a circle

**Key words**
$\pi$ (pronounced pi)
circumference
diameter
radius

## Round and round

Find six cylindrical objects – bottles, cans, tubes, or piping will do. You also need about 2 m of string.

Copy this table so that you can fill it in as you do this activity.

| Object number | Diameter | Circumference | Circumference Diameter |
|---|---|---|---|
| 1 | | | |
| 2 | | | |
| 3 | | | |
| 4 | | | |
| 5 | | | |
| 6 | | | |

Measure, as accurately as you can, the **diameter** of the first object. Write this measurement in your table.

Wrap the string around the object 10 times, as shown in the diagram. Make sure you start and finish along the *same line*. Mark clearly the point on the string where the tenth wrap ends.

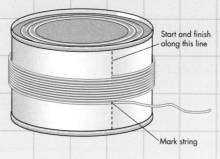

Start and finish along this line

Mark string

Then measure, as accurately as you can, the length of your 10 wraps. This should be the distance from the start end of the string to the mark you made on it.

Next, divide this length of string by 10. You have now found the length of the **circumference** of the first object. Write this in the table.

Repeat this procedure for each of the remaining objects.

Finally, complete the last column in the table by using your calculator to divide the circumference by the diameter. In each case, round your answer to two decimal places.

If your measurements have been accurate, all the numbers you get should be about 3.14.

This is the well-known number that is represented by the Greek letter $\pi$. You can obtain a very accurate value for $\pi$ by pressing the $\boxed{\pi}$ key on your calculator. Try it and see how close your numbers are to it.

You calculate the circumference, $C$, of a circle by multiplying its diameter, $d$, by $\pi$, and then rounding your answer to one or two decimal places.

The value of $\pi$ is found on all scientific calculators, with $\pi = 3.141\,592\,654$, but if it is not on your calculator, then take $\pi = 3.142$.

The circumference of a circle is given by the formula:

circumference $= \pi \times$ diameter    *or*    $C = \pi d$

As the diameter is twice the **radius**, $r$, this formula can also be written as $c = 2\pi r$.

---

**EXAMPLE 2**

Calculate the circumference of the circle with a diameter of 4 cm.

Use the formula:

$C = \pi d$

$\quad = \pi \times 4$

$\quad = 12.6$ cm (rounded to 1 decimal place)

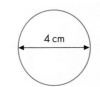

**Remember** The length of the radius of a circle is half the length of its diameter. So, when you are given a radius, in order to find a circumference you must first *double* the radius to get the diameter.

---

**EXAMPLE 3**

Calculate the diameter of a circle that has a circumference of 40 cm.

$C = \pi \times d$

$40 = \pi \times d$

$d = \dfrac{40}{\pi} = 12.7$ cm (rounded to 1 decimal place)

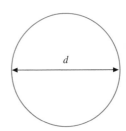

**D**

**1** Calculate the circumference of each circle illustrated below. Give your answers to 1 decimal place.

**a**
8 cm

**b**
5 cm

**c**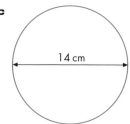
14 cm

**d**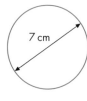
7 cm

**e**
6 cm

**f**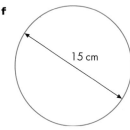
15 cm

**g**
9.2 cm

**h**
4.7 cm

**2** Find the circumference of each of the following coins. Give your answers to 1 decimal place.

**a** 1p coin, diameter 2 cm

**b** 2p coin, diameter 2.6 cm

**c** 5p coin, diameter 1.7 cm

**d** 10p coin, diameter 2.4 cm

**3** Calculate the circumference of each circle illustrated below. Give your answers to 1 decimal place.

**HINTS AND TIPS**

**Remember** to double the radius to find the diameter, or use the formula $C = 2\pi r$.

**a**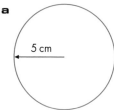
5 cm

**b**
3 cm

**c**
1.5 cm

**d**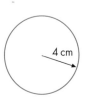
4 cm

**e**
0.9 cm

**f**
2.5 cm

**g**
13 cm

**h**
6.3 cm

**4** The radius of the wheels on Tim's bike is 31.5 cm.

    **a** Calculate the circumference of one of the wheels. Give your answer to the nearest centimetre.

    **b** Tim rides his bike for 1 km. How many complete revolutions does each wheel make?

**FM 5** The diagram represents a race-track on a school playing field. The diameter of each circle is shown.

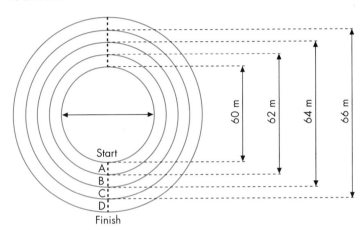

In a race with four runners, each runner starts and finishes on the same inner circle of their lane after completing one circuit.

    **a** Calculate the distance run by each runner in their lane.

    **b** How much further than A does D have to run?

**6** A rope is wrapped eight times round a capstan (cylindrical post), the diameter of which is 35 cm. How long is the rope?

**AU 7** A hamster has a treadmill of diameter 12 cm.

    **a** What is the circumference of the treadmill?

    **b** How many centimetres has the hamster run when the wheel has made 100 complete revolutions?

    **c** Change the answer to part **b** into metres.

    **d** One night, the hamster runs and runs and runs. He turns the wheel 100 000 times. How many kilometres has he run?

**8** A circle has a circumference of 314 cm. Calculate the diameter of the circle.

**9** What is the diameter of a circle if its circumference is 76 cm? Give your answer to 1 decimal place.

**10** What is the radius of a circle with a circumference of 100 cm? Give your answer to 1 decimal place.

**AU** **11** A semicircular protractor has a diameter of 10 cm.

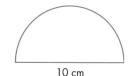

10 cm

Which of the following is the correct length for the perimeter of the protractor?

**a** 15.7 cm      **b** 25.7 cm      **c** 31.4 cm      **d** 41.4 cm

**12** Assume that the human waist is circular.

   **a** What are the distances round the waists of the following people?

   Sue: waist radius of 10 cm            Dave: waist radius of 12 cm

   Julie: waist radius of 11 cm          Brian: waist radius of 13 cm

   **b** Compare differences between pairs of waist circumferences. What connection do they have to π?

   **c** What would be the difference in length between a rope stretched tightly round the Earth and another rope always held 1 m above it?

**13** **a** Calculate the perimeter of each of shapes A and B.

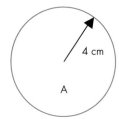

4 cm

A

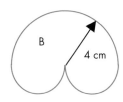

B

4 cm

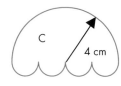

C

4 cm

   **b** Write down the perimeter of shape C.

**PS** **14** A square has sides of length *a* and a circle has radius *r*.

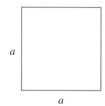

*a*

*a*

*r*

The perimeter of the square is equal to the circumference of the circle.

Show that $r = \dfrac{2a}{\pi}$

**FM** **15** Ben works in a park and wants to buy enough fencing to go round a semicircular flowerbed that has a diameter of 8 m.

The fencing is sold in 2-m lengths. How many lengths does Ben need?

# The area of a circle

This section will show you how to:
- calculate the area of a circle

**Key words**

$\pi$

area

diameter

radius

The **area**, $A$, of a circle is given by the formula:

$$\text{area} = \pi \times \textbf{radius}^2 \quad or \quad A = \pi \times r \times r \quad or \quad A = \pi r^2$$

**Remember**   This formula uses the radius of a circle. So, when you are given the **diameter** of a circle, you must *halve* it to get the radius.

---

**EXAMPLE 4**

**Radius given**

Calculate the area of a circle with a radius of 7 cm.

$$
\begin{aligned}
\text{Area} &= \pi r^2 \\
&= \pi \times 7^2 \\
&= \pi \times 49 \\
&= 153.9 \text{ cm}^2 \text{ (rounded to 1 decimal place)}
\end{aligned}
$$

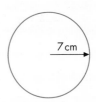

7 cm

---

**EXAMPLE 5**

**Diameter given**

Calculate the area of a circle with a diameter of 12 cm.

First, halve the diameter to get the radius:

$$\text{radius} = 12 \div 2 = 6 \text{ cm}$$

Then, find the area:

$$
\begin{aligned}
\text{area} &= \pi r^2 \\
&= \pi \times 6^2 \\
&= \pi \times 36 \\
&= 113.1 \text{ cm}^2 \text{ (rounded to 1 decimal place)}
\end{aligned}
$$

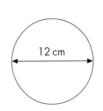

12 cm

**EXERCISE 9C**

**D**

**1** Calculate the area of each circle illustrated below. Give your answers to 1 decimal place.

**a**

5 cm

**b**
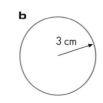
3 cm

**c**
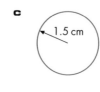
1.5 cm

**d**
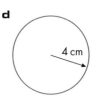
4 cm

**e**
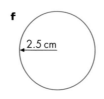
0.9 cm

**f**

2.5 cm

**g**
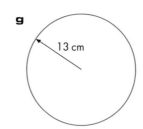
13 cm

**h**
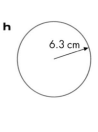
6.3 cm

**2** Find the area of one face of the following coins. Give your answers to 1 decimal place.

  **a**  1p coin, radius 1 cm

  **b**  2p coin, radius 1.3 cm

  **c**  5p coin, radius 0.85 cm

  **d**  10p coin, radius 1.2 cm

**3** Calculate the area of each circle illustrated below.
Give your answers to 1 decimal place.

**HINTS AND TIPS**

**Remember** to halve the diameter to find the radius. The only formula for the area of a circle is $A = \pi r^2$.

**a**

8 cm

**b**
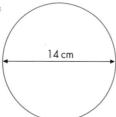
5 cm

**c**
14 cm

**d**

7 cm

**e**

6 cm

**f**
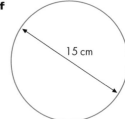
15 cm

**g**
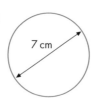
9.2 cm

**h**

4.7 cm

**D**

**AU 4** Milk-bottle tops are stamped from rectangular strips as shown.

Each milk-bottle top is made from a circle of radius 1.7 cm.
Each rectangular strip measures 4 cm by 500 cm.

**a** What is the area of one milk-bottle top?

**b** How many milk-bottle tops can be stamped out of one strip 500 cm long when there is a 0.2 cm gap between adjacent tops?

**c** What is the area of the rectangular strip?

**d** What will be the total area of all the milk-bottle tops stamped out of the one strip?

**e** What waste is produced by one stamping?

**FM 5** A young athlete can throw the discus a distance of 35 m but is never too sure of the direction in which he will throw it. What area of the field should be closed while he is throwing the discus?

**6** Calculate **i** the circumference and **ii** the area of each of these circles. Give your answers to 1 decimal place.

**a**
9 cm

**b**
22 cm

**c**
6.5 cm

**d**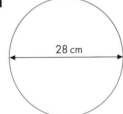
28 cm

**7** A circle has a circumference of 60 cm.

**a** Calculate the diameter of the circle to 1 decimal place.

**b** What is the radius of the circle to 1 decimal place?

**c** Calculate the area of the circle to 1 decimal place.

**8** Calculate the area of a circle with a circumference of 110 cm.

**HINTS AND TIPS**

Because π can be taken as 3.14 or 3.142, answers need not be exact. Examiners usually accept a range of answers.

**C**

**9** Calculate the area of the following shapes. Give your answers to 1 decimal place.

**a**

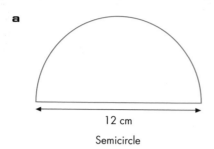

12 cm

Semicircle

**b**

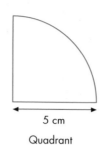

5 cm

Quadrant

**10** Calculate the area of the shaded part of each of these diagrams.

**a**

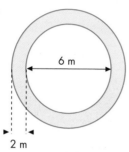

6 m

2 m

**b**

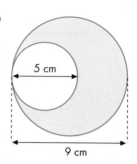

5 cm

9 cm

**HINTS AND TIPS**

In each diagram, subtract the area of the small circle from the area of the large circle.

**c**

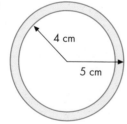

4 cm

5 cm

**11** The diagram shows a circular photograph frame.

Work out the area of the frame. Give your answer to 1 decimal place.

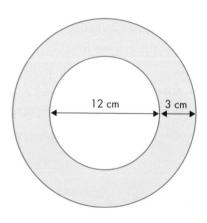

12 cm  3 cm

PS **12** A square has sides of length $a$ and a circle has radius $r$.

The area of the square is equal to the area of the circle.

Show that $r = \dfrac{a}{\sqrt{\pi}}$

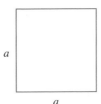

AU **13** A circle fits exactly inside a square of sides 10 cm.

Calculate the area of the shaded region. Give your answer to 1 decimal place.

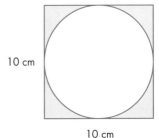

10 cm

10 cm

# 9.4 Answers in terms of π

**This section will show you how to:**

● give answers for circle calculations in terms of π

**Key words**

π
area
circumference
diameter
radius

There are times when you do not want a numerical answer to a circle problem but need to give the answer in terms of π. (The numerical answer could be evaluated later.)

## EXAMPLE 6

What are the **circumference** and **area** of this circle?

Leave your answers in terms of π.

$\text{Circumference} = \pi d = \pi \times 14 = 14\pi$ cm

$\text{Area} = \pi r^2 = \pi \times 7^2 = \pi \times 49 = 49\pi$ cm$^2$

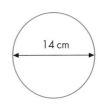

14 cm

If a question asks you to leave an answer in terms of π, it is most likely to be on the non-calculator paper and hence saves you the trouble of using your calculator.

However, if you did, and calculated the numerical answer, you could well lose a mark.

**EXERCISE 9D**

In this exercise, all answers should be given in terms of $\pi$.

**1** A circle has diameter 10 cm.

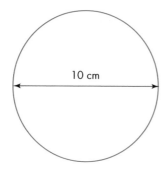

10 cm

State the circumference of the circle.

**2** State the circumference of each of the following circles.

    **a** diameter 4 cm

    **b** radius 10 cm

    **c** diameter 15 cm

    **d** radius 2 cm

**3** State the area of each of the following circles.

    **a** radius 4 cm

    **b** diameter 10 cm

    **c** radius 3 cm

    **d** diameter 18 cm

**4** State the radius of the circle with a circumference of $50\pi$ cm.

**5** State the radius of the circle with an area of $100\pi$ cm$^2$.

**6** State the diameter of a circle with a circumference of 200 cm.

**7** State the radius of a circle with an area of 25 cm$^2$.

**8** Work out the area for each of the following shapes, giving your answers in terms of π.

**a**

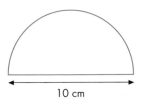

10 cm

**b**

8 cm

**c**

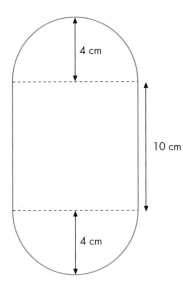

4 cm

10 cm

4 cm

**d**

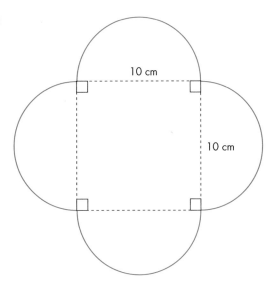

10 cm

10 cm

**9**  **a** Work out the area of a semicircle with radius 8 cm.

8 cm

**b** Work out the area of two semicircles with radii 4 cm.

4 cm

**c** Work out the area of four semicircles with radii 2 cm.

2 cm

**d** By looking at the pattern of areas of the answers to **a**, **b** and **c**, write down the area of eight semicircles with radii 1 cm.

**FM 10** The diagram shows a plan of Mr Green's garden.

The flowerbed is in the shape of a semicircle and has a diameter of 8 m.

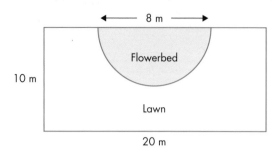

**a** Work out the area of the lawn, giving your answer in terms of π.

**b** His local garden centre sells grass seed in 500 g packets.

If 1 kg of grass seed covers up to 20 m$^2$, how many packets does he need to buy?

**PS 11** A circle fits exactly inside a semicircle of diameter 12 cm.

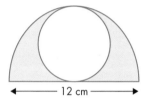

Find the area of the shaded region, giving your answer in terms of π.

**AU 12** A shape is made from a rectangle and a quadrant of a circle.

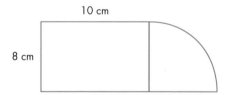

Which of these is the correct value of the area of the shape?

**a** $(80 + 4\pi)$ cm$^2$

**b** $(80 + 8\pi)$ cm$^2$

**c** $(80 + 16\pi)$ cm$^2$

**d** $(80 + 32\pi)$ cm$^2$

## GRADE BOOSTER

**G** You know all the words associated with circles

**G** You can draw a circle if you know the radius

**F** You can draw shapes made from circles

**D** You can calculate the circumference of a circle

**D** You can calculate the area of a circle

**C** You can calculate perimeters and areas of compound shapes made with circles

### What you should know now

- How to draw circles
- All the words associated with circles
- How to calculate the circumference of a circle
- How to calculate the area of a circle

**1** In each diagram, $O$ is the centre of the circle.

**a** Draw a diameter on a copy of this circle. (1)

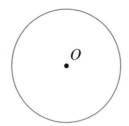

**b** Draw a tangent on a copy of this circle, at $T$. (1)

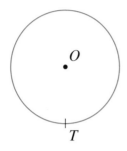

**c** A chord $PQ$ has been drawn on the circle below.

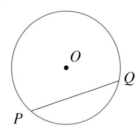

  **i** Mark the midpoint of $PQ$ and label it $M$. (1)

  **ii** Join $OM$.

   What do you notice about the angle between $OM$ and $PQ$? (1)

(Total 4 marks)

*AQA, June 2008, Module 5 Foundation, Question 4*

**2** $O$ is the centre of the circle.

$A$ and $B$ are two points on the circumference.

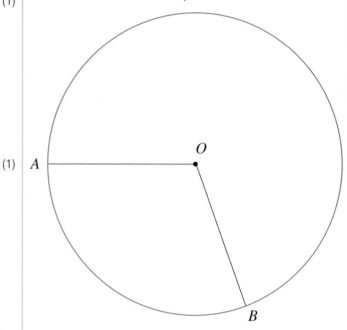

**a** Measure and write down the radius of the circle. (1)

**b** Measure and write down the size of the angle $AOB$. (1)

**c** Draw the line of symmetry of the sector $AOB$. (1)

**d** Draw the tangent to the circle at $A$. (1)

**e** Draw the chord $AB$. (1)

(Total 5 marks)

*AQA, November 2008, Paper 2 Foundation, Question 4*

**3** A wheel of a bicycle is shown.

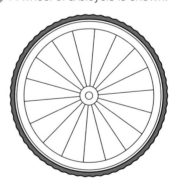

**a** The circumference is 70 cm.

Calculate the diameter. (2)

C  D  F  G

**b** The bicycle travels 50 metres.

How many complete revolutions does the wheel make? (3)

(Total 5 marks)

*AQA, November 2008, Module 5 Higher, Question 1*

  **4** The diagram shows a circle of radius 5.4 metres.

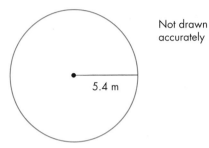

Not drawn accurately

5.4 m

Calculate the area of the circle.

State the units of your answer. (3)

(Total 3 marks)

*AQA, June 2008, Module 5 Foundation, Question 16*

**5**

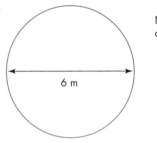

Not drawn accurately

6 m

Calculate the area of a circle of diameter 6 metres.

Give your answer in terms of $\pi$. (2)

(Total 2 marks)

 **6** The diagram shows a running track, made up of a rectangle plus two semicircles.

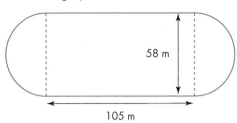

58 m

105 m

Not drawn accurately

Joel runs once round the perimeter of the track.

How far does he run? (4)

(Total 4 marks)

*AQA, June 2007, Module 5 Foundation, Question 16*

**7** The diagram shows a square and two quarter circles.

The square has sides of 6 cm.

The radius of each circle is 3 cm.

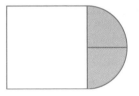

Not drawn accurately

**a** Find the area of the shaded region. (3)

**b** Jane says that because a square has four lines of symmetry, the shaded area also has four lines of symmetry.

Is Jane correct?

Give a reason for your answer. (1)

(Total 4 marks)

*AQA, June 2009, Paper 2 Foundation, Question 24*

## Worked Examination Questions

**1**  A circular pond has a radius of 2.2 m.

    **a**  Calculate the circumference of the pond.

    **b**  Calculate the area of the pond.

**a**  $r = 2.2$, so $d = 4.4$ m

    $c = \pi d$

       $= \pi \times 4.4$ — 1 method mark is available for setting up an equation.

       $= 13.8$ m (1 decimal place) — You get 1 mark for accuracy for the correct answer.

2 marks

**b**  $A = \pi r^2$

       $= \pi \times 2.2^2$ — 1 method mark is available for the first step of solving the equation. $\pi \times 4.84$ would also be acceptable.

       $= \pi \times 4.84$

       $= 15.2$ m$^2$ (1 decimal place) — You get 1 mark for accuracy for the correct answer.

2 marks

**Total:** 4 marks

In an examination, the answers could be given to any number of decimal places as the question does not state the accuracy required.

**2**  A semicircular flowerbed has a diameter of 2.6 m.

Calculate the area of the flowerbed.

Give your answer to one decimal place.

State the units of your answer.

Area of whole circle is $\pi \times 1.3^2$ — You get 1 method mark for setting up an equation, remembering to halve the diameter.

So area of semicircle is $\pi \times \dfrac{1.3^2}{2}$ — You get 1 method mark for realising that the area of a semicircle must therefore divide $\pi \times 1.3^2$ by 2. You must write this equation down to get the mark. Now work this out on your calculator.

Area = 2.6546 ... — You get 1 mark for accuracy for the answer to this equation. Now round the answer from your calculator display.

Area = 2.7 — You get 1 mark for accuracy for the correct, rounded answer.

Area = 2.7 m$^2$ — You can get 1 mark is given for the correct units, even if the answer is wrong.

**Total:** 5 marks

## Worked Examination Questions

**PS** **3** Four identical circles fit exactly in a square with side length $x$.

Work out the area of the shaded region.

Give your answer in terms of $\pi$.

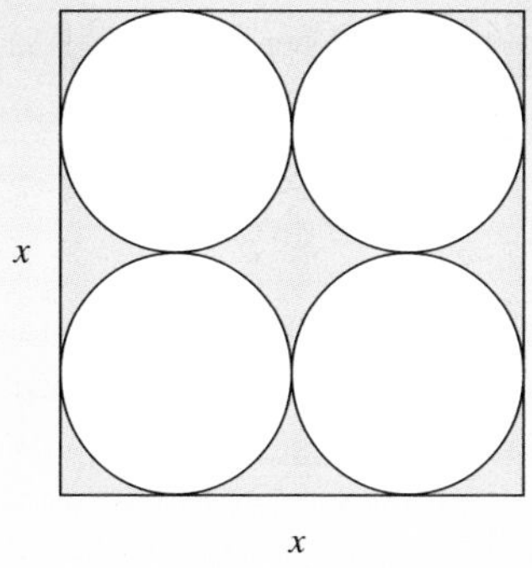

Area of square = $x^2$

Radius of each circle = $\dfrac{x}{4}$

> You get 2 method marks for writing down the correct formulas.

Area of each circle = $\dfrac{\pi x^2}{16}$

> You get 1 method mark for setting up the calculation to find the area of the circles.
>
> Note $\dfrac{x}{4} \times \dfrac{x}{4} = \dfrac{x^2}{16}$

Area of four squares = $\dfrac{\pi x^2}{4}$

So area of shaded region = $x^2 - \dfrac{\pi x^2}{4}$

> You get 1 method mark for setting up the calculation to find the area of the squares.
>
> Note $4 \times \dfrac{\pi x^2}{16} = \dfrac{\pi x^2}{4}$

**Total:** 5 marks

> You get 1 mark for accuracy for the final calculation. Note that if you make one error in the solution, then you would only lose 1 mark.

Circular shapes form the basis of many of the objects that we see and use every day. For example, we see circular shapes in DVDs, wheels, coins and jewellery. Where else do you see circles?

Given how frequently circles appear in our lives, it is important that we understand them mathematically.

In this task you will investigate angles in circles, using mathematical investigation to help you understand this shape more fully.

### Getting started

- List the mathematical vocabulary that you know, that is related to circles. Explain each of the words you think of to a classmate.
- Select one fact that you know, that is related to circles. Explain your fact to your partner.
- Select a real-life object that is in the shape of a circle.

  What mathematical questions could you ask about this object?

**Your task**

Here are four statements about circles.

1 The sum of the opposite angles of a cyclic quadrilateral is 180°.

So, angles $a + c = 180°$ and angles $b + d = 180°$.

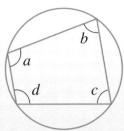

2 A radius bisects a chord at 90°.

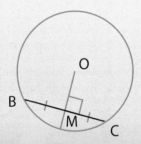

**Your task (continued)**

3 An angle subtended by a chord at the centre is twice the angle subtended by the chord at the circumference. So, angle $b$ is twice the size of angle $a$.

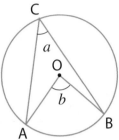

4 Angles subtended at the circumference in the same segment of a circle are equal.

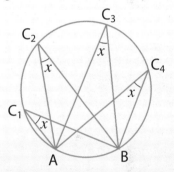

(You might like to think about what's special about angles subtended by the diameter)

Working in pairs, choose one or two of these statements and show whether you think it is true or false.

Write a presentation to explain your findings to the class. In your presentation you must:

- describe the approach that you took to the investigation
- explain your findings
- represent your findings mathematically, using expressions and diagrams
- support your findings with suitable measurements, calculations and diagrams
- explain what is meant by mathematical 'truth'.

# Why this chapter matters

You see transformations every day whether it is a reflection in a mirror or a miniature version of an object. 2D shapes can also be transformed. The activity below will give you a chance to try a transformation yourself.

## How many sides does a strip of paper have?

Take a strip of paper, about 20 cm by 2 cm.

How many sides does it have? Easy! You can see that this has two sides, a top and an underside. If you were to draw a line along one side of the strip, you would have one side with a line 20 cm long on it and one side blank.

Now mark the ends A and B and put a single twist in the strip of paper and tape (or glue) the two ends together as shown.

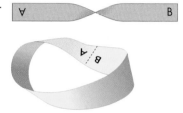

How many sides does this strip of paper have now?

Take a pen and draw a line on the paper, starting at any point you like. Continue the line along the length of the paper – you will eventually come back to your starting point. Your strip has only one side now. There is no blank side.

You have transformed a two-sided piece of paper into a one-sided piece of paper.

This curious shape is called a Möbius strip. It is named after August Ferdinand Möbius, a 19th century German mathematician and astronomer. Möbius, along with others, caused a revolution in geometry.

Möbius strips have a number of surprising applications that exploit this remarkable property of one-sidedness, including conveyer belts in industry as well as in domestic vacuum cleaners.

The Möbius strip has become the universal symbol of recycling. The symbol was created in 1970 by Gary Anderson, who was a senior at the University of Southern California, as part of a contest sponsored by a paper company.

The Möbius strip is one form of transformation. In this chapter, you will look at some other transformations of shapes.

This conveyor belt is used in salt mining.

# Geometry: Transformations

**1** Congruent shapes

**2** Tessellations

**3** Translations

**4** Reflections

**5** Rotations

**6** Enlargements

## This chapter will show you ...

- **G** how to recognise congruent shapes
- **E** how 2D shapes tessellate
- **D** what is meant by a transformation
- **D** how to translate 2D shapes
- **D** how to reflect 2D shapes
- **D** how to rotate 2D shapes
- **D** how to enlarge 2D shapes

## Visual overview

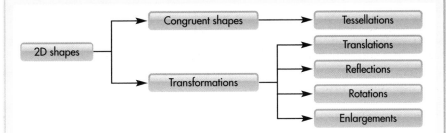

## What you should already know

- How to find the lines of symmetry of a 2D shape
  (KS3 level 3, GCSE grade F)
- How to find the order of rotational symmetry of a 2D shape
  (KS3 level 4, GCSE grade F)
- How to find the equation of a line (KS3 level 6, GCSE grade E)

## Quick check

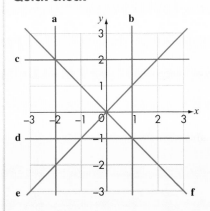

Write down the equations of the lines drawn on the grid.

# Congruent shapes

This section will show you how to:
- recognise congruent shapes

**Key word**
congruent

Two-dimensional shapes that are exactly the *same* size and shape are said to be **congruent**. For example, although they are in different positions, the triangles below are congruent, because they are all exactly the same size and shape.

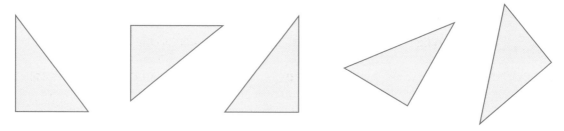

Congruent shapes fit exactly on top of each other. So, one way to see whether shapes are congruent is to trace one of them and check that it covers the other shapes exactly. For some of the shapes, you may have to turn your tracing paper over.

**EXAMPLE 1**

Which of these shapes is not congruent to the others?

a      b      c      d

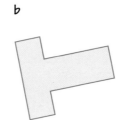
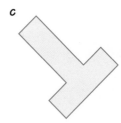
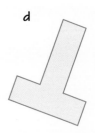

Trace shape **a** and check whether it fits exactly on top of the others.

You should find that shape **b** is not congruent to the others.

     **FM** Functional Maths   **AU** (AO2) Assessing Understanding   **PS** (AO3) Problem Solving

## EXERCISE 10A

**1** State whether the shapes in each pair, **a** to **f** are congruent or not.

**a**

**b**

**c**

**d**

**e**

**f**

**2** Which figure in each group, **a** to **c**, is not congruent to the other two?

**a i**

**ii**

**iii**

**b i**

**ii**

**iii**

**c i**
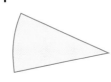

**ii**

**iii**

**3** For each of the following sets of shapes, write down the numbers of the shapes that are congruent to each other.

**a**

**1**        **2**         **3**        **4**

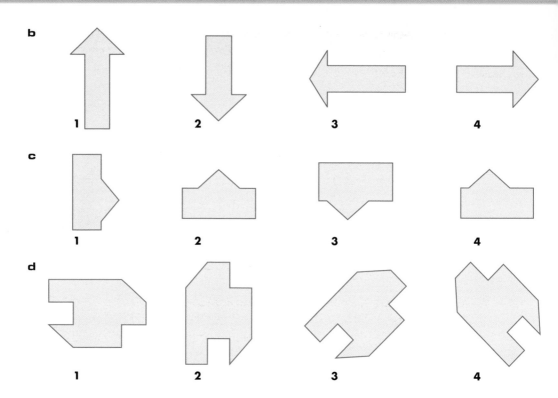

**PS 4** There are three letters of the alphabet that are all congruent to each other.

What are they?

**AU 5** Billy said, "I have two congruent shapes on my T-shirt, but one is bigger than the other."

What is wrong with Billy's statement?

**6** Draw a square PQRS. Draw in the diagonals PR and QS. Which triangles are congruent to each other?

**7** Draw a rectangle EFGH. Draw in the diagonals EG and FH. Which triangles are congruent to each other?

**8** Draw a parallelogram ABCD. Draw in the diagonals AC and BD. Which triangles are congruent to each other?

**9** Draw an isosceles triangle ABC where AB = AC. Draw the line from A to the midpoint of BC. Which triangles are congruent to each other?

**PS 10** A chessboard is made up of 64 small squares. The area of each square is 1 cm$^2$.

a How many squares on the board are congruent to a square:

i 2 cm by 2 cm ii 3 cm by 3 cm iii 4 cm by 4 cm?

b How many different-sized squares are there altogether on the chessboard?

# Tessellations

This section will show you how to:

- tessellate a 2D shape

**Key words**

tessellate
tessellation

## ACTIVITY

### Tiling patterns

You need centimetre-squared paper and some card in several different colours.

Make a template for each of the following shapes on the centimetre-squared paper.

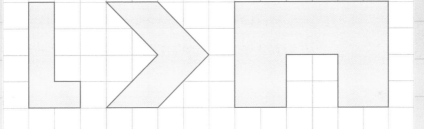

Use your template to make about 20 card tiles for each shape, using different colours.

For each shape, put all the tiles together to create a tiling pattern without any gaps.

What do you find?

From this activity you should have found that you could cover as much space as you wanted, using the *same* shape in a repeating pattern. You can say that the shape **tessellates**.

So, a **tessellation** is a regular pattern made with identical plane shapes, which fit together exactly, without overlapping and leaving no gaps.

**EXAMPLE 2**

Draw tessellations using each of these shapes.

a    b 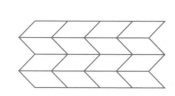   c

These patterns show how each of the shapes tessellates.

a   b   c

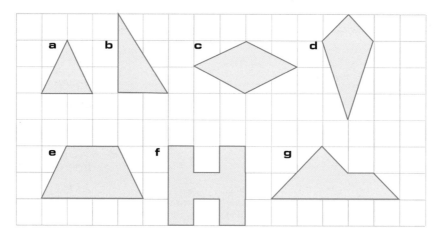

**EXERCISE 10B**

**1** On squared paper, show how each of these shapes tessellates.

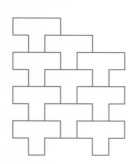

**2** Invent some of your own tessellating patterns.

**PS 3** 'Every quadrilateral will form a tessellation.' Investigate this statement to see whether it is true.

**AU 4** Explain why equilateral triangles, squares and regular hexagons tessellate.

**PS 5** Tania says, "It's impossible to tessellate a five-sided shape."

Investigate this statement to see if you think it may be true.

D

**AU** **6** A semi-regular tessellation is made, using two basic shapes.

Explain how this is possible if one of the shapes is a circle.

**FM** **7** A brick wall is an example of a tessellation.

Bricklayers sometimes like to make interesting patterns in their brickwork.

Using a brick that is three times as long as it is high, sketch a new tessellation that would also give a strong design.

## 10.3 Translations

| This section will show you how to: | Key words |
|---|---|
| • translate a 2D shape | image |
| | object |
| | transformation |
| | translate |
| | translation |
| | vector |

A **transformation** changes the position or the size of a 2D shape in a particular way. You will deal with the four basic ways of using transformations to change a shape: **translation**, reflection, rotation and enlargement.

When a transformation is carried out, the shape in its original position is called the **object** and in its 'new' position it is called the **image**. For translations, reflections and rotations, the object and image are congruent.

A translation is the movement of a shape from one position to another without reflecting it or rotating it. It is sometimes called a 'sliding' transformation, since the shape appears to slide from one position to another.

Every point in the shape moves in the same direction and through the same distance. The object shape **translates** to the image position.

---

**EXAMPLE 3**

Describe the following translations.

   **a**   Triangle A to triangle B

   **b**   Triangle A to triangle C

   **c**   Triangle A to triangle D

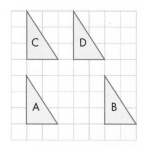

**a**   Triangle A has been transformed into triangle B by a translation of 5 squares right.

**b**   Triangle A has been transformed into triangle C by a translation of 4 squares up.

**c**   Triangle A has been transformed into triangle D by a translation of 3 squares right and 4 squares up.

---

A translation can also be described by using a **vector**. (This is sometimes called a 'column vector'.)

A vector is written in the form $\begin{pmatrix} a \\ b \end{pmatrix}$, where $a$ describes the horizontal movement and $b$ describes the vertical movement.

---

**EXAMPLE 4**

Find the vectors for the following translations.

   **a**   A to B         **b**   B to C         **c**   C to D         **d**   D to A

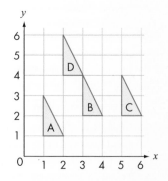

**a**   The vector describing the translation from A to B is $\begin{pmatrix} 2 \\ 1 \end{pmatrix}$.

**b**   The vector describing the translation from B to C is $\begin{pmatrix} 2 \\ 0 \end{pmatrix}$.

**c**   The vector describing the translation from C to D is $\begin{pmatrix} -3 \\ 2 \end{pmatrix}$.

**d**   The vector describing the translation from D to A is $\begin{pmatrix} -1 \\ -3 \end{pmatrix}$.

**EXERCISE 10C**

**D**

**1** Copy each of these shapes onto squared paper and draw its image, using the given translation.

**a**

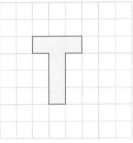

3 squares right

**b**

3 squares up

**c**

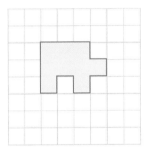

3 squares down

**d**

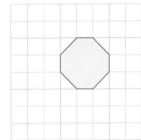

3 squares left

**2** Copy each of these shapes onto squared paper and draw its image, using the given translation.

**a**

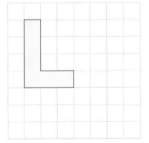

4 squares right and
3 squares down

**b**

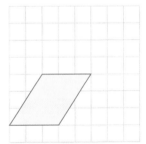

3 squares right and
3 squares up

**c**

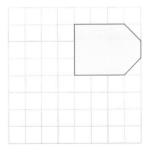

4 squares left and
3 squares down

**d**

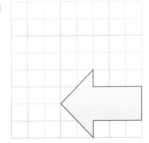

1 square left and
4 squares up

**3** Use vectors to describe these translations.

**a  i** A to B  **ii** A to C  **iii** A to D  **iv** A to E  **v** A to F  **vi** A to G

**b  i** B to A  **ii** B to C  **iii** B to D  **iv** B to E  **v** B to F  **vi** B to G

**c  i** C to A  **ii** C to B  **iii** C to D  **iv** C to E  **v** C to F  **vi** C to G

**d  i** D to E  **ii** E to B  **iii** F to C  **iv** G to D  **v** F to G  **vi** G to E

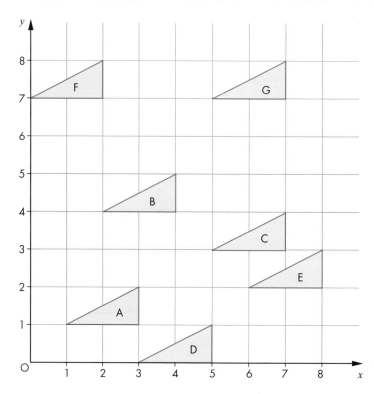

**4** Draw a coordinate grid for $-1 \leqslant x \leqslant 6$ and $-4 \leqslant y \leqslant 6$.

**a** Draw the triangle with coordinates A(1, 1), B(2, 1) and C(1, 3).

**b** Draw the image of triangle ABC after a translation with vector $\begin{pmatrix} 2 \\ 3 \end{pmatrix}$. Label this P.

**c** Draw the image of triangle ABC after a translation with vector $\begin{pmatrix} -1 \\ 2 \end{pmatrix}$. Label this Q.

**d** Draw the image of triangle ABC after a translation with vector $\begin{pmatrix} 3 \\ -2 \end{pmatrix}$. Label this R.

**e** Draw the image of triangle ABC after a translation with vector $\begin{pmatrix} -2 \\ -4 \end{pmatrix}$. Label this S.

**5** Using your diagram from question 4, use vectors to describe the following translations.

**a** P to Q  **b** Q to R  **c** R to S  **d** S to P

**e** R to P  **f** S to Q  **g** R to Q  **h** P to S

**PS** **6** Use a 10 × 10 grid and draw the triangle with coordinates A(0, 0), B(1, 0) and C(0, 1). How many different translations are there that use integer values only and will move the triangle ABC to somewhere in the grid? (Do not draw them all.)

**7** In a game of Snakes and ladders, the snakes and ladders can each be described by a translation.

Use the following vectors.

Ladders $\begin{pmatrix} 1 \\ 2 \end{pmatrix}, \begin{pmatrix} 2 \\ 5 \end{pmatrix}, \begin{pmatrix} -3 \\ 4 \end{pmatrix}, \begin{pmatrix} -2 \\ 3 \end{pmatrix}, \begin{pmatrix} 3 \\ 2 \end{pmatrix}$

Snakes $\begin{pmatrix} 1 \\ -3 \end{pmatrix}, \begin{pmatrix} 3 \\ -4 \end{pmatrix}, \begin{pmatrix} -2 \\ -2 \end{pmatrix}, \begin{pmatrix} -1 \\ -3 \end{pmatrix}, \begin{pmatrix} 2 \\ -5 \end{pmatrix}$

Put all five ladders and all five snakes onto a 10 × 10 grid to design a Snakes and ladders game board.

**AU** **8** If a translation is given by:

$$\begin{pmatrix} x \\ y \end{pmatrix}$$

describe the translation that would take the image back to the original.

## 10.4 Reflections

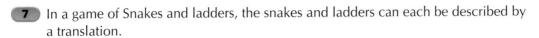

This section will show you how to:

● reflect a 2D shape in a mirror line

Key words

image
mirror line
object
reflect
reflection

A **reflection** is a transformation of a 2D shape so that it becomes the mirror **image** of itself.

Notice that each point on the image is the same perpendicular distance from the **mirror line** as the corresponding point on the **object**.

So, if you could fold the whole diagram along the mirror line, every point on the object would coincide with its reflection.

Object

Mirror line ————————————

Image

**EXAMPLE 5**

    **a**  **Reflect** the triangle ABC in the $x$-axis. Label the image P.

    **b**  Reflect the triangle ABC in the $y$-axis. Label the image Q.

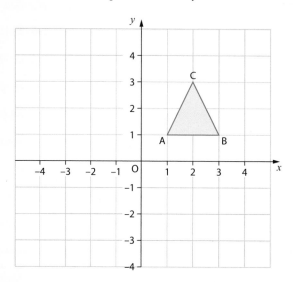

**a**  The mirror line is the $x$-axis. So, each vertex on triangle P will be the same distance from the $x$-axis as the corresponding vertex on the object.

**b**  The mirror line is the $y$-axis. So, each vertex on triangle Q will be the same distance from the $y$-axis as the corresponding vertex on the object.

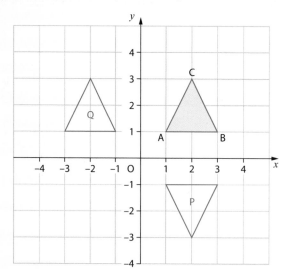

**EXERCISE 10D**

**1** Copy each shape onto squared paper and draw its image after a reflection in the given mirror line.

**a**

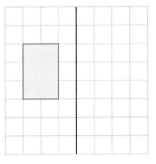

**b**

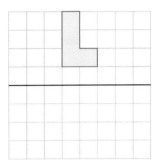

**c**

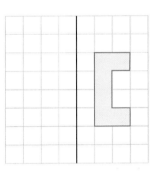

**d**

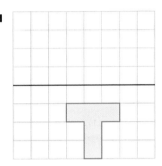

**2** Copy these figures onto squared paper and then draw the reflection of each in the given mirror line.

**a**

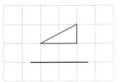

**b**

**c**

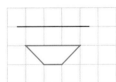

**d**

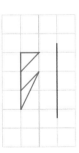

**e**

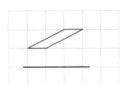

**f**

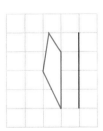

**g**

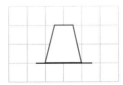

**3** Copy these figures onto squared paper and then draw the reflection of each in the given mirror line.

a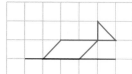

b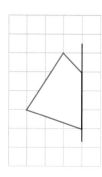

c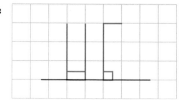

**4** Copy this diagram onto squared paper.

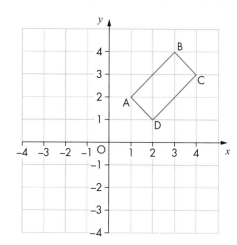

a Reflect the rectangle ABCD in the x-axis. Label the image R.

b Reflect the rectangle ABCD in the y-axis. Label the image S.

c What special name is given to figures that are exactly the same shape and size?

**5** a Draw a coordinate grid for $-5 \leqslant x \leqslant 5$ and $-5 \leqslant y \leqslant 5$.

b Draw the triangle with coordinates A(1, 1), B(3, 1) and C(4, 5).

c Reflect triangle ABC in the x-axis. Label the image P.

d Reflect triangle P in the y-axis. Label the image Q.

e Reflect triangle Q in the x-axis. Label the image R.

f Describe the reflection that will transform triangle ABC onto triangle R.

**6** Copy this diagram onto squared paper.

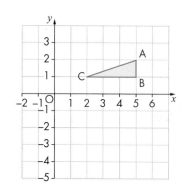

**HINTS AND TIPS**

**Remember** that x-lines are parallel to the y-axis and y-lines are parallel to the x-axis.

a Reflect triangle ABC in the line $x = 2$. Label the image X.

b Reflect triangle ABC in the line $y = -1$. Label the image Y.

**7** Draw these figures on squared paper and then draw the reflection of each in the given mirror line.

**a** **b**

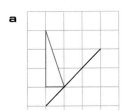

**c**

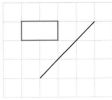

**8** Draw these figures on squared paper and then draw the reflection of each in the given mirror line.

**a** **b**

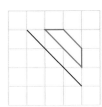

**c**

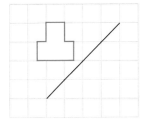

**9** A designer used the following instructions to create a design.

- Start with any rectangle ABCD.
- Reflect the rectangle ABCD in the line AC.
- Reflect the rectangle ABCD in the line BD.

Draw a rectangle and use the above to create a design.

**PS** **10** By using any one of the squares as a starting square ABCD, describe how to keep reflecting the shape to get the final shape in the diagram.

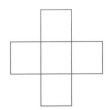

**AU** **11** If Gill reflects shape T in a line, then reflects the image of T in the same line, explain why the final image is in the same position as the original shape.

**12** **a** Draw a pair of axes for $-5 \le x \le 5$ and $-5 \le y \le 5$. Then draw the lines $y = x$ and $y = -x$, as shown below.

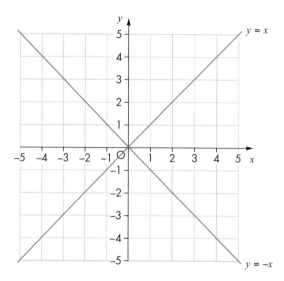

**b** Draw the triangle with coordinates A(2, 1), B(5, 1) and C(5, 3).

**c** Draw the reflection of triangle ABC in the $x$-axis and label the image P.

**d** Draw the reflection of triangle P in the line $y = -x$ and label the image Q.

**e** Draw the reflection of triangle Q in the $y$-axis and label the image R.

**f** Draw the reflection of triangle R in the line $y = x$ and label the image S.

**g** Draw the reflection of triangle S in the $x$-axis and label the image T.

**h** Draw the reflection of triangle T in the line $y = -x$ and label the image U.

**i** Draw the reflection of triangle U in the $y$-axis and label the image W.

**j** What single reflection will move triangle W to triangle ABC?

**13** **a** Repeat the steps of question 12 but start with any shape you like.

**b** Is your answer to part **j** the same as before?

**c** Would your answer to part **j** always be the same, no matter what shape you started with?

# Rotations

This section will show you how to:
- rotate a 2D shape about a point

**Key words**

angle of rotation
anticlockwise
centre of rotation
clockwise
image
object
rotate
rotation

A **rotation** transforms a 2D shape to a new position by turning it about a fixed point, called the **centre of rotation**.

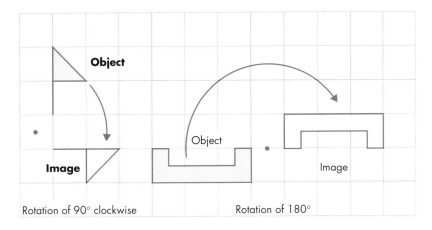

Rotation of 90° clockwise          Rotation of 180°

**Note:**

- The turn is called the **angle of rotation** and the direction is expressed as **clockwise** or **anticlockwise**.

- The position of the centre of rotation is always specified.

- The angles of rotation that occur in GCSE examinations are a $\frac{1}{4}$-turn or 90°, a $\frac{1}{2}$-turn or 180° and a $\frac{3}{4}$-turn or 270°.

- The rotations 180° clockwise and 180° anticlockwise are the same.

**EXAMPLE 6**

Draw the **image** of this shape after it has been rotated through 90° clockwise about the point X.

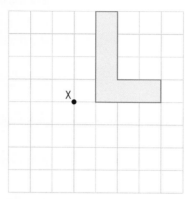

Using tracing paper is always the easiest way to tackle rotations.

First trace the **object** shape and fix the centre of rotation with a pencil point. Then **rotate** the tracing paper through 90° clockwise.

The tracing now shows the position of the image.

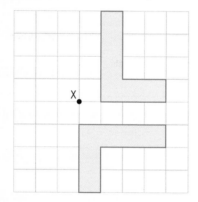

**EXERCISE 10E**

**1** Copy each of these diagrams onto squared paper. Draw each image, using the given rotation about the centre of rotation, X.

a

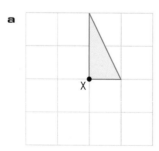

$\frac{1}{2}$-turn

b

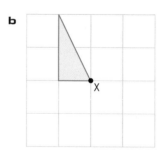

$\frac{1}{4}$-turn clockwise

**c**

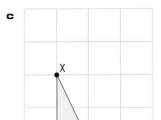

$\frac{1}{4}$-turn anticlockwise

**d**

$\frac{3}{4}$-turn clockwise

**2** Copy each of these diagrams onto squared paper. Draw each image, using the given rotation about the centre of rotation, X.

**a**

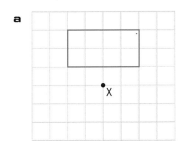

$\frac{1}{2}$-turn

**b**

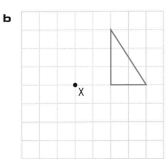

$\frac{1}{4}$-turn clockwise

**c**

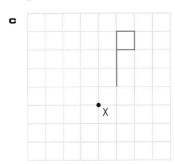

$\frac{1}{4}$-turn anticlockwise

**d**

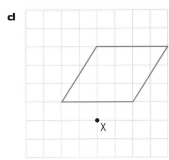

$\frac{3}{4}$-turn clockwise

**3** Copy this diagram onto squared paper.

**a** Rotate the shape through 90° clockwise about the origin O. Label the image P.

**b** Rotate the shape through 180° clockwise about the origin O. Label the image Q.

**c** Rotate the shape through 270° clockwise about the origin O. Label the image R.

**d** What rotation takes R back to the original shape?

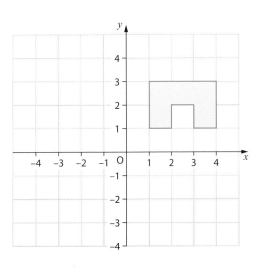

**D**

**4** Copy this diagram onto squared paper.

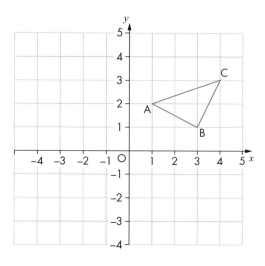

**a** Write down the coordinates of the vertices of the triangle ABC.

**b** Rotate the triangle ABC through 90° clockwise about the origin O. Label the image S.

Write down the coordinates of the vertices of triangle S.

**c** Rotate the triangle ABC through 180° clockwise about the origin O. Label the image T.

Write down the coordinates of the vertices of triangle T.

**d** Rotate the triangle ABC through 270° clockwise about the origin O. Label the image U.

Write down the coordinates of the vertices of triangle U.

**e** What do you notice about the coordinates of the four triangles?

**5** On squared paper, copy these shapes and their centres of rotation.

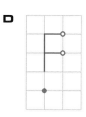

**a** Rotate each shape about its centre of rotation as follows.

**i** first by 90° anticlockwise

**ii** then by a further 180°.

**b** Describe, in each case, the transformation that would take the original shape to the final image.

**6** A graphic designer used the following instructions for creating a design.

• Start with a triangle ABC.

• Reflect the triangle in the line AB.

• Rotate the whole shape about point C clockwise 90°, then a further clockwise 90°, then a further clockwise 90°.

From any triangle of your choice, use the above instructions to create a design.

**PS 7** By using any one of the squares as a starting square ABCD, describe how to keep rotating the shape to get the final diagram shown.

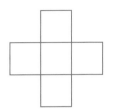

**AU 8** I rotate a shape S about point P, through 90° clockwise to give an image S'.

I repeat the same rotation on S' to give S''.

I repeat the rotation on S'' to give S'''.

I repeat the rotation on S''' to give S''''.

Explain why S'''' is in the same position as S.

**9** Copy this diagram onto squared paper.

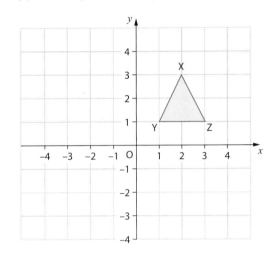

> **HINTS AND TIPS**
>
> Use tracing paper for part **c** and try out different centres until you find the correct one.

**a** Rotate triangle XYZ through 90° anticlockwise about the point (1, −2). Label the image P.

**b** Reflect triangle P in the *x*-axis. Label this triangle Q.

**c** Describe the transformation that maps triangle Q onto triangle XYZ.

**10 a** Draw a coordinate grid, labelling both axes from −5 to 5.

**b** Draw the triangle with vertices A(2, 1), B(3, 1) and C(3, 5).

**c** Reflect triangle ABC in the *x*-axis, then reflect the image in the *y*-axis. Label the final position A'B'C'.

**d** Describe the single transformation that maps triangle ABC onto triangle A'B'C'.

**e** Will this always happen no matter what shape you start with?

**f** Will this still happen if you reflect in the *y*-axis first, then reflect in the *x*-axis?

This section will show you how to:

● enlarge a 2D shape by a scale factor

**Key words**

centre of
    enlargement
enlarge
enlargement
image
object
scale factor

An **enlargement** is a transformation that changes the size of a 2D shape to give a similar **image**. It always has a **centre of enlargement** and a **scale factor**.

The length of each side of the enlarged shape will be:

    length of each side of the **object** × scale factor

The distance of each image point on the enlargement from the centre of enlargement will be:

    distance of original point from centre of enlargement × scale factor

There are two distinct ways to **enlarge** a shape: the ray method and the coordinate method.

---

**EXAMPLE 7**

Enlarge the object triangle ABC by a scale factor 3 about O to give the image triangle A'B'C'.

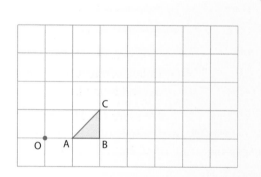

The image triangle A'B'C' is shown below.

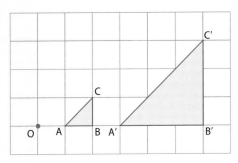

### Note

- The length of each side on the enlarged triangle A'B'C' is three times the corresponding length of each side on the original triangle, so that the sides are in the ratio 1 : 3.

- The distance of any point on the enlarged triangle from the centre of enlargement is three times the corresponding distance from the original triangle.

## Ray method

This is the *only* way to construct an enlargement when the diagram is not on a grid. The following example shows how to enlarge a triangle ABC by scale factor 3 about a centre of enlargement O by the ray method.

### EXAMPLE 8

Enlarge triangle ABC using O as the centre of enlargement and with scale factor 3.

Draw rays from the centre of enlargement, O, to each vertex of the triangle ABC and extend beyond.

Measure the distance from each vertex on triangle ABC to the centre of enlargement and multiply it by 3 to give the distance of each image vertex from the centre of enlargement for triangle A'B'C'.

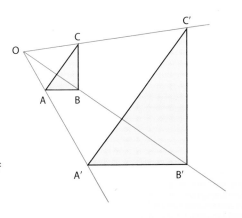

Once each image vertex has been found, the whole image shape can then be drawn.

Check the measurements and see for yourself how the calculations have been done. Notice again that each line is three times as long in the enlargement.

## Coordinate method

Triangle A'B'C' is an enlargement of triangle ABC by scale factor 2, with the origin, O, as the centre of enlargement.

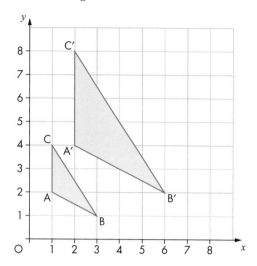

The coordinates of A are (1, 2) and the coordinates of A' are (2, 4). Notice that the coordinates of A' are the coordinates of A multiplied by 2, which is the scale factor of enlargement.

Check that the same happens for the other vertices.

This is a useful method for enlarging shapes on a coordinate grid, when the origin, O, is the centre of enlargement.

---

**EXAMPLE 9**

Enlarge the square by scale factor 3, using the origin as the centre of enlargement.

The coordinates of the original square are (1, 1), (2, 1), (2, 2) and (1, 2).

The enlarged square will have these coordinates multiplied by 3.

The coordinates are, therefore, (3, 3), (6, 3), (6, 6) and (3, 6), as shown on the diagram.

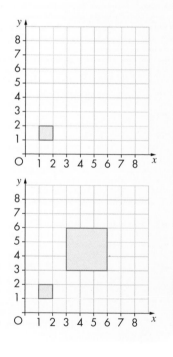

---

**Note**: This only works for enlargements centred on the origin. It is not always the case that the origin is the centre of enlargement. Always read the question carefully.

## Counting squares

### EXAMPLE 10

Enlarge triangle ABC by a scale factor 2, with the point P(O, 1) as the centre of enlargement.

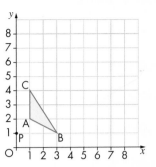

The point A is one square right and one square up from P. As the scale factor is 2, mark A′ two squares right and two squares up from P (2 × 1 = 2).

The point B is three squares right from P, so mark B′ six squares right from P (2 × 3 = 6).

The point C is one square right and three squares up from P, so mark C′ two squares right and six squares up from P (2 × 1 = 2, 2 × 3 = 6).

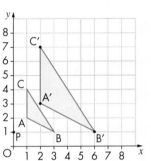

### EXERCISE 10F

**1** Copy each of these figures, with its centre of enlargement. Then enlarge it by the given scale factor, using the ray method.

**a**

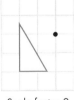

Scale factor 2

**b**

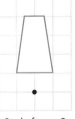

Scale factor 3

**c**

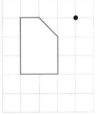

Scale factor 2

**d**

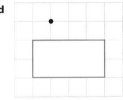

Scale factor 3

D

**2** Copy each of these diagrams onto squared paper and enlarge it by scale factor 2, using the origin as the centre of enlargement.

**a**

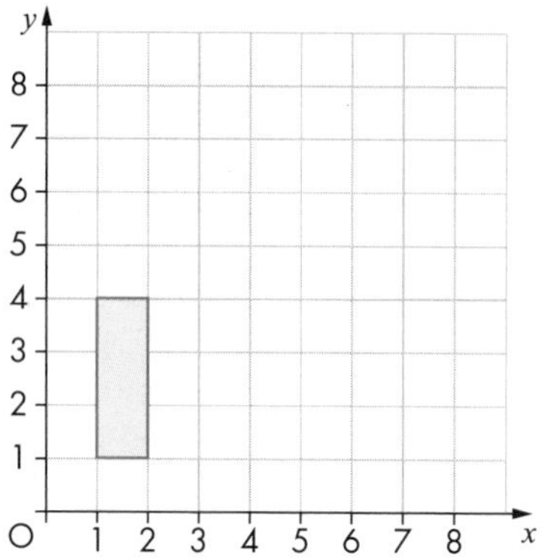


**b**

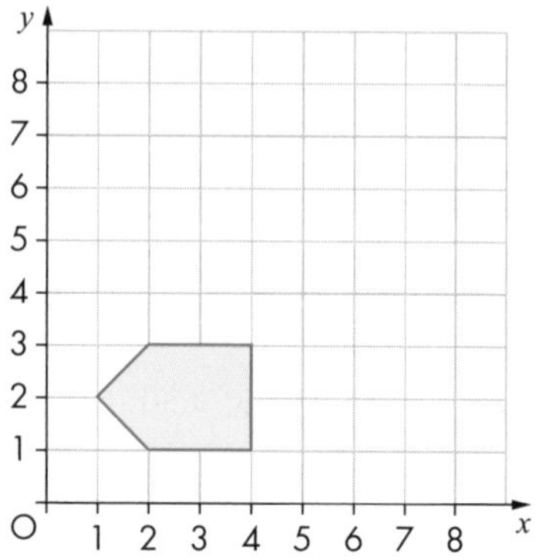


**c**

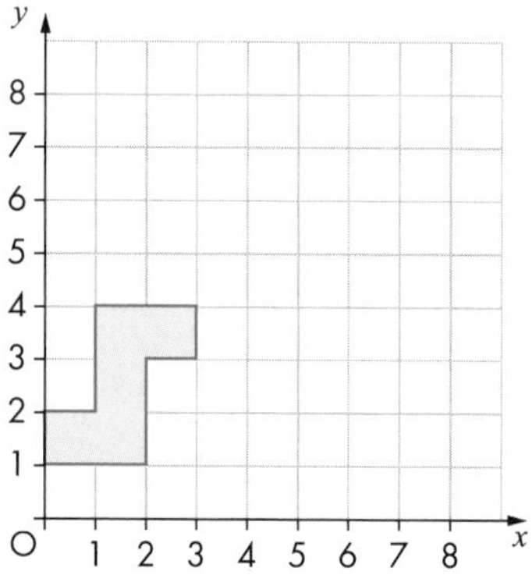


**HINTS AND TIPS**

Even if you are using a counting square method, you can always check by using the ray method.

**3** Copy each of these diagrams onto squared paper and enlarge it by scale factor 2, using the given centre of enlargement.

**a**

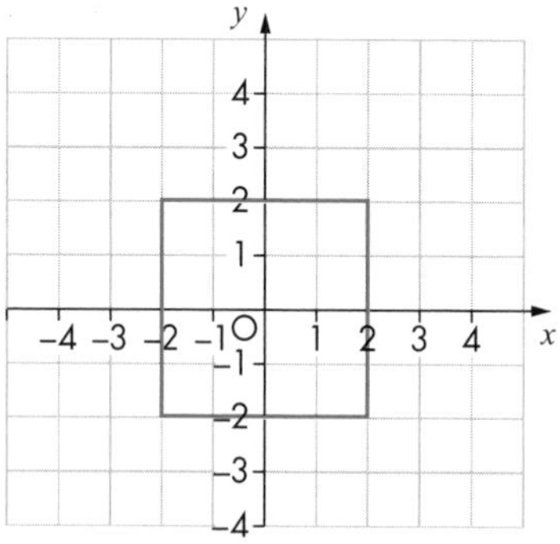


Centre of enlargement (–1, 1)

**b**

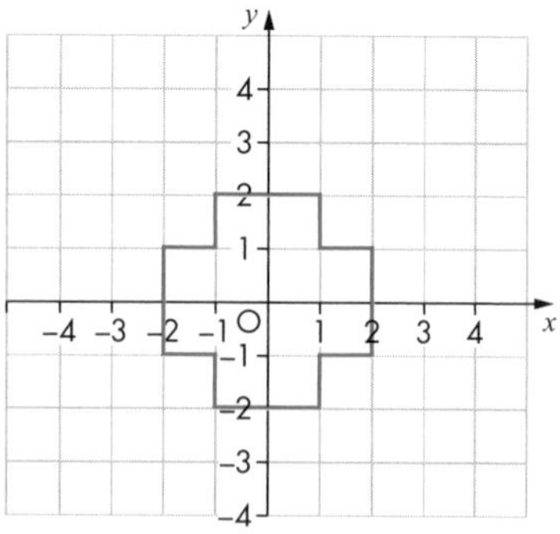


Centre of enlargement (–2, –3)

**4** **a** Draw a triangle ABC on squared paper.

**b** Mark four different centres of enlargement on your diagram:

one above your triangle
one to the left of your triangle
one below your triangle
one to the right of your triangle.

**c** From each centre of enlargement, draw an enlargement by scale factor 2.

**d** What do you notice about each enlarged shape?

**5** A designer is told to use the following routine.

- Start with a rectangle ABCD.

- Reflect ABCD in the line AC.

- Rotate the whole new shape about C through 180°.

- Enlarge the whole shape by scale factor 2, centre of enlargement point A.

Start with any rectangle of your choice and create the design above.

**AU 6** If I enlarge a shape with scale factor 2, the new shape is congruent to the first.

Is this true? Explain your answer.

**PS 7** If I enlarge a shape by scale factor 3, how many times bigger will the area of the new shape be?

**8** 'Strange but true'... you can have an enlargement in mathematics that is actually smaller than the original shape! This happens when you 'enlarge' a shape by a fractional scale factor. For example, triangle ABC on the right has been enlarged by scale factor $\frac{1}{2}$ about the centre of enlargement, O, to give the image triangle A'B'C'.

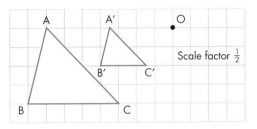

Copy the shape below onto squared paper and enlarge it by scale factor $\frac{1}{2}$ about the centre of enlargement, O.

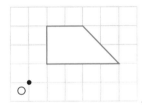

**9** Copy this diagram onto squared paper.

**a** Enlarge the rectangle A by scale factor $\frac{1}{3}$ about the point (−2, 1). Label the image B.

**b** Write down the ratio of the lengths of the sides of rectangle A to the lengths of the corresponding sides of rectangle B.

**c** Work out the ratio of the perimeter of rectangle A to the perimeter of rectangle B.

**d** Work out the ratio of the area of rectangle A to the area of rectangle B.

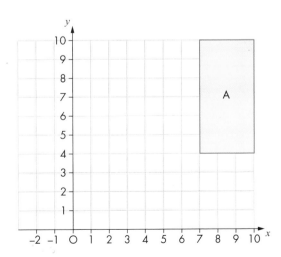

## GRADE BOOSTER

**G** You can recognise congruent shapes

**E** You know how to tessellate a 2D shape

**E** You can reflect a 2D shape in the $x$-axis or the $y$-axis

**D** You can translate a 2D shape

**D** You can reflect a 2D shape in a line $x = a$ or $y = b$

**D** You can rotate a 2D shape about the origin

**D** You can enlarge a 2D shape by a whole-number scale factor

**C** You can translate a 2D shape by a vector

**C** You can reflect a 2D shape in the line $y = x$ or $y = -x$

**C** You can rotate a 2D shape about any point

**C** You can enlarge a 2D shape about any point

### What you should know now

- How to recognise congruent shapes
- How to tessellate a 2D shape
- How to translate a 2D shape
- How to reflect a 2D shape
- How to rotate a 2D shape
- How to enlarge a 2D shape

**1** Some of these shapes are congruent to each other.

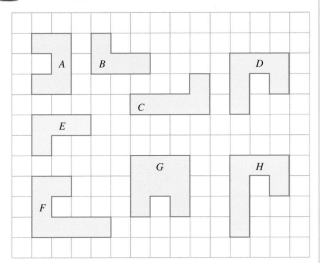

**a** Find a shape that is congruent to *B*. (1)

**b** Find another pair of congruent shapes. (1)

(Total 2 marks)

*AQA, June 2007, Module 5 Foundation, Question 6*

**2** Shapes *A*, *B*, *C* and *D* are made from squares of sides 1 cm.

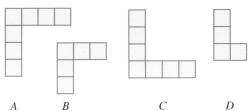

| *A* | *B* | *C* | *D* |

**a** Which **two** shapes are congruent? (1)

**b** Shape *D* is drawn on the grid.

Reflect shape *D* in the mirror line. (2)

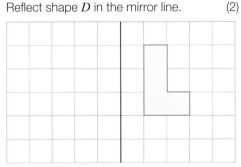

Mirror line

(Total 3 marks)

*AQA, November 2008, Paper 2 Foundation, Question 9*

**3** The diagram shows two shapes, *A* and *B*.

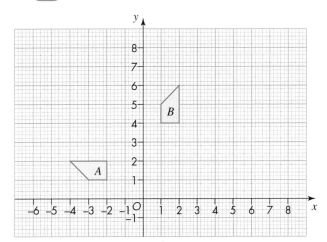

**a** Describe fully the single transformation that takes shape *A* onto shape *B*. (3)

**b** Enlarge shape *B* by scale factor 2, with (0, 7) as the centre of enlargement. (3)

(Total 6 marks)

*AQA, June 2006, Paper 1 Intermediate, Question 14*

**4** This question is about transformations of triangle *A*.

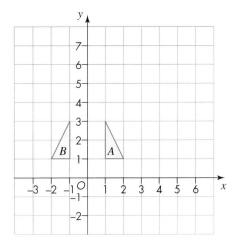

**a** Describe fully the single transformation that takes triangle *A* onto triangle *B*. (2)

**b** Translate triangle *A*, 2 units to the left and 3 units down.

Label the new triangle *C*. (1)

**c** Enlarge triangle *A* by a scale factor of 3, centre (0, 1).

Label the new triangle *D*. (3)

(Total 6 marks)

*AQA, June 2007, Paper 2 Intermediate, Question 10*

**5**

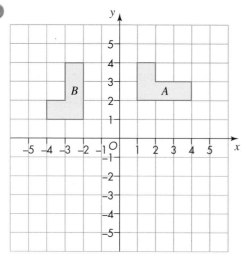

**a** Describe the **single** transformation that takes shape *A* to shape *B*. (3)

**b** Reflect shape *B* in the line $y = -1$. (2)

(Total 5 marks)

*AQA, June 2008, Paper 2 Foundation, Question 22*

**6** The diagram shows a shaded flag.

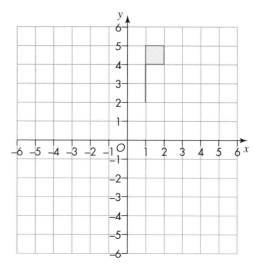

**a** Rotate the shaded flag 90° anticlockwise about the origin.

Label this new flag with the letter *A*. (3)

**b** Reflect the original shaded flag in the line $y = 1$.

Label this new flag with the letter *B*. (2)

**c** Rotate the original shaded flag by a quarter-turn clockwise about (0, 2).

Label this new flag with the letter C. (2)

(Total 7 marks)

*AQA, Paper 2 Intermediate, June 2005, Question 12*

# Worked Examination Questions

**1** The grid shows several transformations of the shaded triangle.

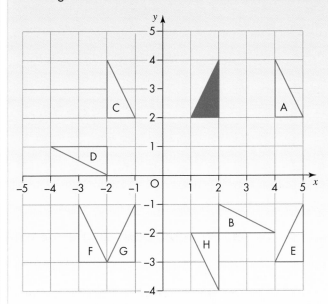

**a** Write down the letter of the triangle:

    **i** after the shaded triangle is reflected in the line $x = 3$

    **ii** after the shaded triangle is translated by the vector $\begin{pmatrix} 3 \\ -5 \end{pmatrix}$

    **iii** after the shaded triangle is rotated 90° clockwise about O.

**b** Describe fully the single transformation that takes triangle F onto triangle G.

**a i** A

    $x = 3$ is the vertical line passing through $x = 3$ on the $x$-axis.
The correct answer receives 1 mark.

  **ii** E

  **iii** B

(3 marks)

    Move the triangle 3 squares to the right and 5 squares down.
The correct answer receives 1 mark.

**b** A reflection in the line $x = -2$.

(2 marks)

(**Total:** 5 marks)

    Use tracing paper to help you. Trace the shaded triangle, pivot the paper on O holding it in place with your pencil point, and rotate the paper through 90° clockwise.
The correct answer receives 1 mark.

    The vertical mirror line passes through $x = -2$ on the $x$-axis.
You get 1 method mark for identifying the reflection and 1 accuracy mark for the mirror line.

## Worked Examination Questions

**FM** **2** Dan went to the local gardening store and saw different paving stones. He looked at some octagonal ones that he thought he would use to pave his back garden.

When he got them back home he found they didn't tessellate.

**a** Explain why the regular octagon does not tessellate.

**b** What can he now do to pave his back garden all over?

a Regular octagons placed next to each other will leave gaps but tessellations do not have gaps. The interior angle of the regular octagon is 135° and 360 is not a multiple of 135.

( 1 mark )

You get 1 mark for stating that there will be gaps or for stating that 360 is not a multiple of 135, or equivalent wording.

b The gap in between the regular octagons is in fact a square, so he should buy some square paving stones to fill the gap.

( 1 mark )

You get 1 mark for indicating that the gap is a square.

**Note:** Diagrams could have been drawn here; as long as these are interpreted with some words, the marks would be awarded.

( **Total:** 2 marks )

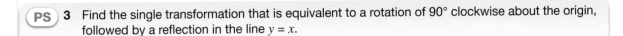

**3** Find the single transformation that is equivalent to a rotation of 90° clockwise about the origin, followed by a reflection in the line $y = x$.

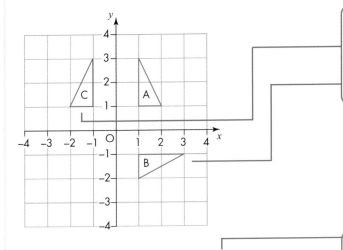

Start with a simple shape on the grid, triangle A.

You get 1 accuracy mark for correctly reflecting triangle B to C.

You get 1 accuracy mark for correctly rotating triangle A to B.

Single transformation is a reflection in the $y$-axis.

You get 1 method mark for identifying this is a reflection and 1 accuracy mark for identifying the mirror line as the $y$-axis.

**Total:** 4 marks

Tessellations are used in art.

M C Escher used repeating patterns and tessellations to create many of his designs, as you can see below. You too can create a design based on tessellations.

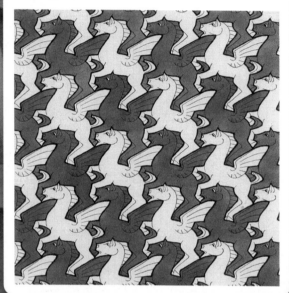

**Getting started**

Answer the questions below:

- What are the four transformations? Give an example of each transformation.
- What is rotational symmetry?
- Draw a shape that has rotational symmetry of order two.
- What polygon has rotational symmetry of order four?

## Your task

In this task you are going to link tessellations with transformations, and then look at creating a design using tessellating shapes.

**Fact: Every triangle and quadrilateral tessellates**

1 Explain why this is true (using diagrams may be helpful).

2 Using triangles and quadrilaterals, create your own tessellating design. Use the guidance given in the box below to help you.

3 Explain the transformations used in your tessellating design.

## Creating a new tessellation

**Step 1:** Draw any triangle.

**Step 2:** On any one of the sides, draw a design that has rotational symmetry.

**Step 3:** Repeat step 2 on the other two sides of the triangle.

By replacing each side of the original triangle with your symmetrical designs, you now have a shape that will tessellate.

## Handy hints

● Use a card template to help create a tessellating pattern.

● When you draw your tessellations you need to be fairly accurate or it will not tessellate. Remember, the line you draw will be bigger than the template.

● Esher created many tessellating designs. You can find a number of these on the internet.

# Why this chapter matters

For anything, from a bridge to a landscape gardening project, the designer needs to construct plans accurately, to be sure that everything will fit together properly. This will also give the people putting it together a blueprint to work from.

The need for accurate drawings is clear in bridge construction. Bridge engineers are responsible for producing practical bridge designs to meet the requirements of their employers. For example, a bridge intended to carry traffic over a newly constructed railway needs to be strong enough to bear the weight of the traffic and stable enough to counteract the effects of the moving traffic and strong winds. The designers produce a blueprint that has all the measurements, including heights, weights and angles, clearly marked on it. Construction workers then use this blueprint to build the bridge to the exact specifications set by the designers and engineers.

Generally, the construction workers work on both ends of the bridge at the same time, meeting in the middle. The blueprints are therefore essential for making sure that the bridge is safe and that the bridge meets in the middle.

Accurately-drawn blueprints were essential in the construction of the Golden Gate Bridge, which crosses the San Francisco Bay. When it was constructed in the 1930s, it was the longest suspension bridge in the world. The bridge engineers had to draw precise blueprints to make sure that they had all the information necessary to build this innovative bridge and that it would be built correctly.

By contrast, a bridge built at a stadium for the Maccabiah Games in Israel was built without proper planning and without accurate blueprints. This led to the bridge collapsing soon after its construction in 1997, killing four athletes and injuring 64 people.

Just like a bridge engineer, you must be accurate in your construction, working with a freshly sharpened pencil and a good pair of compasses, measuring and drawing angles carefully and drawing construction lines as faintly as possible.

In this chapter you will start with simple constructions of triangles, moving on to more complex bisectors and then to plotting loci, which are paths of whole sets of points obeying certain rules or criteria.

# Geometry: Constructions

**1** Constructing triangles

**2** Bisectors

**3** Loci

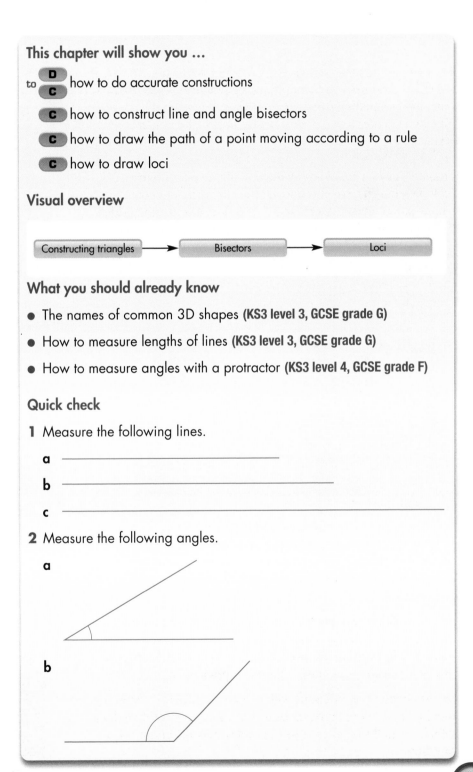

### This chapter will show you ...

to **D** **C** how to do accurate constructions

**C** how to construct line and angle bisectors

**C** how to draw the path of a point moving according to a rule

**C** how to draw loci

### Visual overview

Constructing triangles → Bisectors → Loci

### What you should already know

- The names of common 3D shapes **(KS3 level 3, GCSE grade G)**
- How to measure lengths of lines **(KS3 level 3, GCSE grade G)**
- How to measure angles with a protractor **(KS3 level 4, GCSE grade F)**

### Quick check

**1** Measure the following lines.

a _____

b _____

c _____

**2** Measure the following angles.

a

b

# Constructing triangles

This section will show you how to:
- construct triangles, using compasses, a protractor and a straight edge

**Key words**
angle
compasses
construct
side

There are three ways of **constructing** a triangle. Which one you use depends on what information you are given about the triangle.

## All three sides known

**EXAMPLE 1**

Construct a triangle with **sides** that are 5 cm, 4 cm and 6 cm long.

- **Step 1:** Draw the longest side as the base. In this case, the base will be 6 cm, which you draw using a ruler. (The diagrams in this example are drawn at half-size.)

- **Step 2:** Deal with the second longest side, in this case the 5 cm side. Open the **compasses** to a radius of 5 cm (the length of the side), place the point on one end of the 6 cm line and draw a short faint arc, as shown here.

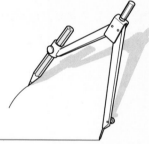

- **Step 3:** Deal with the shortest side, in this case the 4 cm side. Open the compasses to a radius of 4 cm, place the point on the other end of the 6 cm line and draw a second short faint arc to intersect the first arc, as shown here.

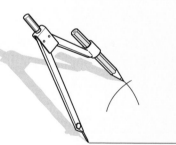

- **Step 4:** Complete the triangle by joining each end of the base line to the point where the two arcs intersect.

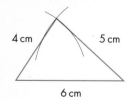

4 cm     5 cm

6 cm

**Note:** The arcs are construction lines and so are always drawn lightly. They must be left in an answer to an examination question to show the examiner how you constructed the triangle.

   **FM** Functional Maths   **AU** (AO2) Assessing Understanding   **PS** (AO3) Problem Solving

# Two sides and the included angle known

**EXAMPLE 2**

Draw a triangle ABC, where AB is 6 cm, BC is 5 cm and the included **angle** ABC is 55°. (The diagrams in this example are drawn at half-size.)

- **Step 1:** Draw the longest side, AB, as the base. Label the ends of the base A and B.

A ——————————— B

- **Step 2:** Place the protractor along AB with its centre on B and make a point on the diagram at the 55° mark.

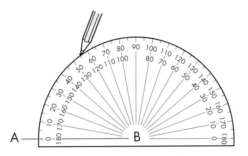

- **Step 3:** Draw a *faint* line from B through the 55° point. From B, using a pair of compasses, measure 5 cm along this line.

- Label the point where the arc cuts the line as C.

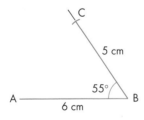

- **Step 4:** Join A and C and make AC and CB into bolder lines.

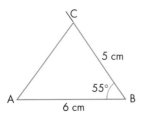

**Note:** The construction lines are drawn lightly and left in to demonstrate how the triangle has been constructed.

# Two angles and a side known

When you know two angles of a triangle, you also know the third.

**EXAMPLE 3**

Draw a triangle ABC, where AB is 7 cm, angle BAC is 40° and angle ABC is 65°.

- **Step 1:** As before, start by drawing the base, which here has to be 7 cm. Label the ends A and B.

A ———————————————————————— B

- **Step 2:** Centre the protractor on A and mark the angle of 40°. Draw a faint line from A through this point.

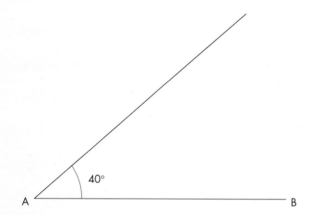

- **Step 3:** Centre the protractor on B and mark the angle of 65°. Draw a faint line from B through this point, to intersect the 40° line drawn from A. Label the point of intersection as C.

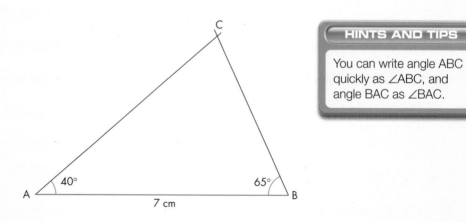

> **HINTS AND TIPS**
>
> You can write angle ABC quickly as ∠ABC, and angle BAC as ∠BAC.

- **Step 4:** Complete the triangle by making AC and BC into bolder lines.

**EXERCISE 11A**

**1** Draw the following triangles accurately and measure the sides and angles not given in the diagram.

**HINTS AND TIPS**

Always make a sketch if one is not given in the question.

**a**

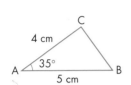

**b**

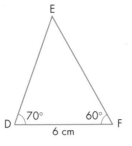

**c**

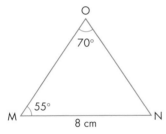

**d**

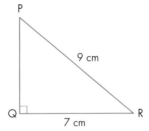

**e**

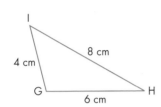

**f**

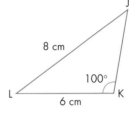

**2 a** Draw a triangle ABC, where AB = 7 cm, BC = 6 cm and AC = 5 cm.

**b** Measure the sizes of ∠ABC, ∠BCA and ∠CAB.

**HINTS AND TIPS**

Sketch the triangle first.

**3** Draw an isosceles triangle that has two sides of length 7 cm and the included angle of 50°.

**a** Measure the length of the base of the triangle.

**b** What is the area of the triangle?

**4** A triangle ABC has ∠ABC = 30°, AB = 6 cm and AC = 4 cm. There are two different triangles that can be drawn from this information.

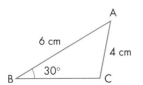
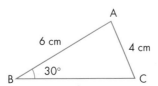

What are the two different lengths that BC can be?

**D**

**5** Construct an equilateral triangle of side length 5 cm.

    **a** Measure the height of the triangle.    **b** What is the area of this triangle?

**6** Construct a parallelogram with sides of length 5 cm and 8 cm and with an angle of 120° between them.

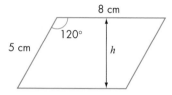

    **a** Measure the height of the parallelogram.

    **b** What is the area of the parallelogram?

**7** Groundsmen painting white lines on a sports field may use a knotted rope, like this one.

It has 12 equally spaced knots. It can be laid out to give a triangle, like this.

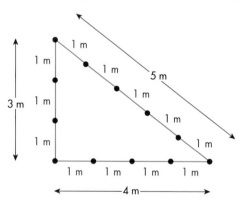

This will always be a right-angled triangle. This helps the groundsmen to draw lines perpendicular to each other.

Here are two more examples of such ropes.

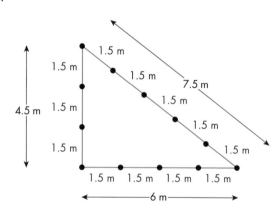

    **a** Show, by constructing each of the above triangles (use a scale of 1 cm ≡ 1 m), that each is a right-angled triangle.

    **b** Choose a different triangle that you think might also be right-angled. Use the same knotted-rope idea to check.

**AU 8** Gabriel says that, as long as he knows all three angles of a triangle, he can draw it. Explain why Gabriel is wrong.

**PS 9** Construct the triangle with the largest area, which has a total perimeter of 12 cm.

# Bisectors

This section will show you how to:
- construct the bisectors of lines and angles
- construct angles of 60° and 90°

**Key words**

angle bisector

bisect

line bisector

perpendicular
    bisector

To **bisect** means to divide in half. So a bisector divides something into two equal parts.

- A **line bisector** divides a straight line into two equal lengths.

- An **angle bisector** is the straight line that divides an angle into two equal angles.

## To construct a line bisector

It is usually more accurate to construct a line bisector than to measure its position (the midpoint of the line).

- **Step 1:** Here is a line to bisect.

- **Step 2:** Open your compasses to a radius of about three-quarters of the length of the line. Using each end of the line as a centre, and without changing the radius of your compasses, draw two intersecting arcs.

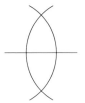

- **Step 3:** Join the two points at which the arcs intersect.

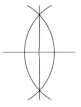

This line is the **perpendicular bisector** of the original line.

## To construct an angle bisector

It is much more accurate to construct an angle bisector than to measure its position.

- **Step 1:** Here is an angle to bisect.

- **Step 2:** Open your compasses to any reasonable radius that is less than the length of the shorter line. If in doubt, go for about 3 cm. With the vertex of the angle as centre, draw an arc through both lines.

- **Step 3:** With centres at the two points at which this arc intersects the lines, draw two more arcs so that they intersect. (The radius of the compasses may have to be increased to do this.)

- **Step 4:** Join the point at which these two arcs intersect to the vertex of the angle.

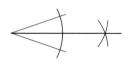

This line is the **angle bisector**.

## To construct an angle of 60°

It is more accurate to construct an angle of 60° than to measure and draw it with a protractor.

- **Step 1:** Draw a line and mark a point on it.

- **Step 2:** Open the compasses to a radius of about 4 centimetres. Using the point you have marked as the centre, draw an arc that crosses the line and extends almost above the point.

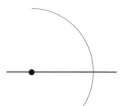

- **Step 3:** Keep the compasses set to the same radius. Using the point where the first arc crosses the line as a centre, draw another arc that intersects the first one.

- **Step 4:** Join the original point to the point where the two arcs intersect.

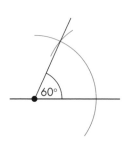

- **Step 5:** Use a protractor to check that the angle is 60°.

## To construct a perpendicular from a point on a line

This construction will produce a perpendicular from a point A on a line.

- Open your compasses to about 2 or 3 cm.
  With point A as centre, draw two short arcs to intersect the line at each side of the point.

- Now extend the radius of your compasses to about 4 cm. With centres at the two points at which the arcs intersect the line, draw two arcs to intersect at X above the line.

- Join AX.
  AX is perpendicular to the line.

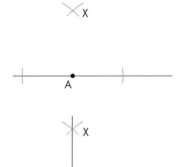

**Note:** If you needed to construct a 90° angle at the end of a line, you would first have to extend the line.

You could be even more accurate by also drawing two arcs *underneath* the line, which would give three points in line.

## To construct a perpendicular from a point to a line

This construction will produce a perpendicular from a point A to a line.

- With point A as centre, draw an arc to intersect the line at two points.

- With centres at these two points of intersection, draw two arcs to intersect each other both above and below the line.

- Join the two points at which the arcs intersect. The resulting line passes through point A and is perpendicular to the line.

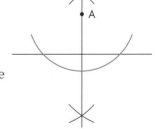

**Examination note:** When a question says *construct*, you must *only* use compasses – no protractor. When it says *draw*, you may use whatever you can to produce an accurate diagram. But also note that, when constructing, you may use your protractor to check your accuracy.

**EXERCISE 11B**

**1** Draw a line 7 cm long and bisect it. Check your accuracy by seeing if each half is 3.5 cm.

**2** Draw a circle of about 4 cm radius.

Draw a triangle inside the circle so that the corners of the triangle touch the circle.

Bisect each side of the triangle.

The bisectors should all meet at the same point, which should be the centre of the circle.

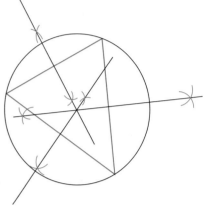

> **HINTS AND TIPS**
>
> **Remember** that examiners want to see your construction lines.

**3 a** Draw any triangle with sides of length between 5 cm and 10 cm.

**b** On each side construct the line bisector.

All your line bisectors should intersect at the same point.

**c** Using this point as the centre, draw a circle that goes through each vertex of the triangle.

**4** Repeat question 3 with a different triangle and check that you get a similar result.

**5 a** Draw this quadrilateral.

**b** Construct the line bisector of each side. These all should intersect at the same point.

**c** Use this point as the centre of a circle that goes through the quadrilateral at each vertex. Draw this circle.

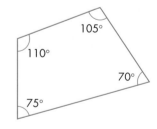

**6 a** Draw an angle of 50°.

**b** Construct the angle bisector.

**c** Check how accurate you have been by measuring each half. Both should be 25°.

**7** Draw a circle with a radius of about 3 cm.

Draw a triangle so that the sides of the triangle are tangents to the circle.

Bisect each angle of the triangle.

The bisectors should all meet at the same point, which should be the centre of the circle.

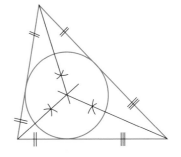

**8 a** Draw any triangle with sides of length between 5 cm and 10 cm.

**b** At each angle construct the angle bisector.
All three bisectors should intersect at the same point.

**c** Use this point as the centre of a circle that just touches the sides of the triangle.

**9** Repeat question 8 with a different triangle.

**FM 10** Pete and Babs have children living in Bristol and Norwich. Pete is about to start a new job in Birmingham. They are looking on a map of Britain for places they might move to.

Babs says, "I want to be the same distance from both children."
Pete says, "I want to be as close to Birmingham as possible."

Find a city that would suit both Pete and Babs.

Use a map of the UK to help you.

**PS 11** Draw a circle with radius of about 4 cm.

Draw a quadrilateral, **not** a rectangle, inside the circle so that each vertex is on the circumference.

Construct the bisector of each side of the quadrilateral.

Where is the point where these bisectors all meet?

**AU 12** Write down instructions to explain how you would construct a triangle with angles 90°, 60° and 30°.

# Loci

This section will show you how to:

- draw loci

**Key words**

equidistant

loci

locus

## What is a locus?

A **locus** (plural **loci**) is the movement of a point according to a rule.

For example, a point that moves so that it is always at a distance of 5 cm from a fixed point, A, will have a locus that is a circle of radius 5 cm.

This is expressed mathematically as:

The locus of the point P is such that AP = 5 cm

Another point moves so that it is always **equidistant** or the same distance from two fixed points, A and B.

This is expressed mathematically as:

The locus of the point P is such that AP = BP

This is the same as the bisector of the line AB, which you have met in lesson 11.2.

Another point moves so that it is always 5 cm from a line AB. The locus of the point P is given as a 'racetrack' shape. This is difficult to express mathematically.

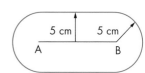

The three examples of loci just given occur frequently.

Imagine a grassy, flat field in which a horse is tied to a stake by a rope that is 10 m long. What is the shape of the area that the horse can graze?

In reality, the horse may not be able to reach the full 10 m if the rope is tied round its neck but you can ignore fine details like that. The situation is 'modelled' by saying that the horse can move around in a 10 m circle and graze all the grass within that circle.

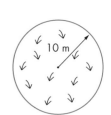

In this example, the locus is the whole of the area inside the circle.

This is expressed mathematically as:

The locus of the point P is such that AP ≤ 10 m

**EXERCISE 11C**

**1** A is a fixed point. Sketch the locus of the point P for these situations.

  **a** AP = 2 cm

  **b** AP = 4 cm

  **c** AP = 5 cm

> **HINTS AND TIPS**
>
> Sketch the situation before doing an accurate drawing.

**2** A and B are two fixed points 5 cm apart. Sketch the locus of the point P for the following situations.

  **a** AP = BP

  **b** AP = 4 cm and BP = 4 cm

  **c** P is always within 2 cm of the line AB.

> **HINTS AND TIPS**
>
> If AP = BP this means the bisector of A and B.

**FM 3** **a** A horse is tied in a field by a rope 4 m long. Describe or sketch the area that the horse can graze.

  **b** The same horse is still tied by the same rope but there is now a long, straight fence running 2 m from the stake. Sketch the area that the horse can now graze.

**4** ABCD is a square of side 4 cm. In each of the following loci, the point P moves only inside the square. Sketch the locus in each case.

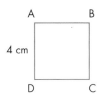

4 cm

  **a** AP = BP

  **b** AP < BP

  **c** AP = CP

  **d** CP < 4 cm

  **e** CP > 2 cm

  **f** CP > 5 cm

**5** One of the following diagrams is the locus of a point on the rim of a bicycle wheel as it moves along a flat road. Which is it?

  **a**

  **b**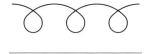

  **c**

  **d**

**6** Draw the locus of the centre of the wheel for the bicycle in question 5.

**PS 7** On a piece of plain paper, mark three points A, B and C, all about 5 cm to 7 cm away from each other. Find the locus of point P where:

**a** P is always closer to point A than point B

**b** P is always equidistant from points B and C.

**AU 8** You do not have a pair of compasses or a protractor – only a ruler.

Explain how you could construct an equilateral triangle, with sides of length 3 cm.

## Practical problems

Most of the loci problems in your GCSE examination will be of a practical nature, as shown in the next three examples.

---

**EXAMPLE 4**

Imagine that a radio company wants to find a site for a transmitter.
The transmitter must be the same distance from both Doncaster and Leeds,
and within 20 miles of Sheffield.

In mathematical terms, this means you are
concerned with the perpendicular bisector between
Leeds and Doncaster, and the area within a circle of
radius 20 miles from Sheffield.

The map, drawn to a scale of 1 cm = 10 miles,
illustrates the situation and shows that the
transmitter can be built anywhere along the thick
green line.

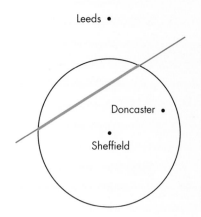

---

## EXAMPLE 5

A radar station in Birmingham has a range of 150 km (that is, it can pick up any aircraft within a radius of 150 km). Another radar station in Norwich has a range of 100 km.

Can an aircraft be picked up by both radar stations at the same time?

The situation is represented by a circle of radius 150 km around Birmingham and another circle of radius 100 km around Norwich. The two circles overlap, so an aircraft could be picked up by both radar stations when it is in the overlap.

## EXAMPLE 6

A dog is tied by a rope, 3 m long, to the corner of a shed, 4 m by 2 m. What is the area that the dog can guard effectively?

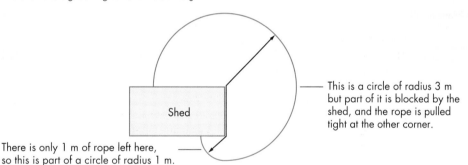

This is a circle of radius 3 m but part of it is blocked by the shed, and the rope is pulled tight at the other corner.

There is only 1 m of rope left here, so this is part of a circle of radius 1 m.

## EXERCISE 11D

For questions 1 to 7, you should start by sketching the picture given in each question on a 6 × 6 grid, each square of which is 2 cm by 2 cm. The scale for each question is given.

**1** A goat is tied to a stake by a rope, 7 m long, in a corner of a field with a fence at each side. What is the locus of the area that the goat can graze? Use a scale of 1 cm ≡ 1 m.

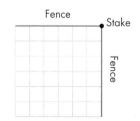

**C**

**2** A horse in a field is tied to a stake by a rope 6 m long. What is the locus of the area that the horse can graze? Use a scale of 1 cm ≡ 1 m.

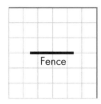

**3** A cow is tied to a rail at the top of a fence 6 m long. The rope is 3 m long. Sketch the area that the cow can graze. Use a scale of 1 cm ≡ 1 m.

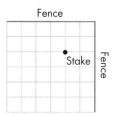

**4** A horse is tied to a stake near a corner of a fenced field, at a point 4 m from each fence. The rope is 6 m long. Sketch the area that the horse can graze. Use a scale of 1 cm ≡ 1 m.

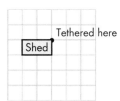

**5** A horse is tied to a corner of a shed, 2 m by 1 m. The rope is 2 m long. Sketch the area that the horse can graze. Use a scale of 2 cm ≡ 1 m.

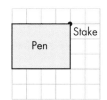

**6** A goat is tied by a 4 m rope to a stake at one corner of a pen, 4 m by 3 m. Sketch the area of the pen on which the goat cannot graze. Use a scale of 2 cm ≡ 1 m.

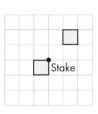

**7** A puppy is tied to a stake by a rope, 1.5 m long, on a flat lawn on which are two raised brick flower beds. The stake is situated at one corner of a bed, as shown. Sketch the area in which the puppy is free to roam. Use a scale of 1 cm ≡ 1 m.

**FM** **8** The diagram, which is drawn to scale, shows two towns, A and B, which are 8 km apart.

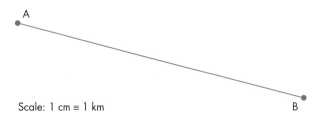

Scale: 1 cm ≡ 1 km

A phone company wants to erect a mobile phone mast.

It must be within 5 km of town A and within 4 km of town B.

Copy the diagram accurately.

Show the possible places where the mast could be.

**FM  9** The map shows a field that is 100 m by 100 m.

There are two large trees in the field and a power line runs across it.

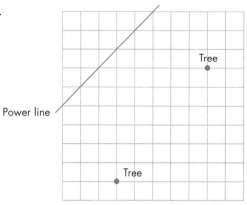

**a** Make an accurate scale drawing of the field, using a scale of 1 cm ≡ 10 m.

**b** Bernice wants to fly a kite.

She cannot fly the kite within 50 m of the power line.

She cannot fly the kite within 30 m of a tree.

Show the area where she can fly the kite.

**FM  10** A radio station broadcasts from London on a frequency of 1000 kHz with a range of 300 km. Another radio station broadcasts from Glasgow on the same frequency with a range of 200 km.

**a** Sketch the area to which each station can broadcast. (See the map on the next page.)

**b** Will they interfere with each other?

**c** If the Glasgow station increases its range to 400 km, will they then interfere with each other?

**FM  11** The radar at Leeds airport has a range of 200 km. The radar at Exeter airport has a range of 200 km. (See the map on the next page.)

**a** Will a plane flying over Glasgow be detected by the radar at Leeds?

**b** Sketch the area where a plane can be picked up by both radars at the same time.

**FM  12** A radio transmitter is to be built according to the following rules.

**i** It has to be the same distance from York and Birmingham. (See the map on the next page.)

**ii** It must be within 350 km of Glasgow.

**iii** It must be within 250 km of London.

> **HINTS AND TIPS**
>
> The same distance from York and Birmingham means on the bisector of the line joining York and Birmingham.

**a** Sketch the line that is the same distance from York and Birmingham.

**b** Sketch the area that is within 350 km of Glasgow and 250 km of London.

**c** Show clearly the possible places at which the transmitter could be built.

Use a copy of this map, if you need to, to answer questions 10 to 17.

For each question, trace the map and mark on those points that are relevant to that question.

**FM 13** A radio transmitter centred at Birmingham is designed to give good reception in an area greater than 150 km and less than 250 km from the transmitter. Sketch the area of good reception.

**FM 14** Three radio stations pick up a distress call from a boat in the Irish Sea. The station at Glasgow can tell from the strength of the signal that the boat is within 300 km of the station. The station at York can tell that the boat is between 200 km and 300 km from York. The station at London can tell that it is less than 400 km from London. Sketch the area where the boat could be.

**15** Sketch the area that is between 200 km and 300 km from Newcastle-upon-Tyne, and between 150 km and 250 km from Bristol.

**16** The shape of Wathsea Harbour is as shown in the diagram. A boat sets off from point A and steers so that it keeps the same distance from the sea-wall and the West Pier. Another boat sets off from B and steers so that it keeps the same distance from the East Pier and the sea-wall. Copy the diagram and, on your diagram, show accurately the path of each boat.

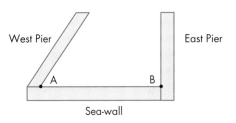

**PS 17** Trevor wanted to fly from the Isle of Wight north, towards Scotland. He wanted to stay the same distance from London as Bristol as far as he could.

Once he is past London and Bristol, which city should he aim towards, to keep him, as accurately as possible, the same distance from London and Bristol? Use the map to help you.

**AU 18** A distress call is heard by coastguards in both Newcastle and Bristol. The signal strength suggests that the call comes from a ship the same distance from both places. Explain how the coastguards could find the area of sea to search.

## GRADE BOOSTER

**D** You can construct diagrams accurately, using compasses, a protractor and a straight edge

**C** You can construct line and angle bisectors, and draw the loci of points moving according to a rule

### What you should know now

- How to draw scale diagrams and construct accurate diagrams, using mathematical instruments

- How to draw loci of sets of points

**1** Here is a sketch of a triangle.

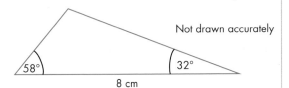

Not drawn accurately

Make an accurate drawing of the triangle. (3)

(Total 3 marks)

*AQA, June 2006, Paper 1 Foundation, Question 13*

**2** In this question, you should use a ruler and compasses only.

**a** Copy this diagram and construct the perpendicular bisector of the line joining the points A and B. (2)

**b** Copy the diagram and bisect the angle ABC. (2)

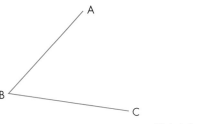

(Total 4 marks)

 **3** The diagram shows a scale drawing of a straight road.

A walker is at point P.

P

Road
_____

Scale: 1 cm represents 0.5 km

**a** Use a ruler and compasses to copy the diagram and construct the perpendicular from the point P to the road.

You **must** show all your construction lines and arcs. (3)

**b** Find the shortest real distance from the walker to the road. (2)

(Total 5 marks)

*AQA, November 2007, Paper 2 Intermediate, Question 14*

 **4 a** Using a ruler and compasses only, construct an angle of 60°.

Show all your construction lines and arcs. (2)

**b** Two lifeboat stations A and B receive a distress call from a boat.

The boat is within 6 kilometres of station A.

The boat is within 8 kilometres of station B.

Shade the possible area in which the boat could be. (2)

Scale: 1 cm represents 1 km

(Total 4 marks)

*AQA, November 2005, Paper 2 Intermediate, Question 22*

**5** The positions of towns *A* and *B* are shown on the diagram.

The diagram is drawn to scale.

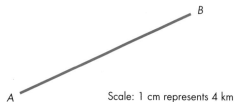

Scale: 1 cm represents 4 km

**a** Work out the actual distance between towns *A* and *B*. (3)

**b** A town *C* is 16 kilometres from *A* and 16 kilometres from *B*.

Using compasses only, mark the **two** possible positions of town *C* on the diagram. (2)

(Total 5 marks)

*AQA, November 2007, Module 5, Paper 1 Intermediate, Question 4*

 **6** The diagram shows an L shape.

Copy the diagram and draw the locus of all points 2 cm from the L shape. (3)

(Total 3 marks)

*AQA, June 2005, Paper 1 Intermediate, Question 15*

 **7** Use a ruler and compasses to construct a rhombus that has sides of 6 cm and whose shorter diagonal is 4 cm. (4)

(Total 4 marks)

*AQA, June 2006, Paper 2 Foundation, Question 24*

 **8** The diagram, which is drawn to scale, shows a garden bordered by a house wall.

On the wall there is an electricity outlet (E) and a water outlet (W).

Ramesh is installing a pond.

The centre of the pond must be within 4 metres of the electricity outlet and within 6 metres of the water outlet.

Scale: 1 cm to 1 metre

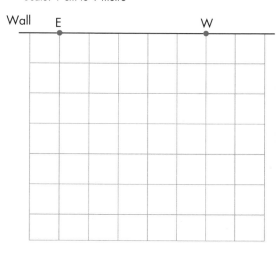

Find the area within which the centre of the pond may be located.

# Worked Examination Questions

**1** Here is a sketch of a triangle. PR = 6.4 cm, QR = 7.7 cm and angle R = 35°.

**a** Make an accurate drawing of the triangle.

**b** Measure the size of angle Q on your drawing.

P

6.4 cm

35°

R

7.7 cm

Q

Make an accurate drawing, using these steps.

**a** **Step 2:** Measure the angle at R as 35°.
Draw a faint line at this angle.

You get 1 accuracy mark for creating an angle between 34° and 35°.

**Step 3:** Using a pair of compasses, draw an arc 6.4 cm long from R. Where this crosses the line from Step 2, make this P.

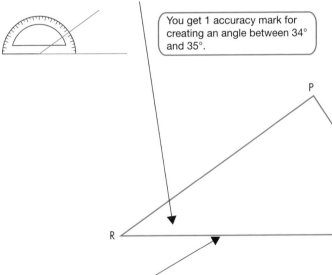

You get 1 accuracy mark for this arc being within 1 mm.

P

R

Q

**Step 4:** Join P to Q.

No marks are awarded for this step.

**Step 1:** Draw the base as a line 7.7 cm long.
You can draw this and measure it with a ruler, although a pair of compasses is more accurate.

No marks are awarded for this step.

2 marks

**b** 56°

1 mark

**Total:** 3 marks

You get 1 accuracy mark for measuring this angle as 56°, ± 2°. If your actual angle was not 56° but you measured it accurately, then you would still get the mark.

You already know that architects and engineers must construct accurate diagrams, to be certain that the buildings and constructions they have designed will be built correctly. However, did you know that the same principles used by architects and engineers to construct diagrams are also used when planning sports pitches, whether it is your local playing field or a Premier League football club?

In this task you will take on the role of the grounds staff of a football pitch. You will need to negotiate many variables to ensure that the pitch is drawn up correctly and can be maintained thoroughly.

### Your task

As a member of the grounds staff you have been asked to prepare the pitch ready for the new football season.

The club needs the pitch designed according to FIFA's specifications.

1 Construct a scale drawing of the football pitch, to be used in laying out the pitch on the football field. Be sure to label all the dimensions of the pitch.

2 The pitch will need to be regularly watered in order to keep it in good condition. For this, you will need to design a comprehensive sprinkler system. On a copy of your drawing of the pitch, mark up where the sprinklers should go, ensuring that the maximum possible area of the pitch is watered at any one time.

### Getting started
Discuss these questions with a partner.

- What shapes do you see on sports fields? Do these shapes vary, depending on the sports that take place on these pitches?
- What angles do you see on sports fields?
- How are shapes drawn on to sports fields?

## FIFA specifications

### The field

The field of play must be rectangular, divided into two halves by a halfway line. The centre mark is indicated at the midpoint of the halfway line and a circle with a radius of 9.15 m (10 yards) is marked around it.

The field dimensions should be as follows.

|        | Minimum                   | Maximum                    |
|--------|---------------------------|----------------------------|
| Length | 90 m (approx. 100 yards)  | 120 m (approx. 130 yards)  |
| Width  | 45 m (approx. 50 yards)   | 90 m (approx. 100 yards)   |

### The goal area

The goal mouth is 7.3 metres (8 yards) wide. The goal area is 5.5 m (6 yards) wide by 18.3 m (12 yards) long.

### The penalty area

The penalty area is 16.5 m (18 yards) wide by 40.3 m (44 yards) long.

Within each penalty area there is a penalty mark 11 m (12 yards) from the midpoint between the goalposts and equidistant from them. An arc with a radius of 9.15 m (10 yards) from each penalty mark is drawn outside the penalty area.

### The corner arc

A flagpost is placed in each corner. A quarter-circle with a radius of 1 m (approximately 1 yard) is drawn at each corner flag post, inside the field of play.

**Hint:** Use the internet to research football pitches and FIFA's specifications further.

# Why this chapter matters

The biggest moveable volume on Earth is water. There are about 1.4 billion cubic kilometres (km³) of water on our planet. This water is essential for the natural processes that create and sustain life on Earth. Volume can help us to assess whether the planet has enough of one of the natural resources that is vital to our daily diet as well as to the survival of our whole planet's ecosystem.

The volume of water on Earth is actually increasing as a result of condensation from volcanoes and from comets that enter the Earth's atmosphere. These processes happen all the time, but they add only about a cubic metre (1 m³) of water every year.

So, just where can we find the total volume of water on our planet?

The table below shows where it is to be found and how it is used by humans, animals and plants.

About 70% of the Earth's surface area is covered in water!

| | Volume (km³) | Comment |
|---|---|---|
| Oceans | 1 338 000 000 | Salt water in oceans, seas and bays |
| Ice | 24 364 000 | Ice caps, glaciers, snow and ground ice |
| Groundwater | 23 400 000 | Fresh and salt water underground and in deep wells |
| Lakes and reservoirs | 176 400 | Fresh and salt water stored on the Earth's surface and often used for drinking, irrigation and recreation |
| Soil moisture | 16 500 | Used by crops, trees and surface vegetation |
| Water vapour in the atmosphere | 12 900 | Including clouds, fog and dew |
| Rivers | 2120 | Drinking, irrigation and recreation |
| Swamp water | 11 470 | Temporary and permanent wetland areas |

As you can see most of the total volume of water on Earth is in our oceans. The Atlantic, Pacific, Indian, Arctic and Southern oceans hold 97.3% of the total water on Earth.

Within the waters of the ocean there are over 1 million kilograms of gold, currently worth £61 billion. That is £9 for every person on Earth.

The volumes of water on Earth are very large and difficult to measure. In comparison, the volumes of most shapes we need to measure are much easier to work out.

This chapter leads you through the process of calculating the volumes and surface areas of a variety of shapes.

# 12

# Geometry: Surface area and volume of 3D shapes

**1** Units of volume

**2** Surface area and volume of a cuboid

**3** Surface area and volume of a prism

**4** Volume of a cylinder

## This chapter will show you ...

**G** the units used when finding the volume of 3D shapes

**E** how to calculate the surface area and volume of a cuboid

**C** how to calculate the surface area and volume of prisms

**C** how to calculate the volume of a cylinder

## Visual overview

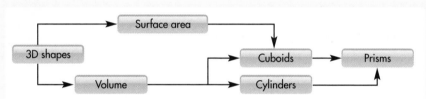

## What you should already know

- How to find the area of a rectangle and a triangle (see Chapter 6) **(KS3 level 5, GCSE grade E)**

- The units used with area **(KS3 level 5, GCSE grade E)**

- The names of basic 3D shapes **(KS3 level 3, GCSE grade G)**

- What is meant by the term 'volume' **(KS3 level 5, GCSE grade G)**

## Quick check

What are the mathematical names of these 3D shapes?

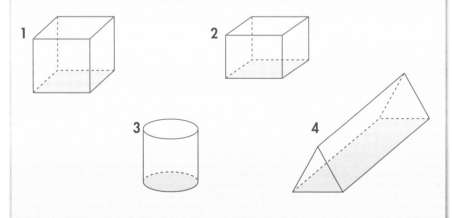

# Units of volume

This section will show you how to:
● use the correct units with volume

**Key words**
cubic centimetre
cubic metre
cubic millimetre
edge
face
vertex
volume

**Volume** is the amount of space taken up inside a 3D shape.
Volume is measured in **cubic millimetres** (mm³), **cubic centimetres** (cm³) or **cubic metres** (m³).

## Length, area and volume

A cube with an **edge** of 1 cm has a volume of 1 cm³ and each **face** has an area of 1 cm².

A cube with an edge of 2 cm has a volume of 8 cm³ and each face has an area of 4 cm².

A cube with an edge of 3 cm has a volume of 27 cm³ and each face has an area of 9 cm².

1 cm

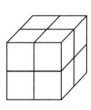
2 cm

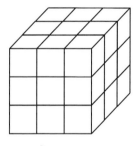
3 cm

---

**EXAMPLE 1**

How many cubes, each 1 cm by 1 cm by 1 cm, have been used to make these steps? What volume do they occupy?

When you count the cubes, do not forget to include those hidden at the back.

You should count:

6 + 4 + 2 = 12

The volume of each cube is 1 cm³.

So, the volume of the steps is:

12 × 1 = 12 cm³

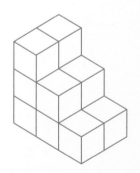

---

**FM** Functional Maths **AU** (AO2) Assessing Understanding **PS** (AO3) Problem Solving

## Area and volume

For shape A and shape B work out the area of the front face and the volume.
Then copy out the sentences and fill in the missing numbers.

| Shape A | Shape B | |
|---|---|---|
|  | 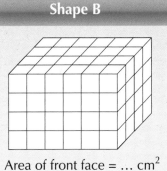 | Each side of shape B is … times as big as each side of shape A. The area of the front face of shape B is … times as big as the front face of shape A. The volume of shape B is …. times as big as the volume of shape A. |
| Area of front face = … cm$^2$<br>Volume = … cm$^3$ | Area of front face = … cm$^2$<br>Volume = … cm$^3$ | |
| 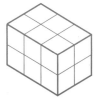 | 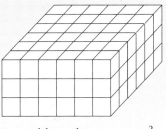 | Each side of shape B is … times as big as each side of shape A. The area of the front face of shape B is … times as big as the front face of shape A. The volume of shape B is …. times as big as the volume of shape A. |
| Area of front face = … cm$^2$<br>Volume = … cm$^3$ | Area of front face = … cm$^2$<br>Volume = … cm$^3$ | |

## EXERCISE 12A

**1** Find the volume of each 3D shape, if the edge of each cube is 1 cm.

**a**

**b**

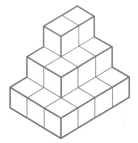

c

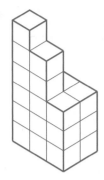

d

**AU 2** Zoe says, "there are a 100 cubes in the shape."
Explain how she might have calculated this.

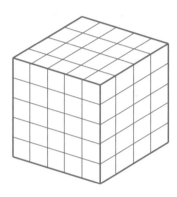

**PS 3** Each of the blocks in this diagram are centimetre cubes.
What is the total visible surface area of the cubes?

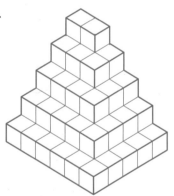

**4** David was asked to pack the display of packets,
shown opposite into cartons. All the packets are the
same size, with volume 100 cm$^3$. Each carton
will contain 24 of the packets. How many cartons
will David need?

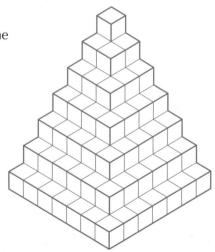

# ACTIVITY

## Many-faced shapes

All 3D shapes have **faces**, **vertices** and **edges**.
(**Note:** Vertices is the plural of vertex.)

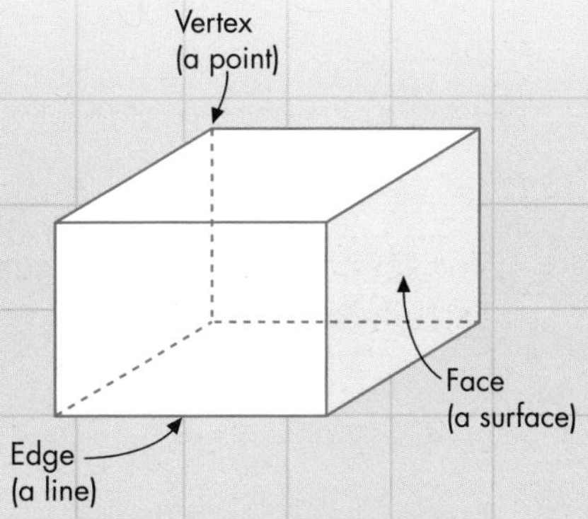

Look at the shapes in the table below and on the next page. Then copy the table and fill it in.

Remember that there are hidden faces, vertices and edges. These are shown with dashed lines.

Look at the numbers in the completed table.

- For each shape, can you find the connection between the following properties?

  - The number of faces, $F$
  - The number of vertices, $V$
  - The number of edges, $E$

- Find some other solid shapes. Does your connection also hold for those?

| Shape | Name | Number of faces ($F$) | Number of vertices ($V$) | Number of edges ($E$) |
|---|---|---|---|---|
| 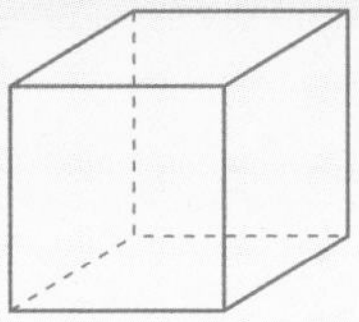 | Cuboid | | | |
| 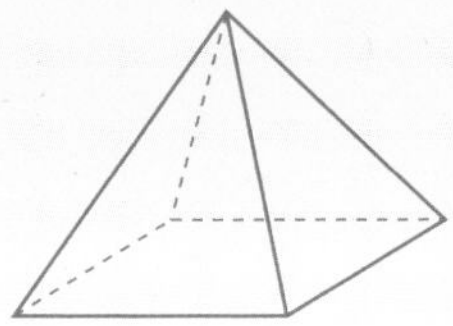 | Square-based pyramid | | | |
| 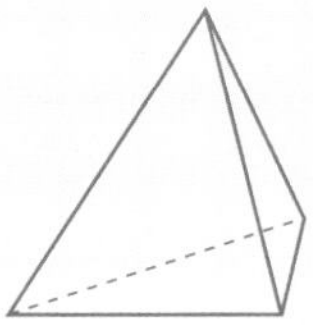 | Triangular-based pyramid (or tetrahedron) | | | |

| Shape | Name | Number of faces ($F$) | Number of vertices ($V$) | Number of edges ($E$) |
|---|---|---|---|---|
| | Octahedron | | | |
| | Triangular prism | | | |
| | Hexagonal prism | | | |
| | Hexagon-based pyramid | | | |

This section will show you how to:
- calculate the surface area and volume of a cuboid

**Key words**

capacity
height
length
litre
surface area
volume
width

A cuboid is a box shape, all six faces of which are rectangles.

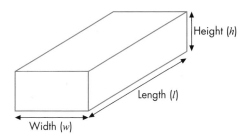

Every day you will come across many examples of cuboids, such as breakfast cereal packets, shoe boxes, DVD players – and even this book.

The **volume** of a cuboid is given by the formula:

volume = **length** × **width** × **height**   *or*   $V = l \times w \times h$   *or*   $V = lwh$

The **surface area** of a cuboid is calculated by finding the total area of the six faces, which are rectangles. Notice that each pair of opposite rectangles have the same area. So, from the diagram above:

area of top and bottom rectangles = 2 × length × width = $2lw$

area of front and back rectangles = 2 × height × width = $2hw$

area of two side rectangles = 2 × height × length = $2hl$

Hence, the surface area of a cuboid is given by the formula:

surface area = $A = 2lw + 2hw + 2hl$

**EXAMPLE 2**

Calculate the volume and surface area of this cuboid.

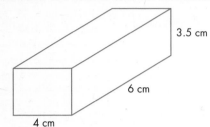

3.5 cm

6 cm

4 cm

Volume = $V = lwh = 6 \times 4 \times 3.5 = 84$ cm$^3$

Surface area = $A = 2lw + 2hw + 2hl$

$\qquad = (2 \times 6 \times 4) + (2 \times 3.5 \times 4) + (2 \times 3.5 \times 6)$

$\qquad = 48 + 28 + 42 = 118$ cm$^2$

**Note:**

1 cm$^3$ = 1000 mm$^3$ and 1 m$^3$ = 1 000 000 cm$^3$

The word '**capacity**' is often used for the volumes of liquids or gases.

The unit used for measuring capacity is the **litre**, l, with:

$\qquad$ 1000 millilitres (ml) = 1 litre

$\qquad$ 100 centilitres (cl) = 1 litre

$\qquad$ 1000 cm$^3$ = 1 litre

$\qquad$ 1 m$^3$ = 1000 litres

**EXERCISE 12B**

**1** Find **i** the volume and **ii** the surface area of each of these cuboids.

**a**

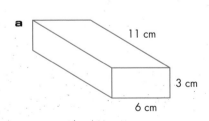

11 cm

3 cm

6 cm

**b**

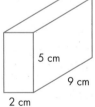

5 cm

9 cm

2 cm

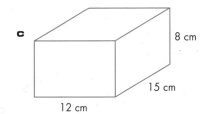

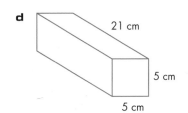

**2** Find the capacity of a fish-tank with dimensions: length 40 cm, width 30 cm and height 20 cm. Give your answer in litres.

**3** Find the volume of the cuboid in each of the following cases.

   **a** The area of the base is 40 cm$^2$ and the height is 4 cm.

   **b** The base has one side 10 cm and the other side 2 cm longer, and the height is 4 cm.

   **c** The area of the top is 25 cm$^2$ and the depth is 6 cm.

**4** Calculate **i** the volume and **ii** the surface area of each of the cubes with these edge lengths.

   **a** 4 cm           **b** 7 cm           **c** 10 mm

   **d** 5 m            **e** 12 m

**FM 5** Safety regulations say that in a room where people sleep there should be at least 12 m$^3$ for each person. A dormitory is 20 m long, 13 m wide and 4 m high. What is the greatest number of people who can safely sleep in the dormitory?

**6** Complete the table below for cuboids **a** to **e**.

| | Length | Width | Height | Volume |
|---|---|---|---|---|
| **a** | 8 cm | 5 cm | 4.5 cm | |
| **b** | 12 cm | 8 cm | | 480 cm$^3$ |
| **c** | 9 cm | | 5 cm | 270 cm$^3$ |
| **d** | | 7 cm | 3.5 cm | 245 cm$^3$ |
| **e** | 7.5 cm | 5.4 cm | 2 cm | |

**7** A tank contains 32 000 litres of water. The base of the tank measures 6.5 m by 3.1 m. Find the depth of water in the tank. Give your answer to one decimal place.

**8** A room contains 168 m$^3$ of air. The height of the room is 3.5 m. What is the area of the floor?

**9** What are the dimensions of cubes with these volumes?

   **a** 27 cm$^3$        **b** 125 m$^3$        **c** 8 mm$^3$        **d** 1.728 m$^3$

**D**

**10** Calculate the volume of each of these shapes.

**a**

2 cm
3 cm
6 cm
2 cm
10 cm
7 cm

**b**

3 cm
9 cm
10 cm
8 cm
2 cm

**AU 11** A cuboid has volume of 125 cm³ and a total surface area of 160 cm².

Is it possible that this cuboid is a cube? Give a reason for your answer.

**C**

**PS 12** The volume of a cuboid is 1000 cm³. What is the smallest surface area it could have?

# 12.3 Surface area and volume of a prism

**This section will show you how to:**
- calculate the surface area and volume of a prism

**Key words**

cross-section
prism
surface area
volume

A **prism** is a 3D shape that has the same **cross-section** running all the way through it, whenever it is cut perpendicular to its length. Here are some examples.

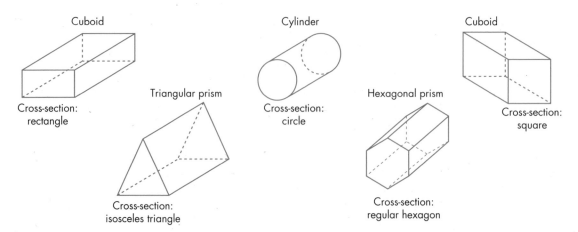

Cuboid
Cross-section: rectangle

Cylinder
Cross-section: circle

Cuboid
Cross-section: square

Triangular prism
Cross-section: isosceles triangle

Hexagonal prism
Cross-section: regular hexagon

The **volume** of a prism is found by multiplying the area of its cross-section by the length of the prism (or height if the prism is stood on end), that is:

volume of prism = area of cross-section × length *or* $V = Al$

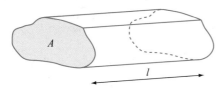

---

**EXAMPLE 3**

Calculate the **surface area** and the volume of the triangular prism below.

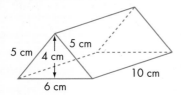

The surface area is made up of three rectangles and two isosceles triangles.

Area of the three rectangles = $10 \times 5 + 10 \times 5 + 10 \times 6 = 50 + 50 + 60 = 160 \text{ cm}^2$

Area of one triangle = $\dfrac{6 \times 4}{2} = 12$, so area of two triangles = $24 \text{ cm}^2$

Therefore, the total surface area = $184 \text{ cm}^2$

Volume of the prism = $Al$

Area of the cross-section = area of the triangle = $12 \text{ cm}^2$

So, $V = 12 \times 10 = 120 \text{ cm}^3$

---

**EXERCISE 12C**

**1** For each prism shown:

   **i** sketch the cross-section

   **ii** calculate the area of the cross-section

   **iii** calculate the volume.

> **HINTS AND TIPS**
>
> Look back at page 131 to remind yourself how to calculate the areas of compound shapes.

**a**

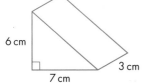

**b**

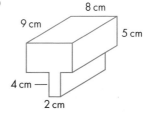

**c**

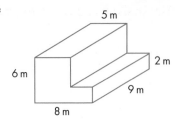

**d**

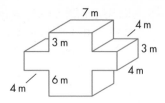

**e**

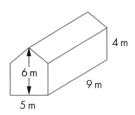

**f**

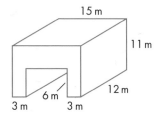

**2** Each of these prisms has a constant cross-section in the shape of a right-angled triangle.

   **a** Find the volume of each prism.     **b** Find the total surface area of each prism.

**i**

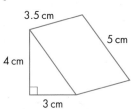

**ii**

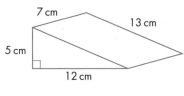

**3** The uniform cross-section of a swimming pool is a trapezium with parallel sides of lengths 1 m and 2.5 m, with a perpendicular distance of 30 m between them. The width of the pool is 10 m. How much water is in the pool when it is full? Give your answer in litres.

**4** Which of these 3D shapes has the greater volume?

**a**

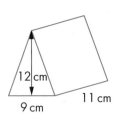

**b**

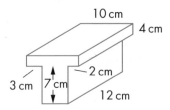

FM **5** Sandra had a swimming pool in her garden. The shallow end is 1 m deep and the deep end 2 m deep, as shown in the diagram.

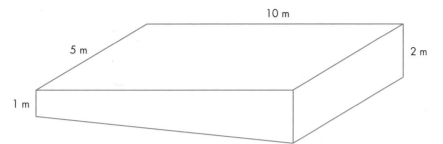

**a** What is the volume of the pool?

**b** How many litres of water will it take to fill the pool?

**c** Sandra has a hosepipe that will deliver water to the pool at the rate of 5 gallons a minute.

How long will it take to fill the pool? Give your answer in days, hours and minutes.

PS **6** The metal cuboid shown in the diagram is melted down and cast into a cube.

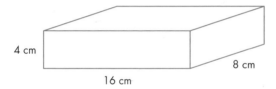

What is the surface area of the cube?

AU **7** Kira needs to find the weight of a metal lintel above a door.

She has calculated the volume of the lintel to be 22 500 cm$^3$.

She knows the weight of 1 cm$^3$ of this metal.

Explain how she can find the approximate weight of the lintel while it is still in place above the door.

This section will show you how to:
- calculate the volume of a cylinder

**Key words**

π
cylinder
height
length
radius
volume

The **volume** of a **cylinder** is found by multiplying the area of its circular cross-section by its **height**, that is:

volume = area of circle × height    *or*   $V = \pi r^2 h$

where $r$ is the **radius** of the cylinder and $h$ is its height or **length**.

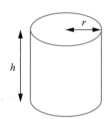

**EXAMPLE 4**

Calculate the volume of a cylinder with a radius of 5 cm and a height of 12 cm.

Volume $= \pi r^2 h = \pi \times 5^2 \times 12 = 942.5$ cm$^3$ (to 1 decimal place)

**EXERCISE 12D**

**1** Find the volume of each of these cylinders. Round your answers to a sensible degree of accuracy.

   **a** base radius 4 cm and height 5 cm

   **b** base diameter 9 cm and height 7 cm

   **c** base diameter 13.5 cm and height 15 cm

   **d** base radius 1.2 m and length 5.5 m.

**2** Find the volume of each of these cylinders. Round your answers to a sensible degree of accuracy.

   **a**

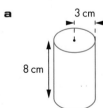

   **b**

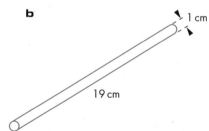

**c**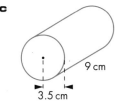

9 cm

3.5 cm

**d**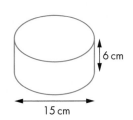

6 cm

15 cm

**FM** **3** The diameter of a cylindrical marble column is 60 cm and its height is 4.2 m. The cost of making this column is quoted as £67.50 per cubic metre. What is the estimated total cost of making the column?

**4** A cylindrical container is 65 cm in diameter. Water is poured into the container until it is 1 m deep. How much water is in the container? Give your answer to the nearest litre.

**5** A cylindrical can of soup has a diameter of 7 cm and a height of 9.5 cm. How much soup does it hold?

**6** A metal bar is 1 m long and has a diameter of 6 cm. What is the volume of the metal bar?

**7** What are the volumes of the following cylinders? Give your answers in terms of π.

**a** with a base radius of 6 cm and a height of 10 cm

**b** with a base diameter of 10 cm and a height of 12 cm.

**PS** **8** Copper wire is made by softening and rolling a copper ingot (a piece of cast metal) measuring 15 cm by 15 cm by 60 cm.

What length of wire of radius 0.5 mm can be rolled from the copper ingot? Give your answer in kilometres.

**AU** **9** Explain how you can tell which of the two cylinders has the larger volume without actually calculating their volumes.

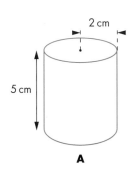

2 cm

5 cm

**A**

1 cm

20 cm

**B**

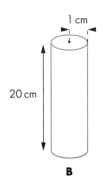

## GRADE BOOSTER

**G** You can find the volume of a 3D shape by counting cubes

**F** You can find the surface area of 3D shapes by counting squares on faces

**E** You know the formula $V = lbh$ to find the volume of a cuboid

**E** You can find the surface area of a cuboid

**C** You can find the surface area and volume of a prism

**C** You can find the volume of a cylinder

### What you should know now

- The units used when finding volume
- How to find the surface area and volume of a cuboid
- How to find the surface area and volume of a prism
- How to find the volume of a cylinder

**1** The diagram shows a solid shape made from four 1-centimetre cubes.

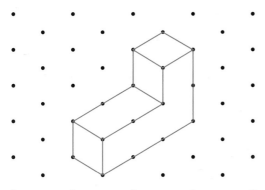

a What is the volume of the solid shape? (2)

b What is the surface area of the solid shape? (3)

(Total 5 marks)

**2** A cuboid is made from centimetre cubes.
The area of the base of the cuboid is 5 cm².
The volume of the cuboid is 10 cm³.
Work out the surface area of the cuboid. (3)

(Total 3 marks)

*AQA, November 2005, Paper 1 Intermediate, Question 17*

 **3** A cuboid has a volume of 75 cm³.

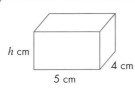

The length is 5 cm.
The width is 4 cm.
Find the height, *h* cm. (2)

(Total 2 marks)

*AQA, June 2008, Paper 2 Foundation, Question 15*

 **4** Jasmin has a pond in her garden.
The surface of the pond is a semicircle of radius 1.4 m.

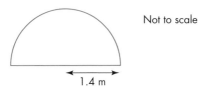

Not to scale

1.4 m

a Calculate the area of a semicircle of radius 1.4 m.
Give your answer to a sensible degree of accuracy.
You **must** show your working. (3)

b The pond is 50 cm deep.
The sides of the pond are vertical.
Calculate the volume of the pond.
Give your answer in cubic metres. (2)

(Total 5 marks)

*AQA, November 2005, Paper 2 Intermediate, Question 17*

**5** The diagram shows a cylinder with a height of 5 cm and a diameter of 16 cm.

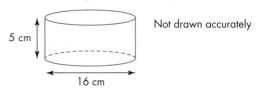

Not drawn accurately

5 cm

16 cm

Calculate the volume of the cylinder.
Give your answer in terms of π.
State the units of your answer. (4)

(Total 4 marks)

*AQA, May 2008, Paper 1 Foundation, Question 26*

**6** A triangular prism has dimensions as shown.

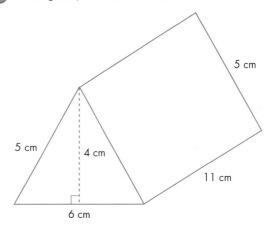

5 cm

5 cm

4 cm

11 cm

6 cm

a Calculate the total surface area of the prism.

b Calculate the volume of the prism.

# Worked Examination Questions

**(FM) 1** A baker uses square and circular tins to make his cakes.

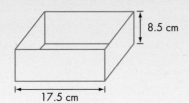

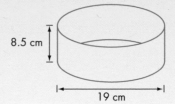

**a** The edge of the base of the square tin is 17.5 cm. Its height is 8.5 cm. Calculate the volume of the tin.

**b** The diameter of the circular tin is 19 cm. Its height is 8.5 cm. Calculate the volume of the circular tin.

**a** $V = lbh$

$\quad = 17.5 \times 17.5 \times 8.5$

$\quad = 2600 \text{ cm}^3$ (to the nearest ten)

You earn 1 method mark for correctly setting up the calculation of $17.5 \times 17.5 \times 8.8$.
You also earn 1 accuracy mark for an answer that could round to 2600.

( 2 marks )

**b** $V = \pi r^2 h$

The diameter is 19 cm, so $r = 9.5$ cm.

So, $V = \pi \times 9.5^2 \times 8.5$

$\quad = 2410 \text{ cm}^3$ (to the nearest ten)

You earn 1 method mark for correctly setting up the calculation of $9.5 \times 9.5 \times 8.5$.
You also earn 1 accuracy mark for an answer that could round to 2410.

( 2 marks )

( **Total:** 4 marks )

There could also be a mark for rounding your numbers to a sensible degree of accuracy. Here this would be to either the nearest ten or the nearest unit.
In some examinations, there could also be a mark for giving the correct units.

# Worked Examination Questions

**FM** **2** A firm makes small rods that are cylinders of radius 5 mm and length 10 cm.

These are all made from blocks of metal measuring 60 cm by 60 cm by 2 m.

How many rods can be created from one block of metal?

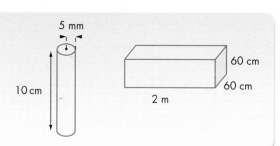

Volume of block = 200 cm × 60 cm × 60 cm

            = 720 000 cm$^3$

> You get 1 method mark for converting to common units and 1 method mark for the calculation 200 × 60 × 60.

Volume of a rod = π × 0.5$^2$ × 10

            = 2.5π cm$^3$

> You get 1 accuracy mark for finding 720 000.

Number of rods = $\dfrac{720\,000}{2.5\pi}$

> You get 1 method mark for converting to common units and 1 method mark for the calculation π × 0.5$^2$ × 10.

         = 91 673.247 22

         = 91 673

> You get 1 accuracy mark for 2.5π or 7.853 981 634. However, this mark could be lost for rounding too soon in this calculation.

**Total: 9 marks**

> You get 1 method mark for the calculation 720 000 ÷ 2.5π.

> 1 accuracy mark is available for 91673.2 …. (… means the number continues.)

> You get 1 mark for accuracy for a final integer value 91 673.
> Note that an important part of solving this problem is that you do not round until the end, otherwise you may get an inaccurate result; for example, if you took the volume of the rod to be 7.85 then you would get a result of 91 719.

**AU** **3** Isaac is asked to find the area of a circle with diameter 2 m. He says it is about 6 m$^2$. Explain how you can tell he is wrong.

If diameter is 2 m then the radius is 1 m

Area = π × 1$^2$

> 1 method mark is available for recognising radius = 1 m.

π is approximately 3, so this works out to be 3 m$^2$ and not 6 m$^2$.

> You also get 1 method mark for realising that area = π × 1$^2$.

**Total: 3 marks**

> You get 1 mark for accuracy for saying π is approximately 3.
> Note that if you calculated the area of the circle exactly, you would not get the last mark.

Farmers have to do mathematical calculations almost every day. For example, an arable farmer may need to know how much seed to buy, how much water is required to irrigate the field each day, how much wheat they expect to grow and how much storage space they need to store wheat once it is harvested.

Farming can be filled with uncertainties, including changes in weather, crop disease and changes in consumption. It is therefore important that farmers correctly calculate variables that are within their control, to minimise the impact of changes that are outside their control.

### Grain storage

Wheat is stored in large containers called silos. These are usually big cylinders but can also be various other shapes.

### Important information about wheat crops (yield data)

- A 1 kg bag of seeds holds 26 500 seeds

- A 1 kg bag of seeds costs 50p

- I want to plant 60 bags of seed

- I need to plant 100 seeds in each square metre ($m^2$) of field

- I need to irrigate each square metre of the field with 5 litres of water each day

- I expect to harvest 0.7 kg of wheat from each square metre of the field

- Every cubic metre ($m^3$) of storage will hold 800 kg of wheat

**Your task**

Rufus, a crop farmer, is going to grow his first field of wheat next summer. Using all the information that he has gathered, help him to plan for his wheat crop. You should consider:

- the size of the field that he will require
- how much seed he will need
- how much water he will need to irrigate the crops, per day, and how it will be stored
- how he will store the seeds and wheat
- how much profit he could make if grain is sold at £92.25 per tonne.

**Getting started**

Think about these points to help you create your plan.

- What different shapes and sizes of field could the crops be grown in?
- If Rufus needs a reservoir to hold one day's irrigation water, what size cylinder would he need? How would this change if he chose a cuboid? What other shapes and sizes of reservoir could he use?
- What shapes and sizes could the silos be?

**Handy hints**

Remember: 1000 litres = $1\,m^3$

1000 kg = 1 tonne

# Why this chapter matters

There are many curves that can be seen in everyday life. Did you know that all these curves can be represented mathematically?

Below are a few examples of simple curves that you may have come across. Can you think of any others?

Many road signs are circular.

A chain hanging freely between two supports forms a curve called a catenary.

The examples above both show circular-based curves. However, in mathematics curves can take many shapes. These can be demonstrated using a cone, as shown on the right and below. If you can make a cone out of plasticine or modelling clay, then you can prove this principle yourself. As you look at these curves, try to think of where you have seen them in your own life.

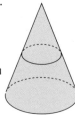

If you slice the cone parallel to the base, the shape you are left with is a **circle**.

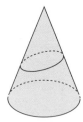

If you slice the cone at an angle to the base, the shape you are left with is an **ellipse**.

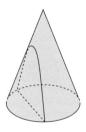

If you slice the cone vertically, the shape you are left with is a **hyperbola**.

The curve that will be particularly important in this chapter is the parabola. Car headlights are shaped like parabolas.

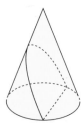

If you slice the cone parallel to its sloping side, the shape you are left with is a **parabola**.

The suspension cables on the Humber Bridge are also parabolas.

All parabolas are quadratic graphs. During the course of this chapter you will be looking at how to use quadratic equations to draw graphs that have this kind of curve.

# 13 Algebra: Quadratic graphs

**1** Drawing quadratic graphs

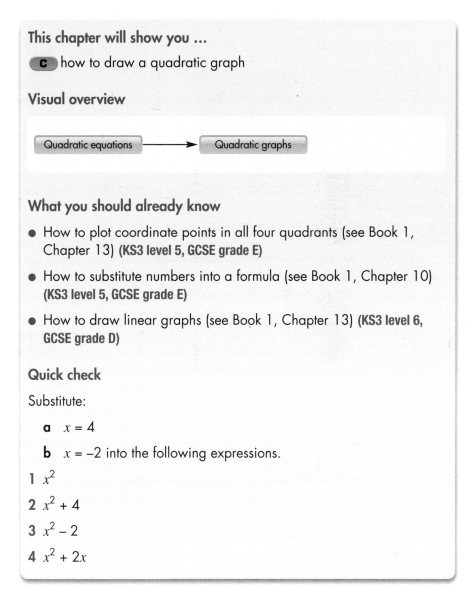

**This chapter will show you ...**

**c** how to draw a quadratic graph

**Visual overview**

Quadratic equations ⟶ Quadratic graphs

**What you should already know**

- How to plot coordinate points in all four quadrants (see Book 1, Chapter 13) **(KS3 level 5, GCSE grade E)**

- How to substitute numbers into a formula (see Book 1, Chapter 10) **(KS3 level 5, GCSE grade E)**

- How to draw linear graphs (see Book 1, Chapter 13) **(KS3 level 6, GCSE grade D)**

**Quick check**

Substitute:

**a** $x = 4$

**b** $x = -2$ into the following expressions.

**1** $x^2$

**2** $x^2 + 4$

**3** $x^2 - 2$

**4** $x^2 + 2x$

# Drawing quadratic graphs

**This section will show you how to:**
- draw a quadratic graph, given its equation

**Key words**
parabola
quadratic equation
quadratic graph

A graph with a ∪ or ∩ shape is a quadratic graph.

A **quadratic graph** has an equation that involves $x^2$.

All of the following are **quadratic equations** and each would produce a quadratic graph.

$y = x^2$

$y = x^2 + 5$

$y = x^2 - 3x$

$y = x^2 + 5x + 6$

$y = x^2 + 2x - 5$

---

**EXAMPLE 1**

Draw the graph of $y = x^2$ for $-3 \leqslant x \leqslant 3$.

First make a table, as shown below.

| $x$ | −3 | −2 | −1 | 0 | 1 | 2 | 3 |
|---|---|---|---|---|---|---|---|
| $y = x^2$ | 9 | 4 | 1 | 0 | 1 | 4 | 9 |

Now draw axes, with $-3 \leqslant x \leqslant 3$ and
$0 \leqslant y \leqslant 9$, plot the points and
join them to make a smooth curve.

This is the graph of $y = x^2$.
This type of graph is often referred
to as a **parabola**.

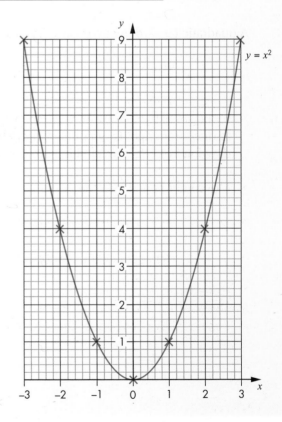

---

**FM** Functional Maths  **AU** (AO2) Assessing Understanding  **PS** (AO3) Problem Solving

Note that although it is difficult to draw accurate curves, examiners work to a *tolerance of only 2 mm.*

Here are some of the more common ways in which marks are lost in an examination.

- When the points are too far apart, a curve tends to 'wobble'.

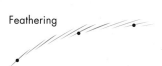

Wobbly curve

- Drawing curves in small sections leads to 'feathering'.

Feathering

- The place where a curve should turn smoothly is drawn 'flat'.

Flat bottom

- A curve is drawn through a point that, clearly, has been incorrectly plotted.

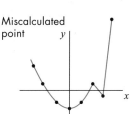

Miscalculated point

A quadratic curve drawn correctly will *always* be a smooth curve.

Here are some tips that will make it easier for you to draw smooth, curved graphs.

- If you are *right-handed*, you might like to turn your piece of paper or your exercise book round so that you draw from left to right. Your hand may be steadier this way than if you try to draw from right to left or away from your body. If you are *left-handed*, you may find drawing from right to left the more accurate way.

- Move your pencil over the points as a practice run without drawing the curve.

- Do one continuous curve and only stop at a plotted point.

- Use a *sharp* pencil and do not press too heavily, so that you may easily rub out mistakes.

Normally in an examination, grids are provided with the axes clearly marked. Remember that a tolerance of 2 mm is all that you are allowed. In the exercises, suitable ranges are suggested for the axes. Usually you will be expected to use 2 mm graph paper to draw the graphs.

**EXAMPLE 2**

   **a** Draw the graph of $y = x^2 + 2x - 3$ for $-4 \leqslant x \leqslant 2$.

   **b** Use your graph to find the value of $y$ when $x = 1.6$.

   **c** Use your graph to find the values of $x$ that give a $y$-value of 1.

   **a** Draw a table as follows to help work each step of the calculation.

| $x$ | −4 | −3 | −2 | −1 | 0 | 1 | 2 |
|---|---|---|---|---|---|---|---|
| $x^2$ | 16 | 9 | 4 | 1 | 0 | 1 | 4 |
| $+2x$ | −8 | −6 | −4 | −2 | 0 | 2 | 4 |
| −3 | −3 | −3 | −3 | −3 | −3 | −3 | −3 |
| $y = x^2 + 2x - 3$ | 5 | 0 | −3 | −4 | −3 | 0 | 5 |

Generally, you do not need to work out all values in a table. If you use a calculator, you need only to work out the $y$-value. The other rows in the table are just working lines to break down the calculation.

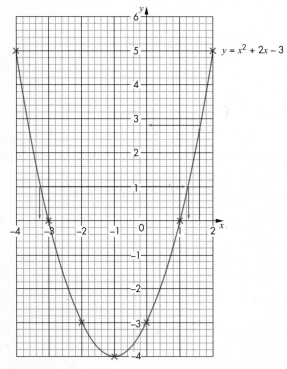

   **b** To find the corresponding $y$-value for any value of $x$, you start on the $x$-axis at that $x$-value, go up to the curve, across to the $y$-axis and read off the $y$-value. This procedure is marked on the graph with arrows.

      Always show these arrows because even if you make a mistake and misread the scales, you may still get a mark.

      So when $x = 1.6$, $y = 2.8$.

   **c** This time start at 1 on the $y$-axis and read off the two $x$-values that correspond to a $y$-value of 1.

      Again, this procedure is marked on the graph with arrows.

      So when $y = 1$, $x = -3.2$ or $x = 1.2$.

**EXERCISE 13A**

**1** Copy and complete the table for the graph of $y = x^2$ for $-5 \leqslant x \leqslant 5$.

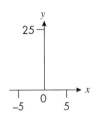

| x | −5 | −4.5 | −4 | −3.5 | −3 | −2.5 | −2 | −1.5 | −1 | −0.5 | 0 |
|---|---|---|---|---|---|---|---|---|---|---|---|
| $y = x^2$ | 25 | 20.25 | 16 | | | | | | 1 | 0.25 | 0 |

As the graph is symmetrical, you do not need to work out the values for 0 to 5.

**2** Copy and complete the table for the graph of $y = 3x^2$ for $-3 \leqslant x \leqslant 3$.

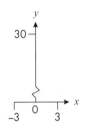

| x | −3 | −2 | −1 | 0 | 1 | 2 | 3 |
|---|---|---|---|---|---|---|---|
| $y = 3x^2$ | 27 | | 3 | | | 12 | |

**3** Copy and complete the table for the graph of $y = x^2 + 2$ for $-5 \leqslant x \leqslant 5$.

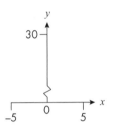

| x | −5 | −4 | −3 | −2 | −1 | 0 | 1 | 2 | 3 | 4 | 5 |
|---|---|---|---|---|---|---|---|---|---|---|---|
| $y = x^2 + 2$ | 27 | | 11 | | | | | 6 | | | |

**4** **a** Copy and complete the table for the graph of $y = x^2 - 3x$ for $-5 \leqslant x \leqslant 5$. Use your table to plot the graph.

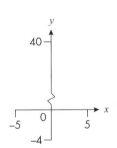

| x | −5 | −4 | −3 | −2 | −1 | 0 | 1 | 2 | 3 | 4 | 5 |
|---|---|---|---|---|---|---|---|---|---|---|---|
| $x^2$ | 25 | | 9 | | | | | 4 | | | |
| $-3x$ | 15 | | | | | | | −6 | | | |
| $y$ | 40 | | | | | | | −2 | | | |

**b** Use your graph to find the value of $y$ when $x = 3.5$.

**c** Use your graph to find the values of $x$ that give a $y$-value of 5.

**5** **a** Copy and complete the table for the graph of $y = x^2 - 2x - 8$ for $-5 \leqslant x \leqslant 5$. Use your table to plot the graph.

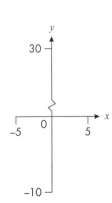

| x | −5 | −4 | −3 | −2 | −1 | 0 | 1 | 2 | 3 | 4 | 5 |
|---|---|---|---|---|---|---|---|---|---|---|---|
| $x^2$ | 25 | | 9 | | | | | 4 | | | |
| $-2x$ | 10 | | | | | | | −4 | | | |
| $-8$ | −8 | | | | | | | −8 | | | |
| $y$ | 27 | | | | | | | −8 | | | |

**b** Use your graph to find the value of $y$ when $x = 0.5$.

**c** Use your graph to find the values of $x$ that give a $y$-value of −3.

**6** **a** Copy and complete the table for the graph of $y = x^2 - 5x + 4$ for $-2 \leqslant x \leqslant 5$. Use your table to plot the graph.

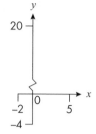

| $x$ | −2 | −1 | 0 | 1 | 2 | 3 | 4 | 5 |
|---|---|---|---|---|---|---|---|---|
| $y$ | 18 | | 4 | | | −2 | | |

**b** Use your graph to find the value of $y$ when $x = -0.5$.

**c** Use your graph to find the values of $x$ that give a $y$-value of 3.

**7** The diagram shows a side elevation of a cone and with a cut parallel to one side.

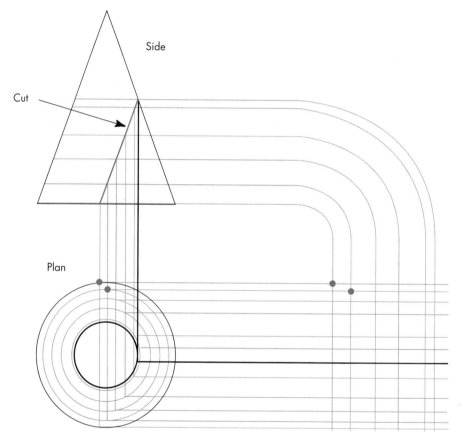

The cone is divided into horizontal sections.

A plan view of the cone is shown.

Construction lines have been drawn to link the elevation and the plan.

Two of the intersecting points have been drawn on the plan.

Two points have also been drawn where the construction lines from the side elevation intersect with the construction lines from the plan.

**a** Plot the rest of the points on the plan and join them with a smooth curve to see the plan view of the parabola.

**b** Plot the rest of the points on the intersecting lines and join them with a smooth curve to see the parabola.

**FM** **8** A car travelling at 30 metres per second, brakes at a set of traffic lights.

After $t$ seconds the speed, $v$, in metres per second, is given by $v = 30 - 3t$.

The distance travelled, $s$, in metres, in time, $t$, after applying the brakes is given by the formula

$$s = 30t - 1.5t^2$$

**a** It takes the car 10 s to stop. How far has it travelled in this time?

**b** Complete the table for the speed and distance travelled for $0 \leqslant t \leqslant 10$.

| $t$ (s) | 1 | 2 | 3 | 4 | 5 | 6 | 7 | 8 | 9 | 10 |
|---|---|---|---|---|---|---|---|---|---|---|
| $v$ (m/s) | 27 | | | | | | | | | |
| $s$ (m) | 28.5 | | | | | | | | | |

**c** Using a horizontal axis for $v$ from 0 to 30 and a vertical axis for $s$ from 0 to 150, plot the graph of $v$ against $s$.

**d** Approximately how far had the car travelled when it had reduced its speed by half?

**9** **a** Copy and complete the table for the graph of $y = x^2 + 2x - 1$ for $-3 \leqslant x \leqslant 3$. Use your table to plot the graph.

| $x$ | −3 | −2 | −1 | 0 | 1 | 2 | 3 |
|---|---|---|---|---|---|---|---|
| $x^2$ | 9 | | | | 1 | 4 | |
| $+2x$ | −6 | | −2 | | | 4 | |
| $-1$ | −1 | −1 | | | | −1 | |
| $y$ | 2 | | | | | 7 | |

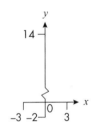

**b** Use your graph to find the $y$-value when $x = -2.5$.

**c** Use your graph to find the values of $x$ that give a $y$-value of 1.

**10** **a** Copy and complete the table to draw the graph of $y = x^2 - 4$ for $-4 \leqslant x \leqslant 4$.

| $x$ | −4 | −3 | −2 | −1 | 0 | 1 | 2 | 3 | 4 |
|---|---|---|---|---|---|---|---|---|---|
| $y$ | 12 | | | −3 | | | | 5 | |

**b** Where does the graph cross the $x$-axis?

**c** Use your graph to find the $y$-value when $x = 1.5$.

**d** Use your graph to find the values of $x$ that give a $y$ value of 8.

**11** **a** Copy and complete the table to draw the graph of $y = x^2 + 4x$ for $-5 \leqslant x \leqslant 2$.

| $x$ | −5 | −4 | −3 | −2 | −1 | 0 | 1 | 2 |
|-----|-----|-----|-----|-----|-----|-----|-----|-----|
| $x^2$ | 25 | | | 4 | | | 1 | |
| $+4x$ | −20 | | | −8 | | | 4 | |
| $y$ | 5 | | | −4 | | | 5 | |

**b** Where does the graph cross the $x$-axis?

**c** Use your graph to find the $y$-value when $x = -2.5$.

**d** Use your graph to find the values of $x$ that give a $y$-value of 3.

**12** **a** Copy and complete the table to draw the graph of $y = x^2 - 6x + 3$ for $-1 \leqslant x \leqslant 7$.

| $x$ | −1 | 0 | 1 | 2 | 3 | 4 | 5 | 6 | 7 |
|-----|-----|-----|-----|-----|-----|-----|-----|-----|-----|
| $y$ | 10 | | | −5 | | | −2 | | |

**b** Where does the graph cross the $x$-axis?

**c** Use your graph to find the $y$-value when $x = 3.5$.

**d** Use your graph to find the values of $x$ that give a $y$-value of 5.

**FM 13** Rae drops objects from different heights and times how long they take to reach the ground.

Here are her results.

| Height (m) | 10 | 30 | 50 | 80 | 125 | 200 |
|-----|-----|-----|-----|-----|-----|-----|
| Time (s) | 1.4 | 2.5 | 3.2 | 4 | 5 | 6.3 |

**a** Draw a graph to show these results, with a horizontal axis for time from 0 to 7 and a vertical axis for height from 0 to 250.

**b** Rae throws an object from the top of a cliff.

It takes 5.5 seconds to reach the base of the cliff.

Use the graph to estimate the height of the cliff.

## GRADE BOOSTER

**c** You can draw a simple quadratic graph

**c** You can draw a more complex quadratic graph

**c** You can find $x$ (or $y$) values from a quadratic graph given the $y$ (or $x$) values

### What you should know now

- How to draw a quadratic graph
- How to read values from a quadratic graph

**1** **a** Complete the table of values for
$y = x^2 - x - 5$ (2)

| $x$ | −2 | −1 | 0 | 1 | 2 | 3 | 4 |
|---|---|---|---|---|---|---|---|
| $y$ | 1 | | −5 | −5 | −3 | 1 | |

**b** On a grid like the one below, draw the graph of $y = x^2 - x - 5$ for values of $x$ from −2 to 4 (2)

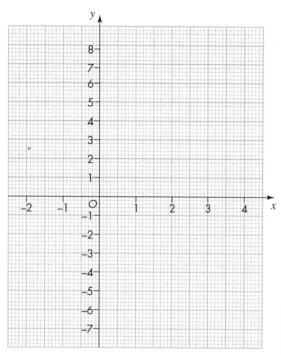

**c** Find the values of $x$ when $y = 0$ (1)

(Total 5 marks)

*AQA, June 2008, Paper 1 Foundation, Question 27*

**2** **a** Complete the table of values for
$y = x^2 - 3$ (1)

| $x$ | −3 | −2 | −1 | 0 | 1 | 2 | 3 |
|---|---|---|---|---|---|---|---|
| $y$ | | 1 | −2 | −3 | −2 | | 6 |

**b** On a grid like the one below, draw the graph of $y = x^2 - 3$ for values of $x$ from −3 to +3 (2)

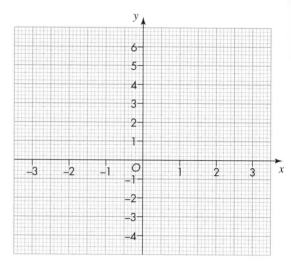

**c** Use your graph to find the values of $x$ when $y = 0$ (2)

(Total 5 marks)

*AQA, November 2005, Paper 1 Intermediate, Question 7*

**3** **a** Complete the table of values for
$y = x(x + 3)$ (2)

| $x$ | −4 | −3 | −2 | −1 | 0 | 1 | 2 |
|---|---|---|---|---|---|---|---|
| $y$ | 4 | 0 | | −2 | 0 | 4 | |

**b** On a grid like the one below, draw the graph of $y = x(x + 3)$ for values of $x$ from −4 to +2 (2)

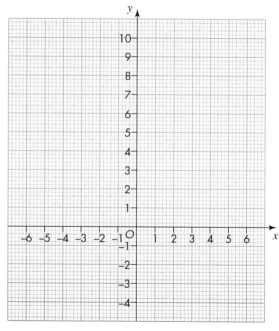

(Total 4 marks)

*AQA, June 2009, Paper 2 Foundation, Question 13*

c

# Worked Examination Questions

**1 a** Complete the table of values for $y = x^2 - 4x + 1$.

| $x$ | −1 | 0 | 1 | 2 | 3 | 4 | 5 |
|---|---|---|---|---|---|---|---|
| $y$ | 6 | | −2 | | −2 | | 6 |

**b** Draw the graph of $y = x^2 - 4x + 1$ for $-1 \leqslant x \leqslant 5$.

**c** Use the graph to find the $x$-value when $y = 2$.

**a** When $x = 0$, $y = (0)^2 - 4(0) + 1 = 0 - 0 + 1 = 1$

When $x = 2$, $y = (2)^2 - 4(2) + 1 = 4 - 8 + 1 = -3$

When $x = 4$, $y = (4)^2 - 4(4) + 1 = 16 - 16 + 1 = 1$

> Substitute numbers into the equation to get 1 mark.

( 1 mark )

**b**

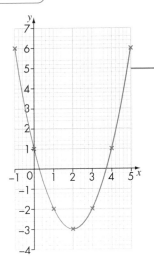

> Plot the points. You get 1 mark for plotting the points and 1 mark for drawing a smooth curve.

( 2 marks )

**c**

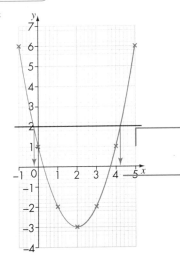

> Draw a line $y = 2$ horizontally to meet the graph at two points.

> Draw lines down to the $x$-axis from these points and read off the values to get 1 mark.

−0.2 and 4.2

( 1 mark )    ( **Total:** 4 marks )

The forms of many suspension bridges are based on quadratic functions. Their shape is a classic quadratic curve.

Quadratic curve

In this task you will investigate the quadratic functions that can be used to describe stable suspension bridges.

## Getting started

Use these questions to familiarise yourself with how quadratic expressions can be used to represent bridges.

● What would you need to know, to be able to describe the shape of a bridge, in terms of a quadratic formula?

● Think about bridges and other landmarks in your local area. How many of these are based on quadratic equations and form parabolas. Use images to illustrate your findings.

## Your task

Below you can see the dimensions of the Clifton Suspension Bridge. Use these dimensions to construct a diagram of the bridge.

Then, using your diagram, estimate the quadratic equation for the curve of the bridge. Represent this equation appropriately.

Write a report explaining the mathematical process that you used to solve this problem. State any assumptions that you made and explain whether you could have found different answers if you had changed your assumptions.

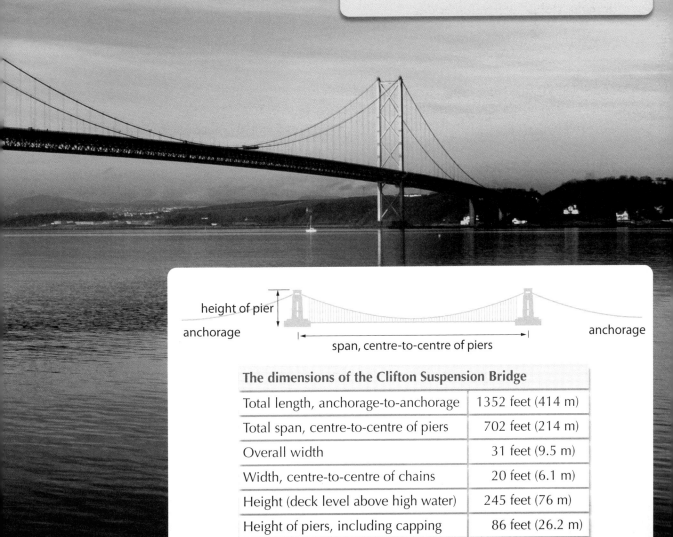

| The dimensions of the Clifton Suspension Bridge | |
| --- | --- |
| Total length, anchorage-to-anchorage | 1352 feet (414 m) |
| Total span, centre-to-centre of piers | 702 feet (214 m) |
| Overall width | 31 feet (9.5 m) |
| Width, centre-to-centre of chains | 20 feet (6.1 m) |
| Height (deck level above high water) | 245 feet (76 m) |
| Height of piers, including capping | 86 feet (26.2 m) |
| Dip of chains | 70 feet (21.3 m) |

# Why this chapter matters

Pythagoras was born on the island of Samos in 568 BC. He has been described as the first pure mathematician and is best known for developing the theorem that bears his name – Pythagoras' theorem.

Pythagoras

The ancient world was filled with war and travel, so this gave Pythagoras the opportunity to visit different countries (sometimes as a prisoner!) and learn about different cultures and systems of knowledge, including different ways of thinking about mathematics.

He learnt from the Egyptians and the Babylonians about science, religion, mathematics and astronomy, and ultimately settled in Italy where he established the Pythagorean Brotherhood (a secret society devoted to politics, mathematics and astronomy). All this helped him to develop the theorem we now know as Pythagoras' theorem.

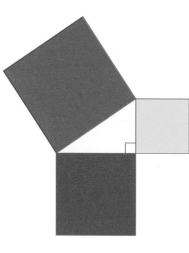

His theorem centres on the fact that squares drawn on the sides of any right-angled triangle have a special relationship with each other – that is, that the smaller squares can be fitted into the larger square. This idea was known to the Babylonians a thousand years earlier, but it was Pythagoras who was the first actually to prove it.

It is said that when he discovered his famous theorem, he was so full of joy that he showed his gratitude to the gods by sacrificing a hundred oxen!

It is interesting to note that Pythagoras was only interested in the idea of the squares being drawn and being able to combine both smaller squares into the larger square. He was not interested in the numbers attached to these squares – this development came later. This may be because Pythagoras was not just a mathematician; he was a philosopher who thought of each new theorem as a platform for developing further and not an end in itself.

Pythagoras' theorem is now used in all sorts of fields, from geography to engineering. It is a cornerstone of much other mathematics and interestingly works in 3D blocks, too (although at GCSE you will only look at the theorem in 2D).

It is, therefore, a vital part of mathematics to get to grips with, both in life and for your GCSE examination.

Pythagoras' theorem can be used to find the height of a mountain.

Pythagoras' theorem can be used to make sure that structures, such as masts, are correctly positioned for maximum strength.

# Geometry: Pythagoras' theorem

**1** Pythagoras' theorem

**2** Finding a shorter side

**3** Solving problems using Pythagoras' theorem

## This chapter will show you ...

**c** how to use Pythagoras' theorem in right-angled triangles

**c** how to solve problems using Pythagoras' theorem

### Visual overview

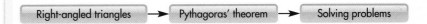

### What you should already know

- How to find the square and square root of a number **(KS3 level 4, GCSE grade F)**
- How to round numbers to a suitable degree of accuracy **(KS3 level 6, GCSE grade D)**

### Quick check

Use your calculator to evaluate the following, giving your answers to 1 decimal place.

**1** $2.3^2$

**2** $15.7^2$

**3** $0.78^2$

**4** $\sqrt{8}$

**5** $\sqrt{260}$

**6** $\sqrt{0.5}$

# Pythagoras' theorem

**This section will show you how to:**

- calculate the length of the hypotenuse in a right-angled triangle

**Key words**

hypotenuse
Pythagoras' theorem

Pythagoras, the mathematician, enjoyed geometry and playing with shapes. He was fascinated with right-angled triangles. He played around with squares on the sides of triangles until he discovered the now-famous Pythagoras' theorem about these squares.

The activity below will lead you to discover this rule for yourself and to show that it actually works.

## ACTIVITY

### Squares on triangles

1 Draw a right-angled triangle with sides of 3 cm and 4 cm, as shown.

2 Measure accurately the long side of the triangle (the **hypotenuse**).

3 Draw four more right-angled triangles, choosing your own lengths for the short sides.

4 When you have done this, measure the hypotenuse for each triangle.

5 Copy and complete the table below for your triangles.

| Short side $a$ | Short side $b$ | Hypotenuse $c$ | $a^2$ | $b^2$ | $c^2$ |
|---|---|---|---|---|---|
| 3 | 4 | 5 | 9 | 16 | 25 |
| | | | | | |
| | | | | | |
| | | | | | |
| | | | | | |

Is there a pattern in your results? Can you see that $a^2$, $b^2$ and $c^2$ are related in some way?

You should spot that the value of $a^2$ added to that of $b^2$ is very close to the value of $c^2$. (Why don't the values add up exactly?)

You have 'rediscovered' **Pythagoras' theorem**. His theorem can be expressed in several ways, two of which are given on the next page.

**FM** Functional Maths   **AU** (AO2) Assessing Understanding   **PS** (AO3) Problem Solving

Consider squares being drawn on each side of a right-angled triangle, with sides 3 cm, 4 cm and 5 cm.

The longest side is called the hypotenuse and is always opposite the right angle.

Pythagoras' theorem can then be stated as follows:

> *For any right-angled triangle, the area of the square drawn on the hypotenuse is equal to the sum of the areas of the squares drawn on the other two sides.*

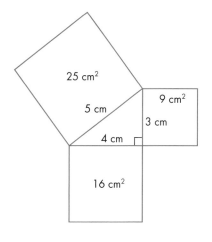

The form in which most of your parents would have learnt the theorem when they were at school – and which is still in use today – is as follows:

> *In any right-angled triangle, the square of the hypotenuse is equal to the sum of the squares of the other two sides.*

Pythagoras' theorem is more usually written as a formula:

$$c^2 = a^2 + b^2$$

**Remember** that Pythagoras' theorem can only be used in right-angled triangles.

## Finding the hypotenuse

---

**EXAMPLE 1**

Find the length of the hypotenuse, marked $x$ on the diagram.

Using Pythagoras' theorem gives:

$$x^2 = 8^2 + 5.2^2$$
$$= 64 + 27.04$$
$$= 91.04$$

So, $x = \sqrt{91.04} = 9.5$ cm (1 decimal place)

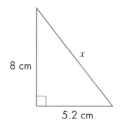

## EXERCISE 14A

**1** For each of the following triangles, calculate the length of the hypotenuse, $x$, rounding your answers to 1 decimal place.

**a**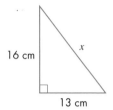
9 cm
$x$
5 cm

**b**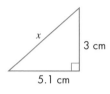
$x$
3 cm
5.1 cm

**c**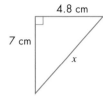
4.8 cm
7 cm
$x$

**d**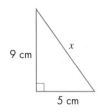
16 cm
$x$
13 cm

**e**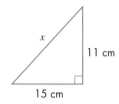
$x$
11 cm
15 cm

> **HINTS AND TIPS**
>
> In these questions you are finding the hypotenuse. Add the squares of the two shorter sides in every case.

**f**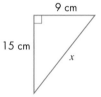
9 cm
15 cm
$x$

**g**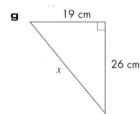
19 cm
$x$
26 cm

**h**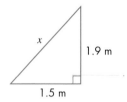
$x$
1.9 m
1.5 m

**i**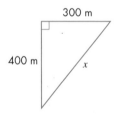
300 m
400 m
$x$

**j**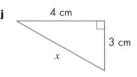
4 cm
3 cm
$x$

**k**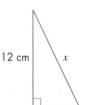
12 cm
$x$
5 cm

**l**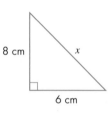
8 cm
$x$
6 cm

**FM 2** Harold, the school groundsman, knew Pythagoras' theorem. He used lengths of rope to help him create right angles for the line markings on pitches.

He had ropes of lengths:

50 cm, 1 m, 1.2 m, 1.25 m, 1.3 m, 1.5 m, 2 m and 2.5 m.

Which of these rope lengths could be used to create a right angle?

**PS 3** Find, by trial and improvement or otherwise, the length of $x$ in this triangle.
Give your answer correct to 1 decimal place.

$x + 2$
$x$
12 cm

**AU 4** Explain how you can tell that a triangle with sides of length 6 cm, 7 cm and 10 cm is not a right-angled triangle.

The last three examples in question 1 give whole-number answers. Sets of whole numbers that obey Pythagoras' theorem are called *Pythagorean triples*. Examples of these are:

3, 4, 5     5, 12, 13     and     6, 8, 10

Note that 6, 8, 10 are respectively multiples of 3, 4, 5.

## 14.2 Finding a shorter side

**This section will show you how to:**
- calculate the length of a shorter side in a right-angled triangle

**Key word**
Pythagoras' theorem

By rearranging the formula for **Pythagoras' theorem**, you can easily calculate the length of one of the shorter sides.

$$c^2 = a^2 + b^2$$

So:    $a^2 = c^2 - b^2$   or   $b^2 = c^2 - a^2$

**EXAMPLE 2**

Find the length $x$.

In the triangle, $x$ is one of the shorter sides.

So, using Pythagoras' theorem gives:

$$x^2 = 15^2 - 11^2$$
$$= 225 - 121$$
$$= 104$$

So:  $x = \sqrt{104} = 10.2$ cm (1 decimal place)

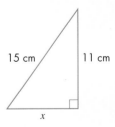

**EXERCISE 14B**

**1** For each of the following triangles, calculate the length $x$ to 1 decimal place.

**a**

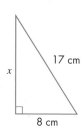

17 cm
$x$
8 cm

**b**

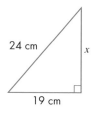

24 cm
$x$
19 cm

**c**

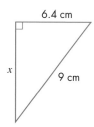

6.4 cm
$x$
9 cm

**d**

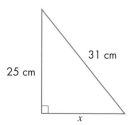

31 cm
25 cm
$x$

**e**

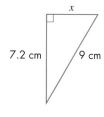

$x$
7.2 cm   9 cm

**f**

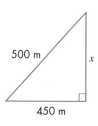

500 m
$x$
450 m

**g**

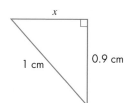

$x$
1 cm   0.9 cm

**h**

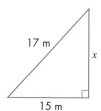

17 m
$x$
15 m

**2** For each of the following triangles, calculate the length $x$ to 1 decimal place.

**a**

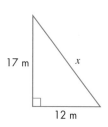

17 m
$x$
12 m

**b**

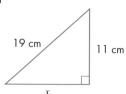

19 cm   11 cm
$x$

**c**

17 m
$x$
23 m

**d**

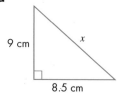

9 cm
$x$
8.5 cm

**e**

34 m
$x$
41 m

**f**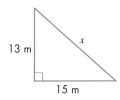

**g**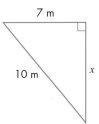

**h**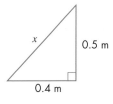

**3** For each of the following triangles, find the length marked $x$.

**a**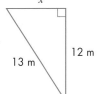

**b**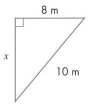

**c**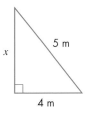

**d**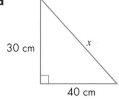

**4** What is the length of the diagonal of the base of the back of the lorry?

**PS 5** Find three possible pairs of lengths for the sides marked $a$ and $b$ in this triangle.

**AU 6** Explain how you can tell that a triangle with sides of length 8 inches, 6 inches and 10 inches is a right-angled triangle.

# Solving problems using Pythagoras' theorem

This section will show you how to:
- use Pythagoras' theorem to solve problems

**Key word**
Pythagoras' theorem

**Pythagoras' theorem** can be used to solve certain practical problems. When a problem involves two lengths only, follow these steps.

- Draw a diagram for the problem, making sure that it includes a right-angled triangle.

- Look at the diagram and decide which side has to be found: the hypotenuse or one of the shorter sides. Label the unknown side $x$.

- If it is the hypotenuse, then square both numbers, add the squares and take the square root of the sum.

- If it is one of the shorter sides, then square both numbers, subtract the smaller square from the larger square and take the square root of the difference.

**EXAMPLE 3**

A plane leaves Manchester airport and heads due east. It flies 160 km before turning due north. It then flies a further 280 km and lands. What is the distance of the return flight if the plane flies straight back to Manchester airport?

First, sketch the situation.

Using Pythagoras' theorem gives:

$$x^2 = 160^2 + 280^2$$
$$= 25\,600 + 78\,400$$
$$= 104\,000$$

So: $x = \sqrt{104\,000} = 322$ km

(nearest whole number)

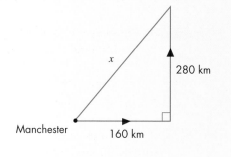

Remember the following tips when solving problems.

- Always sketch the right-angled triangle you need. Sometimes, the triangle is already drawn for you but some problems involve other lines and triangles that may confuse you. So identify which right-angled triangle you need and sketch it separately.

- Label the triangle with necessary information, such as the length of its sides, taken from the question. Label the unknown side $x$.

- Set out your solution as in the last example. Avoid shortcuts, since they often cause errors. You gain marks in your examination for showing clearly how you are applying Pythagoras' theorem to the problem.

- Round your answer to a suitable degree of accuracy.

**EXERCISE 14C**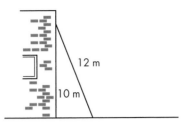

**1** A ladder, 12 m long, leans against a wall. The ladder reaches 10 m up the wall. How far away from the foot of the wall is the foot of the ladder?

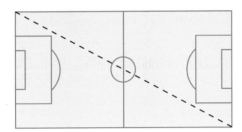

12 m

10 m

**2** A model football pitch is 2 m long and 0.5 m wide. How long is the diagonal?

**3** How long is the diagonal of a rectangle 6 m long and 9 m wide?

**4** How long is the diagonal of a square with a side of 8 m?

**5** In a hockey game, after a pass was made, the ball travelled 7 m up the field and 6 m across the field. How long was the actual pass?

**6** A ship going from a port to a lighthouse steams 15 km east and 12 km north. How far is the lighthouse from the port?

**7** A plane flies from London due north for 120 km before turning due west and flying for a further 85 km and landing at a secret location. How far from London is the secret location?

**8** Some pedestrians want to get from point X on one road to point Y on another. The two roads meet at right angles.

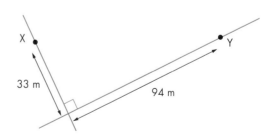

X

Y

33 m

94 m

   **a** If they follow the roads, how far will they walk?

   **b** Instead of walking along the road, they take the shortcut, XY. Find the length of the shortcut.

   **c** How much distance do they save?

**9** At the moment, three towns, A, B and C, are joined by two roads, as in the diagram. The council want to make a road that runs directly from A to C. How much distance will the new road save?

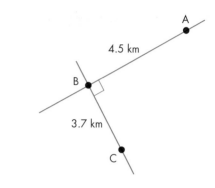

**10** A mast on a sailboat is strengthened by a wire (called a stay), as shown on the diagram. The mast is 35 ft tall and the stay is 37 ft long. How far from the base of the mast does the stay reach?

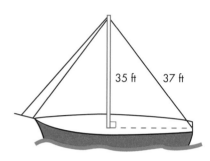

**11** A four-metre ladder is put up against a wall.

    **a** How far up the wall will it reach when the foot of the ladder is 1 m away from the wall?

    **b** When it reaches 3.6 m up the wall, how far is the foot of the ladder away from the wall?

**12** A pole, 8 m high, is supported by metal wires, each 8.6 m long, attached to the top of the pole. How far from the foot of the pole are the wires fixed to the ground?

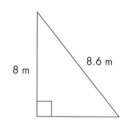

**PS** **13** How long is the line that joins two coordinates A(13, 6) and B(1, 1)?

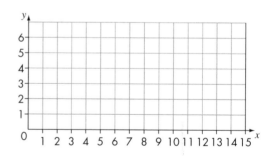

**FM** **14** The regulation for safe use of ladders states that, for a five-metre ladder: *The foot of the ladder must be placed between 1.6 m and 2.1 m from the foot of the wall.*

    **a** What is the maximum height the ladder can safely reach up the wall?

    **b** What is the minimum height the ladder can safely reach up the wall?

**PS** **15** A rectangle is 4.5 cm long. The length of its diagonal is 5.8 cm. What is the area of the rectangle?

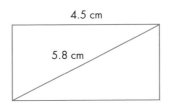

4.5 cm

5.8 cm

> **HINTS AND TIPS**
>
> First find the width, then the area.

**16** Two large trees, 5.5 m and 6.8 m tall, stand 12 m apart. A bird flies directly from the top of one tree to the top of the other. How far has the bird flown?

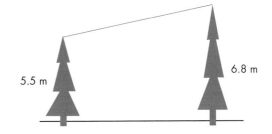

6.8 m

5.5 m

**PS** **17** Is the triangle with sides 7 cm, 24 cm and 25 cm, a right-angled triangle?

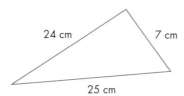

24 cm

7 cm

25 cm

**PS** **18** The formula for Pythagoras' theorem in 3D is

$$a^2 + b^2 + c^2 = d^2$$

where $d$ is the long diagonal through the inside of a cuboid, from one corner to the other.

Find some cuboids to test this theorem.

**AU** **19** If you are told the three sides of a triangle, how can you tell whether it is a right-angled triangle?

**PS** **20**

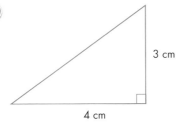

3 cm

4 cm

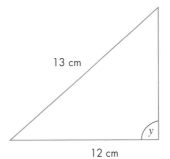

13 cm

12 cm

$y$

Will these triangles fit together exactly along the unknown edge?

Show all your workings.

## GRADE BOOSTER

**c** You can use Pythagoras' theorem in right-angled triangles

**c** You can solve problems in 2D, using Pythagoras' theorem

### What you should know now

- How to use Pythagoras' theorem to find the hypotenuse or one of the shorter sides of a right-angled triangle, given the other two sides
- How to solve problems, using Pythagoras' theorem

**1** Calculate the length, $x$ cm, in the triangle below. (3)

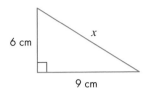

6 cm
$x$
Not drawn accurately
9 cm

(Total 3 marks)

*AQA, June 2008, Paper 2 Foundation, Question 25*

**2** $DEF$ is a right-angled triangle.
$DE = 15$ cm, $DF = 17$ cm

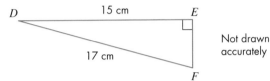

D
15 cm
E
17 cm
Not drawn accurately
F

Calculate the length of the side $EF$. (3)

(Total 3 marks)

**3** In the diagram, ABC is a right-angled triangle.
AC = 19 cm and AB = 9 cm.

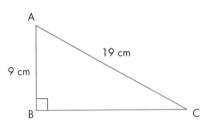

A
19 cm
9 cm
B
C

Calculate the length of BC (in centimetres).

(Total 3 marks)

*AQA, June 2005, Paper 2 Higher, Question 10a*

**4** In the diagram, PQRS is a quadrilateral.
Angles RQS and QSP are right angles.
PS = 4 cm, QR = 12 cm and RS = 13 cm.

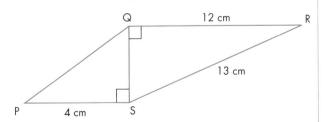

Q
12 cm
R
13 cm
P
4 cm
S

Calculate the length of PQ (in centimetres)

**5** A ladder of length 5 m rests against a wall.
The foot of the ladder is 1.7 m from the base of the wall.

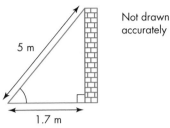

5 m
Not drawn accurately
1.7 m

How far up the wall does the ladder reach? (3)

(Total 3 marks)

*AQA November 2008, Paper 2 Foundation, Question 25*

**6** In triangle $XYZ$, angle $Y = 90°$, $XY = 12.7$ cm and $YZ = 3.5$ cm

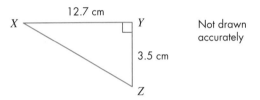

12.7 cm
$X$
$Y$
Not drawn accurately
3.5 cm
$Z$

Calculate $XZ$. (3)

(Total 3 marks)

*AQA, June 2008, Module 5, Paper 2 Foundation, Question 17*

**7** The diagram shows a ship, S, out at sea.
It is 30 kilometres east and 25 kilometres north of a port, P.

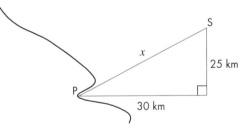

S
$x$
25 km
P
30 km

Calculate the direct distance from the port to the ship. This distance is marked $x$ on the diagram.

Give your answer to 1 decimal place.

# Worked Examination Questions

**1** The sketch shows triangle ABC.
AB = 40 cm, AC = 41 cm and CB = 9 cm.

By calculation, show that triangle ABC is a
right-angled triangle.

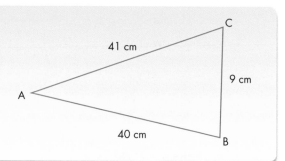

For triangle ABC to be right-angled,
the right angle must be at B and
AC must be the hypotenuse.

$$40^2 + 9^2 = 1681$$

$$41^2 = 1681$$

so $40^2 + 9^2 = 41^2$ making this
a right-angled triangle

**Total:** 3 marks

> Selecting the two smallest squares and adding them together earns 1 method mark.

> Squaring all three numbers will earn 1 method mark.

> Showing that the two smaller squares add up to the largest square, then stating it is a right-angled triangle, earns 1 mark.

**2** By looking at the side lengths of a triangle, how can you tell whether the triangle is:

   **a**  a right-angle triangle

   **b**  an obtuse-angled triangle?

Look at the lengths of the two smaller sides,
$a$ and $b$.

Square them both and add them together,
$a^2 + b^2$.

Square the length of the longest side, $c^2$.

If $a^2 + b^2 = c^2$ then the triangle
is right-angled.

If $a^2 + b^2 < c^2$ then the triangle
is obtuse-angled.

**Total:** 3 marks

> Recognising that you need to use the squares of all three sides earns 1 method mark.

> 1 mark is available for recognising the conditions for a right-angled triangle.

> 1 mark is available for recognising the conditions for an obtuse-angled triangle.

## Worked Examination Questions

**AU** **3** A 3, 4, 5 triangle is a right-angled triangle.

Explain how you know that this is not the only triangle that has a hypotenuse of 5.

Given the hypotenuse is 5.

Suppose one of the smaller sides was, say, 2 cm.

> You earn 1 mark for using another possible side length with the hypotenuse of 5 cm.

I could use Pythagoras' theorem to find the length of the other side as:

$\sqrt{(5^2 - 2^2)} = 4.58$ cm

> 1 mark is available for showing you can have sides that are not 3 and 4.

Total: 2 marks

When you are out walking on the hills it can be very useful to be able to estimate various distances that you have to cover. Of course, you can just use the scale on the map, but another way is by using Pythagoras' theorem with small right-angled triangles.

**Getting started**

- You know that the **square** of 2 is $2^2 = 4$. Write down the **square** of each of these numbers.

  5          0.1          0.4          0.03

  Think of a number that has a square between 0.1 and 0.001.

- You know that the **square root** of 4 is $\sqrt{4} = 2$. Now write down the **square root** of each of these numbers.

  16          81          0.01          0.025

  Think of a number that has a square root between 50 and 60.

- On a set of coordinate axes, draw the points A(1, 2) and B(4, 6).

  What is the distance from point A to point B?

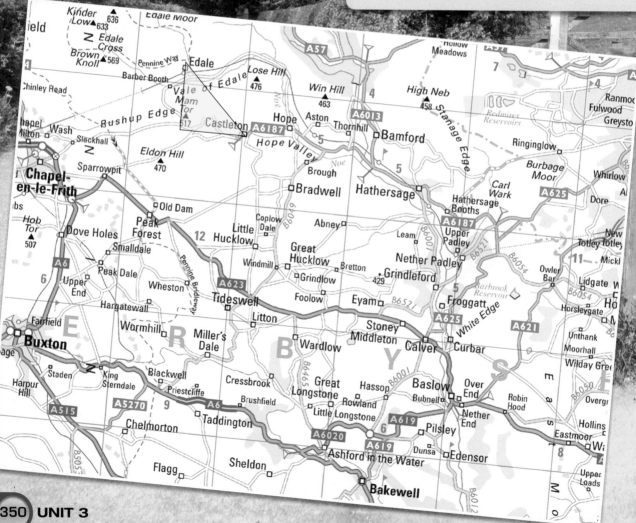

## Your task

Freya and Chris often go out walking in the Peak District. On the left is a copy of the map they use. Use this map extract to complete these tasks.

1   Write five questions similar to the examples given on the right. Swap them with the person next to you.

Answer each other's questions, making sure you show your working clearly.

Now swap again and mark each other's answers. Give constructive feedback.

2   Plan a walk with a circular route that is between 20 and 35 km long.

If the average person walks at approximately 4.5 miles per hour, estimate the time it would take to complete your route.

## Example

Freya and Chris were at Edale. They wanted to know the rough distance to Castleton. Freya decided to set herself a maths problem, using Pythagoras' theorem.

She looked at the map and imagined the yellow right-angled triangle.

Using the fact that each square on the map represents an area 5 km by 5 km, she estimated each small side of the triangle to be 3 km.

Then she applied Pythagoras' theorem.

$3^2 + 3^2 = 9 + 9 = 18$

On the hillside, without a calculator, she estimated the square root of 18 to be just over 4, giving a distance of 4 km.

Another day, Freya and Chris were at Hucklow and wanted to know the distance to Hathersage.

Use Freya's method to estimate the distance from Hucklow to Hathersage.

## Additional information

When working in distances, you need to work in either miles and other imperial units or kilometres and other metric units.

To change between these units there are some key conversion facts. Either use a textbook or the internet to find these.

## Answers to Chapter 1

### 1.1 Basic calculations and using brackets

**Exercise 1A**

**1** **a** 45 **b** 52 **c** 66

**2** **a** 200 **b** 115 **c** 236

**3** **a** 56 **b** 157 **c** 76 **d** 193

**4** **a** 144 **b** 108

**5** **a** 12.54 **b** 27.45

**6** **a** 26.7 **b** 24.5 **c** 145.3 **d** 1.5

**7** Sovereign is 102.47p per litre, Bridge is 102.73p per litre so Sovereign is cheaper.

**8** Abby 1.247, Bobby 2.942, Col 5.333, Donna 6.538
Col is correct.

**9** $31 \times 3600 \div 1610 = 69.31677 \approx 70$

**10** **a** 167.552 **b** 196.48

**11** **a** 2.77 **b** 6

**12** **a** 497.952 **b** 110.978 625

### 1.2 Using a calculator to add and subtract fractions

**Exercise 1B**

**1** **a** $1\frac{11}{20}$ **b** $1\frac{8}{15}$ **c** $1\frac{1}{4}$ **d** $\frac{147}{200}$ **e** $\frac{43}{80}$ **f** $1\frac{63}{80}$

  **g** $\frac{11}{30}$ **h** $\frac{29}{48}$ **i** $\frac{17}{96}$ **j** $\frac{167}{240}$ **k** $\frac{61}{80}$ **l** $\frac{277}{396}$

**2** **a** $6\frac{11}{20}$ **b** $8\frac{8}{15}$ **c** $16\frac{1}{4}$ **d** $11\frac{147}{200}$ **e** $7\frac{43}{80}$ **f** $11\frac{63}{80}$

  **g** $3\frac{11}{30}$ **h** $2\frac{29}{48}$ **i** $3\frac{17}{96}$ **j** $7\frac{167}{240}$ **k** $7\frac{61}{80}$ **l** $1\frac{277}{396}$

**3** $\frac{1}{12}$

**3** **a** $12\frac{1}{4}$ **b** $3\frac{1}{4}$

**5** Use the fraction key to input $\frac{3}{25}$, then key in + and then use the fraction key again to input $\frac{7}{10}$

**6** $\frac{47}{120}$

**7** **a** $-\frac{77}{1591}$ **b** Answer is negative

**8** **a** $\frac{223}{224}$ **b** $\frac{97}{1248}$ **c** $-\frac{97}{273}$

  **d** One negative and one positive so $\frac{5}{7}$ is less than $\frac{14}{39}$ and is less than $\frac{5}{7}$.

**9** **a** Answers will vary
  **b** Yes, always true, unless fractions are equivalent

**10** $18\frac{11}{12}$ cm

**11** $\frac{5}{12}$ (anticlockwise) or $\frac{7}{12}$ (clockwise)

### 1.3 Using a calculator to multiply and divide fractions

**Exercise 1C**

**1** **a** $\frac{3}{5}$ **b** $\frac{7}{12}$ **c** $\frac{9}{25}$ **d** $\frac{27}{200}$

  **e** $\frac{21}{320}$ **f** $\frac{27}{128}$ **g** $5\frac{2}{5}$ **h** $5\frac{1}{7}$

  **i** $2\frac{1}{16}$ **j** $\frac{27}{40}$ **k** $3\frac{9}{32}$ **l** $\frac{11}{18}$

**2** $\frac{1}{6}$ m²

**3** 15

**4** **a** $\frac{27}{64}$ **b** $\frac{27}{64}$

**5** **a** $\frac{4}{5}$ **b** $\frac{4}{5}$ **c** $\frac{16}{21}$ **d** $\frac{16}{21}$

**6** **a** $8\frac{11}{20}$ **b** $18\frac{1}{60}$ **c** $65\frac{91}{100}$ **d** $22\frac{1}{8}$

  **e** $7\frac{173}{320}$ **f** $52\frac{59}{160}$ **g** $2\frac{17}{185}$ **h** $2\frac{22}{103}$

  **i** $1\frac{305}{496}$ **j** $5\frac{17}{65}$ **k** $7\frac{881}{4512}$ **l** $5\frac{547}{1215}$

**7** $18\frac{5}{12}$ m²

**8** $3\frac{11}{32}$ cm³

**9** $90\frac{5}{8}$ miles

**10** 3

**11** 3

### Examination questions

**1** $\frac{14}{3} = 4\frac{2}{3}$ litres milk
So 3 bottles needed.

**2** $73\frac{13}{19}$ or 73.7 mph

**3** 16

**4** $20\frac{5}{12}$ cm²

**5** **a** $\frac{3}{4}$ metre **b** 100 strides
  **c** 2250 metres = 2.25 km

**6** **a** $56\frac{1}{4}$ cm² **b** $10\frac{1}{4}$ cm

**7** **a** 19.85454545… **b** 19.9

**8 a** 23.76153642...  **b** 23.8 or 24

**9 a** 30.94694426...  **b** 30.95

**10 a** 3.586440678...  **b** 3.59

**11 a** 77 cm³
   **b** Two numbers with a product of 20, for example 5 cm and 4 cm

## Answers to Chapter 2

## 2.1  Basic algebra

**Exercise 2A**

**1 a** Stu $3n$; Tamara $n + 5$; Ursula $n - 4$; Vic $3n + 6$  **b** $9n + 7$

**2 a** $35 + z$, $Y + z$

**3 a** $20x$  **b** $3w^2$  **c** $18h^2$  **d** $12x$  **e** $5z$  **f** $7y^2$
   **g** $11a + 5b$  **h** $3x - 2$

**4** 50

**5** Any expressions such as $2 \times 15w$ or $10w + 20w$

**6** 45p

**7 a** $300L + 6S$  **b** 271.2 m

**8 a** 21  **b** 13  **c** 41  **d** 15  **e** −60  **f** 96

**9 a** expression (E)  **b** formula (F)  **c** equation (Q)

**10** Any equivalent expressions such as $6x + 9y + 2x - 12y$

**11 a** £7.10  **b** 4 km  **c** No, he needs £13.10

**12 a** All of them  **b** $\frac{1}{2}$

**13 a** $15 - 5m$  **b** $6x + 21$  **c** $x^2 + 2x$
   **d** $10m - 2m^2$  **e** $5s^2 + 15s$  **f** $3nm - 3np$

**14 a** $3(6 - m)$  **b** $6(x + 2)$  **c** $x(x + 5)$
   **d** $m(10 - m)$  **e** $3(5s^2 + 1)$  **f** $n(3 - p)$

**15 a** $-3x - 8y$  **b** $-2a + 4b$

**16 a** Side AF − side DE = $4x - 1 - x = 3x - 1$
   **b** $14x$  **c** 84 cm

**17** 4 cm × 12 cm

**18** Any values that work, e.g. $x = 8$, $b = 4$, $h = 32$

**19 a** $6 + 3 \times 9 - 15 = 18$  **b** $2 \times 6 - 9 + 3 \times 3 = 12$

**20 a** $\frac{450}{n}$  **b** £390

**21 a** $12p^3 - 4p^2q$  **b** $10t^4 + 35t^2$  **c** $10x^2 + 35xy$
   **d** $10m^2 - 2m^5$  **e** $8s^4 + 24s^3t$  **f** $6nm^3 - 6n^2m^2$

**22 a** $4(t - 2)$ and $4t - 8$  **b** £26

**23 a** $23x + 11$  **b** $9y + 7$  **c** $2x - 8$
   **d** $22x + 9$  **e** $14x^2 - 10x$  **f** $2x^3 + 17x^2 - 9$

**24 a** $3p(3p + 2t)$  **b** $4m(3p - 2m)$  **c** $4ab(4a + 1)$
   **d** $2(2a^2 - 3a + 1)$  **e** $5xy(4y + 2x + 1)$  **f** $4mt(2t - m)$

**25** Darren has added 2 and 3 instead of multiplying and added 2 and −5 instead of multiplying. The correct answer is $6x - 10$

**26 a** $4(2y + 4)$  **b** $3(2z + 1)$

**27** Number off each day continues 81, 243, 729, 2187
   Total number off continues 121, 364, 1093, 3280
   So by the 8th day there are no students left in school.

**28 a** $21f + 21s$  **b** $315f + 504s$  **c** £240 profit

**29** $6(3x + 5) - 2(x - 2) = 18x + 30 - 2x + 4 = 16x + 34$

**30 a** Both calculations give the cost of 5 main courses and 5 deserts.
   **b** Easier to work out as bracket evaluates to 10
   **c** £50

**31 a** B  **b** They do not take out the highest common factor.

**32** No common factors

## 2.2  Substitution using a calculator

**Exercise 2B**

**1 a** 14.3  **b** 38.8  **c** 5.4

**2 a** 7.2  **b** 11.4  **c** 9.7

**3 a** 9.36  **b** 6.69  **c** 3

**4 a** 28  **b** 10.8  **c** 18

**5 a** 7.44  **b** 0.61  **c** 1.16

**6 a** 684  **b** 342  **c** 792

**7 a** 8.6  **b** 4.8  **c** 8.4

**8 a** 4.68  **b** 5.02  **c** −3.1

**9 a** £477.90  **b** £117.90 still owed (debit)

**10 a** One odd value and one even value, different from each other.
   **b** Any valid combination, e.g. $x = 1$, $y = 2$

**11 a** 4.1  **b** 8  **c** 4.525

**12 a** £767.50  **b** £107.50 in debit

**13 a** $x$ must be 2, $y$ can be any other prime number.
   **b** $x$ must be an odd prime, $y$ can be any other prime number.

**14 a** First term is cost of petrol, each mile is a tenth of £0.98. Second term is the hire cost divided by the miles.
   **b** 29.8p per mile

## 2.3    Solving linear equations

**Exercise 2C**

**1 a** 5       **b** 17       **c** $7\frac{1}{2}$       **d** 50

**2 a** $2\frac{1}{2}$    **b** 10    **c** –2    **d** $2\frac{1}{2}$    **e** 20    **f** 60

**3 a** 13    **b** 19    **c** –1    **d** 41

**4 a** –3    **b** $2\frac{1}{2}$    **c** 0    **d** $5\frac{1}{2}$

**5 a** 2    **b** 15    **c** 7    **d** 1

**6 a** –12    **b** 5    **c** –1    **d** 1

## 2.4    Setting up equations

**Exercise 2D**

**1 a** 9       **b** 8

**2 a** $\frac{M}{4} - 5 = 7$       **b** £48

**3** 8 m²

**4 a** $8c - 10 = 56$       **b** £8.25

**5 a** B: 450 cars, C: 450 cars, D: 300 cars    **b** 800    **c** 750

**6** Length: 5.5 m, width: 2.5 m, area: 13.75 m². Carpet costs £123.75

**7** 90p

**8 a** 1.5    **b** 2

**9 a** 1.5 cm **b** 6.75 cm²

**10** 17

**11** 3 years old

**12** 9 years old

**13** 3 cm

**14** 5

**15 a** $4x + 40 = 180$    **b** $x = 35°$

**16 a** 15    **b** –1    **c** $2(n + 3)$, $2(n + 3) - 5$
**d** $2(n + 3) - 5 = n$, $2n + 6 - 5 = n$, $2n + 1 = n$, $n = -1$

**17** No as $x + x + 2 + x + 4 + x + 6 = 360$ gives $x = 87°$ so the consecutive numbers (87, 89, 91, 93) are not even but odd.

**18** $4x + 18 = 3x + 1 + 50$, $x = 33$. Large bottle 1.5 litres, small bottle 1 litre

## 2.5    Trial and improvement

**Exercise 2E**

**1 a** 4 and 5       **b** 4 and 5       **c** 2 and 3

**2** $x = 3.5$

**3** $x = 3.7$

**4** $x = 2.5$

**5** $x = 1.5$

**6 a** $x = 2.4$       **b** $x = 2.8$       **c** $x = 3.2$

**7 a** $x = 7.8$ cm       **b** width is 7.8 cm and length is 12.8 cm

**8** $x = 5.8$

**9** Volume $= x \times 2x(x + 8) = 500$, $x^3 + 8x^2 = 250$, $4 \Rightarrow 192$, $5 \Rightarrow 325$, $4.4 \Rightarrow 240.064$, $4.5 \Rightarrow 253.125$, $4.45 \Rightarrow 246.541125$, so dimensions are 4.5 cm, 9 cm and 12.5 cm

**10 a** Volume of cube is $x^3$, volume of hole is $\frac{x}{2} \times \frac{x}{2} \times 8 = 2x^3$. Cube minus hole is 1500

   **b** $12 \Rightarrow 1440$, $13 \Rightarrow 1859$, $12.1 \Rightarrow 1478.741$, $12.2 \Rightarrow 1518.168$, $12.15 \Rightarrow 1498.368375$ so the value of $x = 12.2$ (to 1 dp)

**11** 2.76 and 7.24

# Examination questions

**1 a** T       **b** T       **c** F

**2 a** 6       **b** $5(x + 2)$

**3 a i** 2 kg    **ii** 1 kg       **b** 2.5 kg

**4 a** 5c
**b i** 12    **ii** 20    **iii** 32    **iv** 2.5

**5 a** $6x + 5$
**b** 15
**c i** $1 \times 3 + 4 = 7$, $1 \times (3 + 4) = 7$
   **ii** $a(b + c) = a \times b + a \times c = ab + ac \neq ab + c$

**6 a** $x + 5$ cm
**b** $x - 2$ cm
**c** $2x$ cm
**d** 90 cm

**7 a** 20.1 cm²
**b i** $3R + S$
   **ii** $2R = S$

**8** –3.34

**9 a** $y + 5$
**b** $2y$
**c** $4y + 5$
**d** $4y + 5 = 77$, $4y = 72$, $y = 18$

**10** $y = 5$, $5z = 20$

**11 a** £220
**b** 250

**12** $\frac{2}{3}$

**13** 2.4

**14** 3.7

Answers to Chapter 3

## 3.1 Systems of measurement

**Exercise 3A**

**1**  **a** metres     **b** kilometres     **c** millimetres
    **d** kilograms or grams   **e** litres     **f** kilograms
    **g** tonnes     **h** millilitres     **i** centilitres
    **j** metres     **k** kilograms     **l** litres
    **m** grams     **n** centilitres     **o** millimetres

**2**  Check individual answers.

**3**  The 5 metre since his height is about 175 cm, the lamp post will be about 525 cm

**4**  Inches, feet and yards are too small as units; this distance is an approximation and so needs to be a large unit as this is a large distance.

## 3.2 Metric units

**Exercise 3B**

**1**  **a** 1.25 m     **b** 8.2 cm     **c** 0.55 m
    **d** 2.1 km     **e** 2.08 m     **f** 1.24 m
    **g** 4.2 kg     **h** 5.75 t     **i** 8.5 cl
    **j** 2.58 l     **k** 3.4 l     **l** 0.6 t
    **m** 0.755 kg     **n** 0.8 l     **o** 2 l
    **p** 63 cl     **q** 8.4 m$^3$     **r** 35 cm$^3$
    **s** 1.035 m$^3$     **t** 0.53 m$^3$     **u** 34 000 m

**2**  **a** 3400 mm     **b** 135 mm     **c** 67 cm
    **d** 7030 m     **e** 7.2 mm     **f** 25 cm
    **g** 640 m     **h** 2400 ml     **i** 590 cl
    **j** 84 ml     **k** 5200 l     **l** 580 g
    **m** 3750 kg     **n** 0.000 94 l     **o** 2160 cl
    **p** 15 200 g     **q** 14 000 l     **r** 0.19 ml

**3**  He should choose the 2000 mm × 15 mm × 20 mm

**4**  as 1 millilitre = 1 cm$^3$ and 1 litre = 1000 cm$^3$

**5**  1 000 000 000 000

## 3.3 Imperial units

**Exercise 3C**

**1**  **a** 24 in     **b** 12 ft     **c** 3520 yd
    **d** 80 oz     **e** 56 lb     **f** 6720 lb
    **g** 40 pt     **h** 48 in     **i** 36 in
    **j** 30 ft     **k** 64 oz     **l** 5 ft
    **m** 70 lb     **n** 12 yd     **o** 224 oz
**2**  **a** 5 miles     **b** 120 pt     **c** 5280 ft
    **d** 8 ft     **e** 7 st     **f** 7 gall
    **g** 2 lb     **h** 5 yd     **i** 5 tons
    **j** 63 360 in     **k** 8 lb     **l** 9 gall
    **m** 10 st     **n** 3 miles     **o** 35 840 oz

**3**  the 32-ounce bag

**4**  4 014 489 600

**5**  1 tonne = 1000 kilograms = 1000 × 2.2 pounds = 2200 pounds; 1 ton = 2240 pounds; 2240 is greater than 2200

## 3.4 Conversion factors

**Exercise 3D**

**1**  **a** 20 cm     **b** 13.2 lb     **c** 48 km
    **d** 67.5 l     **e** 2850 ml     **f** 10 gal
    **g** 12 in     **h** 50 miles     **i** 5 kg
    **j** 3 pints     **k** 160 km     **l** 123.2 lb
    **m** 180 l     **n** 90.9 kg     **o** 1100 yd
    **p** 30 cm     **q** 6.4 kg     **r** 90 cm

**2**  ton. Repeat working of Exercise 3C, question 5.

**3**  1 yard = 36 inches ≈ 36 × 2.5 cm = 90 cm; 1m = 100 cm, so the metre is longer

**4**  **a** **i** 1000 g     **ii** 1 kg
    **b** **i** 4500 g     **ii** 4.5 kg

**5**  **a** 135 miles     **b** 50 mph     **c** 2 h 42 min

**6**  4 hours 10 minutes

**7**  288

## Examination questions

**1**  **a** metres (m)     **b** millimetres (mm)     **c** litres (l)

**2**  **a** centimetres (cm)     **b** litres (l)
    **c** square metres (m$^2$)     **d** tonnes (t)

**3**  40 cm

**4**  **a** 36 litres     **b** 8.89 gallons

**5**  **a** $1\frac{3}{4}$ pints     **b** $4\frac{1}{2}$ litres

**6**  65 mph ≈ 65 × 8 ÷ 5 = 104 km per hour, so Gianni was speeding

**7**  Yes, 16 × 28.33 = 453.28 and 453.28 < 500

**8**  No, 13 inches ≈ $\frac{30}{12}$ = 32.5 cm and 32.5 > 32

## Answers to Chapter 4

### 4.1 Reading scales

**Exercise 4A**

**1 a i** 4     **ii** 16 g     **iii** 38 mph
  **b i** 8 kg     **ii** 66 mph     **iii** 60 g
  **c i** 13 oz     **ii** 85 mph     **iii** 76 kph
  **d i** 26     **ii** 71.6     **iii** 64

**2** **a**   **b**   **c**

  **d**

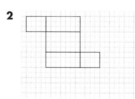

  **e**   **f**

**3 a** 50 °C   **b** 64 °C   **c** −10 °C   **d** 82 °C   **e** −16 °C

**4 a** 8 kg     **b** 29 mph     **c** 230 g     **d** 12.7 kg

**5** 360 g        **b** weigh out 400 g, then weigh out 300 g

**6 a** 1.2 kg     **b** 125 g

**7 a** 125 km/h
  **b** 125 km/h shown on scale marked from 0 to 200 km/h; the scale could go up in 10s, 20s or 25s, discuss this with students

**8** No, it is pointing to 7.48 m; each division is 0.1 ÷ 5 = 0.02

### 4.2 Sensible estimates

**Exercise 4B**

**1** Bicycle about 2 m, bus about 10 m, train about 17 m

**2** Height about 4 m, length about 18 or 19 m

**3** 250 g

**4 a** About 4 m     **b** About 5 m     **c** About 5.5 m

**5** About 9.5 g or 10 g

**6** About 11 m; the ratio of Joel's height in the illustration to his real height must be the same as the ratio of the height on the statue in the illustration to its actual height

**7** About 8 m

### 4.3 Scale drawings

**Exercise 4C**

**1 a** Onions: 40 m × 10 m, soft fruit: 50 m × 10 m, apple trees: 20 m × 20 m, lawn: 30 m × 20 m, potatoes: 50 m × 20 m
  **b** Onions: 400 m², soft fruit: 500 m², apple trees: 400 m², lawn: 600 m², potatoes: 1000 m²

**2 a** 33 cm     **b** 9 cm

**3 a** 30 cm × 30 cm   **b** 40 cm × 10 cm   **c** 20 cm × 15 cm
  **d** 30 cm × 20 cm   **e** 30 cm × 20 cm   **f** 10 cm × 5 cm

**4 a** Student's scale drawing.     **b** 38 or 39

**5 a** 8.4 km     **b** 4.6 km     **c** 6.2 km
  **d** 6.4 km     **e** 7.6 km     **f** 2.4 km

**6 a i** 64 km   **ii** 208 km   **iii** 116 km   **iv** 40 km
  **b i** 84 km   **ii** 196 km   **iii** 152 km   **iv** 128 km

**7 a** 50 km   **b** 35 km   **c** 45 km

**8 c** 7 cm represents 210 m, so 1 cm represents 30 m or 1 cm represents 3000 cm

**9** 1 : 63 360

### 4.4 Nets

**Exercise 4D**

**1 a**   **b**   **c**

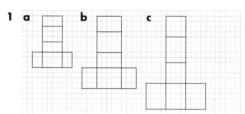

**2**

**3**

**4 a**   **b**

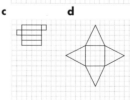

  **c**   **d**

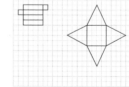

**5**

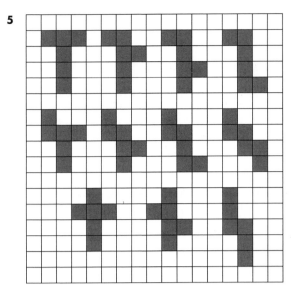

**6 a** and **b**

## 4.5 Using an isometric grid

**Exercise 4E**

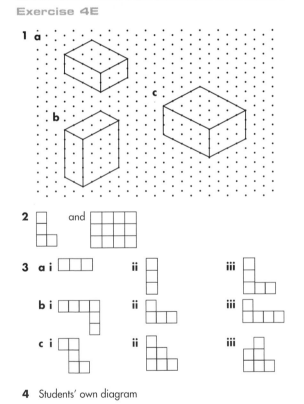

**1 a**

**b**

**c**

**2** and

**3 a i**    **ii**    **iii**

   **b i**    **ii**    **iii**

   **c i**    **ii**    **iii**

**4** Students' own diagram

**5**

**6 a**      **b** 90

## Examination questions

**1 a** 76 cm     **b** 340 kg     **c** 86 mph

**2 a** 5.8 kg
   **b** Check students' diagrams. Each graduation represents 0.2 kg, therefore the arrow should be drawn exactly halfway between the graduations for 3 kg and 3.2 kg.
   **c** 6.6 lb

**3** Check students' diagrams.

**4 a** 1 : 200 000     **b i** 21 km    **ii** 30 cm

**5 a** Check students' answers. Shading should be added to the top faces of the three 'cubes' on the lower surface, to the left of the one already shaded, and the top of the tall column, to indicate what someone looking down directly on the solid would see.

**b**        **c**

### Answers to Chapter 5

## 5.1 Speed, time and distance

**Exercise 5A**

**1** 18 mph

**2** 280 miles

**3** 52.5 mph

**4** 11.50 am

**5** 500 s

**6 a** 75 mph     **b** 6.5 h     **c** 175 miles
   **d** 240 km     **e** 64 km/h     **f** 325 km
   **g** 4.3 h (4 h 18 min)

**7 a** 7.75 h     **b** 52.9 mph

**8 a** 2.25 h     **b** 99 miles

**9 a** 1.25 h     **b** 1 h 15 min

**10 a** 48 mph     **b** 6 h 40 min

**11 a** 120 km     **b** 48 km/h

**12 a** 30 min     **b** 6 mph

**13 a** 10 m/s     **b** 3.3 m/s     **c** 16.7 m/s
   **d** 41.7 m/s     **e** 20.8 m/s

**14 a** 90 km/h     **b** 43.2 km/h     **c** 14.4 km/h
   **d** 108 km/h     **e** 1.8 km/h

**15 a** 64.8 km/h    **b** 28 s    **c** 8.07 (37 min journey)

**16 a** 6.7 m/s    **b** 66 km    **c** 5 minutes
     **d** 133.3 metres

**17** 6.6 minutes

## 5.2    Direct proportion problems

**Exercise 5B**

**1** 60 g

**2** £5.22

**3** 45

**4** £6.72

**5 a** £312.50    **b** 8

**6 a** 56 litres    **b** 350 miles

**7 a** 300 kg    **b** 9 weeks

**8** 40 s

**9 a   i** 100 g margarine, 200 g sugar, 250 g flour, 150 g ground rice
    **ii** 150 g margarine, 300 g sugar, 375 g flour, 225 g ground rice
    **iii** 250 g margarine, 500 g sugar, 625 g flour, 375 g ground rice
   **b** 24

**10** Peter's shop as I can buy 24. At Paul's shop I can only buy 20.

## 5.3    Best buys

**Exercise 5C**

**1 a** £4.50 for a 10-pack    **b** £1.08 for 6
   **c** £2.45 for 1 litre    **d** Same value
   **e** 29p for 250 grams    **f** £1.39 for a pack of 6
   **g** £4 for 3 cartons

**2 a** Large jar    **b** 600 g tin    **c** 5 kg bag
   **d** 75 ml tube    **e** Large box    **f** Large box
   **g** 400 ml bottle

**3 a** £5.11    **b** Large tin

**4 a** 95p    **b** Family size

**5** Bashir's

**6** Mary

**7** Kelly

## Examination questions

**1** £75

**2 a** 60%    **b** 210 ml

**3** Small pack, as £9.60 for 12

**4 a** 14 days    **b** 153 miles

**5 a** 3 hours 35 minutes    **b** 64 mph

**6** Holiday shop 3.2p per ml
   Southern Pharmacy 3p per ml
   Southern Pharmacy is better value

**7 a** $2\frac{1}{2}$ hours    **b** 90 mph    **c** 4 hours

**8 a** 12 mph    **b** 14.4 mph

### Answers to Chapter 6

## 6.1    Perimeter

**Exercise 6A**

**1 a** 10 cm   **b** 8 cm   **c** 14 cm   **d** 12 cm   **e** 16 cm   **f** 6 cm

**2 a** 10 cm   **b** 12 cm   **c** 12 cm   **d** 14 cm   **e** 12 cm   **f** 12 cm

**3** 18 m

**4** No, the perimeter is 30 cm as two sides will touch.

**5** False, it is 28 cm

## 6.2    Area of an irregular shape

**Exercise 6B**

**1 a** 10 cm$^2$   **b** 11 cm$^2$   **c** 13 cm$^2$   **d** 12 cm$^2$ (estimates only)

**2** Student's answer

**3** Student's answer

**4** 18–24 cm$^2$

**5** 26–30 m$^2$

**6** The area of the rectangle around the shape is 24 cm$^2$

## 6.3    Area of a rectangle

**Exercise 6C**

**1 a** 35 cm$^2$, 24 cm    **b** 33 cm$^2$, 28 cm    **c** 45 cm$^2$, 36 cm
   **d** 70 cm$^2$, 34 cm    **e** 56 cm$^2$, 30 cm    **f** 10 cm$^2$, 14 cm

**2 a** 53.3 cm$^2$, 29.4 cm    **b** 84.96 cm$^2$, 38 cm

**3 a** 20 cm, 21 cm$^2$    **b** 18 cm, 20 cm$^2$    **c** 2 cm, 8 cm$^2$
   **d** 3 cm, 15 cm$^2$    **e** 3 mm, 18 mm    **f** 4 mm, 22 mm
   **g** 5 m, 10 m$^2$    **h** 7 m, 24 m

**4** 39

**5 a** 4    **b** 1 h 52 min

**6** £839.40

**7** 40 cm

**8** 96

**9** B, 44 cm$^2$

**10** Never (the area becomes four times greater).

**11 a** 100 mm$^2$
**b i** 300 mm$^2$ **ii** 500 mm$^2$ **iii** 630 mm$^2$

**12 a** 10 000 cm$^2$
**b i** 20 000 cm$^2$ **ii** 40 000 cm$^2$ **iii** 56 000 cm$^2$

## 6.4    Area of a compound shape

**Exercise 6D**

**1 a** 30 cm$^2$        **b** 40 cm$^2$        **c** 51 cm$^2$
**d** 35 cm$^2$        **e** 43 cm$^2$        **f** 51 cm$^2$
**g** 48 cm$^2$        **h** 33 cm$^2$

**2** 24

**3** The correct answer is 44 cm$^2$, the length of the bottom rectangle is 6 cm (10 − 4).

**4** 72 cm$^2$

**5** 48 cm

**6** Yes, the area to paint is 9.1 m$^2$

## 6.5    Area of a triangle

**Exercise 6E**

**1 a** 6 cm$^2$, 12 cm    **b** 120 cm$^2$, 60 cm   **c** 30 cm$^2$, 30 cm

**2** 40 cm$^2$

**3** 84 m$^2$

**4 a** 21 cm$^2$        **b** 55 cm$^2$        **c** 165 cm$^2$

**5 c** 75 cm$^2$

**6** 32 cm, 36 cm$^2$

**7** 108 cm$^2$

**8 a** 5.5 m$^2$        **b** 4

**Exercise 6F**

**1 a** 21 cm$^2$        **b** 12 cm$^2$        **c** 14 cm$^2$
**d** 55 cm$^2$        **e** 90 cm$^2$        **f** 140 cm$^2$

**2 a** 28 cm$^2$        **b** 8 cm          **c** 4 cm
**d** 3 cm           **e** 7 cm          **f** 44 cm$^2$

**3** 64 cm$^2$

**4 a** 40 cm$^2$        **b** 65 m$^2$        **c** 80 cm$^2$

**5 a** 65 cm$^2$        **b** 50 m$^2$

**6** For example: height 10 cm, base 10 cm; height 5 cm, base 20 cm; height 25 cm, base 4 cm; height 50 cm, base 2 cm

**7 a** 1500 cm$^2$        **b** 1800 cm$^2$

**8** Triangle c; a and b each have an area of 15 cm$^2$ but c has an area of 16 cm$^2$.

## 6.6    Area of a parallelogram

**Exercise 6G**

**1 a** 96 cm$^2$        **b** 70 cm$^2$        **c** 20 cm$^2$
**d** 125 cm$^2$        **e** 10 cm$^2$        **f** 112 m$^2$

**2** No, it is 24 cm$^2$, she used the slanting side instead of the perpendicular height.

**3** 16 cm

**4 a** 500 cm$^2$        **b** 15

## 6.7    Area of a trapezium

**Exercise 6H**

**1 a** 30 cm$^2$        **b** 77 cm$^2$        **c** 24 cm$^2$
**d** 42 cm$^2$        **e** 40 cm$^2$        **f** 6 cm
**g** 3 cm

**2 a** 27.5 cm, 36.25 cm$^2$        **b** 33.4 cm, 61.2 cm$^2$
**c** 38.6 m, 88.2 m$^2$

**3** Any pair of lengths that add up to 10 cm
For example: 1 cm, 9 cm; 2 cm, 8 cm; 3 cm, 7 cm; 4 cm, 6 cm; 4.5 cm, 5.5 cm

**4** Shape c. Its area is 25.5 cm$^2$

**5** Shape a. Its area is 28 cm$^2$

**6** a

**7** 2 cm

**8** 1.4 m$^2$

## Examination questions

**1 a** 7 cm$^2$
**b** Check students' diagrams. Rectangles should be either 1 cm × 8 cm or 2 cm × 4 cm.
**c** 12–14 cm$^2$

**2 a** 24 cm          **b** 32 cm$^2$

**3 a** 900 cm$^2$        **b** 50 cm          **c** 60

**4 a** 4.5 squares     **b** 8 squares       **c** 12 squares

**5 a** 10 cm$^2$        **b** 31.5 cm$^2$

**6** 39 cm$^2$

**7** 59.9 cm$^2$

## Answers to Chapter 7

### 7.1 Lines of symmetry

**Exercise 7A**

1 a  b

c  d

e  f  g

2 Discuss students' answers. There are many possibilities.

3 **a i** 5 **ii** 6 **iii** 8 **b** 10

4 a  b  c

5 a  b

c  d

e  f

6 2, 1, 1, 2, 0

7 a

**b** Students' own answers

8 **a** 1 **b** 5 **c** 1 **d** 6

9 Discuss students' answers. There are many possibilities.

10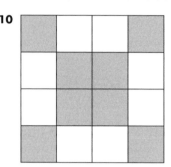

11 No, a triangle may have no lines of symmetry, or one or three, but you cannot draw a triangle with two lines of symmetry.

### 7.2 Rotational symmetry

**Exercise 7B**

1 **a** 4 **b** 2 **c** 2 **d** 3 **e** 6

2 **a** 4 **b** 5 **c** 6 **d** 4 **e** 6

3 **a** 2 **b** 2 **c** 2 **d** 2 **e** 2

4 **a** 4 **b** 3 **c** 8 **d** 2 **e** 4 **f** 2

5 A, B, C, D, E, F, G, J, K, L, M, P, Q, R, T, U, V, W, Y

6 Students' own answers

7 **a** 6 **b** 9 (the small red circle surrounded by nine 'petals' and 12 (the centre pattern)

8 Students' own answers

9 for example:

10

| | | Number of lines of symmetry | | | |
|---|---|---|---|---|---|
| | | 0 | 1 | 2 | 3 |
| **Order of rotational symmetry** | 1 | D | A | | |
| | 2 | E | | B | |
| | 3 | | | | C |

### Examination questions

1 **a** F or N **b** A or E or M
 **c** H **d** H or N

**2 a** Check students' answers    **b** Check students' answers

**3 a** 3    **b**

**4 a**

**b i**        **ii** 4

**5 a** Check students' answers    **b** Check students' answers

## Answers to Chapter 8

## 8.1 Measuring and drawing angles

**Exercise 8A**

**1 a** 40°    **b** 30°    **c** 35°    **d** 43°    **e** 100°    **f** 125°
**g** 340°    **h** 225°

**2** Student's drawings of angles

**3** Student's drawing and calculations

**4** Yes, the angle is 75°

**5** Any angle between 81° and 89°

**6** (c) is an obtuse angle, the others are acute

**7 a** 80°    **b** 50°    **c** 25°

## 8.2 Angle facts

**Exercise 8B**

**1 a** 48°    **b** 307°    **c** 108°    **d** 52°    **e** 59°    **f** 81°
**g** 139°    **h** 51°    **i** 138°    **j** 128°    **k** 47°    **l** 117°
**m** 27°    **n** 45°    **o** 108°    **p** 69°    **q** 135°    **r** 58°
**s** 74°    **t** 23°    **u** 55°    **v** 56°

**2 a** 82°    **b** 105°    **c** 75°

**3** 45° + 125° = 170° and for a straight line it should be 180°.

**4 a** $x = 100°$    **b** $x = 110°$    **c** $x = 30°$

**5 a** $x = 55°$    **b** $x = 45°$    **c** $x = 12.5°$

**6 a** $x = 34°, y = 98°$  **b** $x = 70°, y = 120°$ **c** $x = 20°, y = 80°$

**7** 6 × 60° = 360°; imagine six of the triangles meeting at a point

**8** $x = 35°, y = 75°$; $2x = 70°$ (opposite angles), so $x = 35°$ and $x + y = 110°$ (angles on a line), so $y = 75°$

## 8.3 Angles in a triangle

**Exercise 8C**

**1 a** 70°    **b** 50°    **c** 80°    **d** 60°    **e** 75°    **f** 109°
**g** 38°    **h** 63°

**2 a** No, total is 190°    **b** Yes, total is 180°    **c** No, total is 170°
**d** Yes, total is 180°    **e** Yes, total is 180°    **f** No, total is 170°

**3 a** 80°    **b** 67°    **c** 20°    **d** 43°    **e** 10°    **f** 1°

**4 a** 60°    **b** Equilateral triangle    **c** Same length

**5 a** 70° each    **b** Isosceles triangle
**c** Same length

**6** $x = 50°, y = 80°$

**7 a** 109°    **b** 130°    **c** 135°

**8** 65°

**9** Isosceles triangle; angle DFE = 30° (opposite angles), angle DEF = 75° (angles on a line), angle FDE = 75° (angles in a triangle), so there are two equal angles in the triangle and hence it is an isosceles triangle

**10** $a$ = 80° (opposite angles), $b$ = 65° (angles on a line), $c$ = 35° (angles in a triangle)

**11** Missing angle = $y$, $x + y = 180°$ and $a + b + y = 180°$ so $x = a + b$

## 8.4 Angles in a polygon

**Exercise 8D**

**1 a** 90°    **b** 150°    **c** 80°    **d** 80°    **e** 77°    **f** 131°
**g** 92°    **h** 131°

**2 a** No, total is 350°    **b** Yes, total is 360°    **c** No, total is 350°
**d** No, total is 370°    **e** Yes, total is 360°    **f** Yes, total is 360°

**3 a** 100°    **b** 67°    **c** 120°    **d** 40°    **e** 40°    **f** 1°

**4 a** 90°    **b** Rectangle    **c** Square

**5 a** 120°    **b** 170°    **c** 125°    **d** 136°    **e** 149°    **f** 126°
**g** 212°    **h** 114°

**6** 60° + 60° + 120° + 120° + 120° + 240° = 720°

**7** $y = 360° − 4x$; $2x + y + 2x = 360°$, $4x + y = 360°$, so $y = 360° − 4x$

**8 a** $8x + 40° = 360°$
**b** $x = 40°$, smallest angle is $x + 20 = 60°$

## 8.5 Regular polygons

**Exercise 8E**

**1 a i** 45°    **ii** 8    **iii** 1080°
**b i** 20°    **ii** 18    **iii** 2880°
**c i** 15°    **ii** 24    **iii** 3960°
**d i** 36°    **ii** 10    **iii** 1440°

**2 a i** 172° **ii** 45 **iii** 7740°
 **b i** 174° **ii** 60 **iii** 10 440°
 **c i** 156° **ii** 15 **iii** 2340°
 **d i** 177° **ii** 120 **iii** 21 240°

**3 a** Exterior angle is 7°, which does not divide exactly into 360°
 **b** Exterior angle is 19°, which does not divide exactly into 360°
 **c** Exterior angle is 11°, which does divide exactly into 360°
 **d** Exterior angle is 70°, which does not divide exactly into 360°

**4 a** 7° does not divide exactly into 360°
 **b** 26° does not divide exactly into 360°
 **c** 44° does not divide exactly into 360°
 **d** 13° does not divide exactly into 360°

**5** $x = 45°$, they are the same, true for all regular polygons

**6** Three are 135° and two are 67.5°

**7** 88°; $\dfrac{1440° - 5 \times 200°}{5}$

**8 a** 36° **b** 10

## 8.6 Parallel lines

**Exercise 8F**

**1 a** 40° **b** $b = c = 70°$
 **c** $d = 75°$, $e = f = 105°$ **d** $g = 50°$, $h = i = 130°$
 **e** $j = k = l = 70°$ **f** $n = m = 80°$

**2 a** $a = 50°$, $b = 130°$ **b** $c = d = 65°$, $e = f = 115°$
 **c** $g = i = 65°$, $h = 115°$ **d** $j = k = 72°$, $l = 108°$
 **e** $m = n = o = p = 105°$ **f** $q = r = s = 125°$

**3 a** $a = 95°$ **b** $b = 66°$, $c = 114°$

**4 a** $x = 30°$, $y = 120°$ **b** $x = 25°$, $y = 105°$
 **c** $x = 30°$, $y = 100°$

**5 a** $x = 50°$, $y = 110°$ **b** $x = 25°$, $y = 55°$
 **c** $x = 20°$, $y = 140°$

**6** 290°; $x$ is double the angle allied to 35°, so is $2 \times 145°$

**7** $a = 66°$; angle BDC = 66° (angles in a triangle = 180°) so $a = 66°$ (corresponding angles)

**8** Angle PQD = 64° (alternate angles), so angle DQY = 116° (angles on a line = 180°)

**9** Use alternate angles to see $b$, $a$ and $c$ are all angles on a straight line, and so total 180°

**10** Third angle in triangle equals $q$ (alternative angle), angle sum of triangle is 180°.

## 8.7 Special quadrilaterals

**Exercise 8G**

**1 a** $a = 110°$, $b = 55°$ **b** $c = 75°$, $d = 115°$
 **c** $e = 87°$, $f = 48°$

**2 a** $a = c = 105°$, $b = 75°$ **b** $d = f = 70°$, $e = 110°$
 **c** $g = i = 63°$, $h = 117°$

**3 a** $a = 135°$, $b = 25°$ **b** $c = d = 145°$
 **c** $e = f = 94°$

**4 a** $a = c = 105°$, $b = 75°$ **b** $d = f = 93°$, $e = 87°$
 **c** $g = i = 49°$, $h = 131°$

**5 a** $a = 58°$, $b = 47°$ **b** $c = 141°$, $d = 37°$
 **c** $e = g = 65°$, $f = 115°$

**6** both 129°

**7** Marie, a rectangle must have right angles

**8 a** 65°
 **b** Trapezium, angle A + angle D = 180° and angle B + angle C = 180°

## 8.8 Bearings

**Exercise 8H**

**1 a** 110° **b** 250° **c** 091° **d** 270° **e** 130° **f** 180°

**2** Check students' sketches

**3**

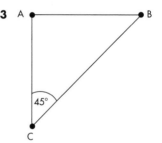

**4 a** 090°, 180°, 270° **b** 000°, 270°, 180°

**5**

| Leg | Actual distance | Bearing |
| --- | --- | --- |
| 1 | 50 km | 060° |
| 2 | 70 km | 350° |
| 3 | 65 km | 260° |
| 4 | 46 km | 205° |
| 5 | 60 km | 130° |

**6 a** 045° **b** 290°

**7 a** 250° **b** 325° **c** 144°

**8 a** 900 m **b** 280° **c** angle NHS = 150° and HS = 3 cm

**9** 108°

**10** 255°

## Examination questions

**1 a** Obtuse **b** Acute **c** Reflex **d** Right

**2 a** 28° **b** 38°

**3 a** A quadrilateral splits into 2 triangles, $2 \times 180° = 360°$
 **b i** $6x + 72 = 360$
 **b ii** $x = 48°$, 132°

**4** **a** rectangle, parallelogram, rhombus
 **b** rectangle, parallelogram
 **c** e.g. rectangle, it has four right angles

**5** **a** 300 m   **b** 215°
 **b** Angle NAC = 130° and AC = 7 cm

**6** **a** 360° ÷ 6 = 60°
 **b** 135°

## Answers to Chapter 9

## 9.1   Drawing circles

Exercise 9A

**1** **a** $1\frac{1}{2}$ cm, 3 cm   **b** 2 cm, 4 cm   **c** 3 cm, 6 cm

**2** Student's circles

**3** **a** diameter   **b** chord   **c** radius
 **d** sector

**4** Student's drawings

**5** Student's drawings

**6** **a–c** Student's drawing   **d** regular hexagon

**7** **a–c** Student's drawing   **d** 90°
 **e** Student's drawings
 **f** A radius is perpendicular to a tangent at a point
 It may be worth some discussion to point out that it is always true that a radius meets a tangent at right angles.

**8** **a** 6 cm   **b** 12 cm

## 9.2   The circumference of a circle

Exercise 9B

**1** **a** 25.1 cm   **b** 15.7 cm   **c** 44.0 cm
 **d** 22.0 cm   **e** 18.8 cm   **f** 47.1 cm
 **g** 28.9 cm   **h** 14.8 cm

**2** **a** 6.3 cm   **b** 8.2 cm   **c** 5.3 cm
 **d** 7.5 cm

**3** **a** 31.4 cm   **b** 18.8 cm   **c** 9.4 cm
 **d** 25.1 cm   **e** 5.7 cm   **f** 15.7 cm
 **g** 81.7 cm   **h** 39.6 cm

**4** **a** 198 cm   **b** 505

**5** **a** A 188.5 m, B 194.8 m, C 201.1 m, D 207.3 m
 **b** 18.7 or 18.8 m

**6** 879.6 or 880 cm

**7** **a** 37.7 cm   **b** 3770 cm   **c** 37.7 m
 **d** 37.7 km

**8** 100 cm

**9** 24.2 cm

**10** 15.9 cm

**11** b, 25.7 cm

**12** **a** Sue 62.8 cm, Julie 69.1 cm, Dave 75.4 cm, Brian 81.7 cm
 **b** The difference between the distances round the waists of two people is 2π times the difference between their radii.
 **c** 6.28 m

**13** **a** Perimeters of shapes A and B are both 25.1 cm
 **b** 25.1 cm

**14** $4a = 2\pi r$, so $2a = \pi r$, therefore $r = \frac{2a}{\pi}$

**15** 11

## 9.3   The area of a circle

Exercise 9C

**1** **a** 78.5 cm$^2$   **b** 28.3 cm$^2$   **c** 7.1 cm$^2$
 **d** 50.3 cm$^2$   **e** 2.5 cm$^2$   **f** 19.6 cm$^2$
 **g** 530.9 cm$^2$   **h** 124.7 cm$^2$

**2** **a** 3.1 cm$^2$   **b** 5.3 cm$^2$   **c** 2.3 cm$^2$
 **d** 4.5 cm$^2$

**3** **a** 50.3 cm$^2$   **b** 19.6 cm$^2$   **c** 153.9 cm$^2$
 **d** 38.5 cm$^2$   **e** 28.3 cm$^2$   **f** 176.7 cm$^2$
 **g** 66.5 cm$^2$   **h** 17.3 cm$^2$

**4** **a** 9.1 cm$^2$   **b** 138   **c** 2000 cm$^2$
 **d** 1255.8 cm$^2$ or 1252.9 cm$^2$ using unrounded answer from **a**
 **e** 744.2 cm$^2$ or 747.1 cm$^2$, using unrounded answer from **a**

**5** 3848.5 m$^2$

**6** **a i** 56.5 cm   **ii** 254.5 cm$^2$
 **b i** 69.1 cm   **ii** 380.1 cm$^2$
 **c i** 40.8 cm   **ii** 132.7 cm$^2$
 **d i** 88.0 cm   **ii** 615.8 cm$^2$

**7** **a** 19.1 cm   **b** 9.5 cm
 **c** 286.5 cm$^2$ (or 283.5 cm$^2$)

**8** 962.9 cm$^2$ (or 962.1 cm$^2$)

**9** **a** 56.5 cm$^2$   **b** 19.6 cm$^2$

**10** **a** 50.3 m$^2$   **b** 44.0 cm$^2$   **c** 28.3 cm$^2$

**11** 141.4 cm$^2$; $A = \pi \times 9^2 - \pi \times 6^2 = 141.4$ cm$^2$

**12** $a^2 = \pi r^2$, so $r^2 = \frac{a^2}{\pi}$, therefore $r = \frac{a}{\sqrt{\pi}}$

**13** 21.5 cm$^2$

## 9.4   Answers in terms of π

Exercise 9D

**1** 10π cm

**2** **a** 4π cm   **b** 20π cm   **c** 15π cm
 **d** 4π cm

**3 a** $16\pi$ cm$^2$     **b** $25\pi$ cm$^2$     **c** $9\pi$ cm$^2$
   **d** $81\pi$ cm$^2$

**4** 25 cm

**5** 10 cm

**6** $\frac{200}{\pi}$ cm

**7** $\frac{5}{\sqrt{\pi}}$ cm

**8 a** $12.5\pi$ cm$^2$     **b** $16\pi$ cm$^2$     **c** $(16\pi + 80)$ cm$^2$
   **d** $(50\pi + 100)$ cm$^2$

**9 a** $32\pi$ cm$^2$     **b** $16\pi$ cm$^2$     **c** $8\pi$ cm$^2$
   **d** $4\pi$ cm$^2$

**10 a** $(200 - 8\pi)$ m$^2$     **b** 18

**11** $9\pi$ cm$^2$; $\frac{1}{2}(\pi \times 6^2) - \pi \times 3^2 = 18\pi - 9\pi = 9\pi$

**12 c**; $80 + \frac{1}{4}(\pi \times 8^2) = 80 + 16\pi$

## Examination questions

**1 a** Check students' diagrams. The diameter should be a straight line drawn from one side of the circle to the other, passing through the centre point, 0.
   **b** Check students' diagrams. The tangent should be a straight line that just touches the circumference at one point only.
   **c i** Check students' diagrams. Ensure midpoint is marked accurately.
      **ii** it is a right angle

**2 a** 4 cm
   **b** 110°
   **c** Check students' diagrams. The line of symmetry should be the bisector of angle A0B (midway between A and B).
   **d** Check students' diagrams. The tangent should touch the circumference at A and be at 90° to A0.
   **e** Check students' diagrams. The chord should be a straight line joining points A and B.

**3 a** 22.3 cm     **b** 224

**4** 91.6 m$^2$

**5** $9\pi$ m$^2$

**6** 392 m

**7 a** 14.1 cm$^2$     **b** No, it has 1 line of symmetry

### Answers to Chapter 10

## 10.1   Congruent shapes

**Exercise 10A**

**1 a** yes     **b** yes     **c** no     **d** yes     **e** no     **f** yes

**2 a** triangle ii     **b** triangle iii     **c** sector i

**3 a** 1, 3, 4     **b** 2, 4     **c** 1, 4     **d** 1, 2, 3, 4

**4** b, d and p

**5** If the shapes are congruent they must be the same size.

**6** 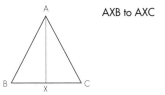 PQR to QRS to RSP to SPQ; SXP to PXQ to QXR to RXS

**7** EGF to FHE to GEH to HFG; EFX to HGX; EXH to FXG

**8** ABC to CDA; BDC to DBA; BXA to DXC; BXC to DXA

**9** AXB to AXC

**10 a i** 49     **ii** 36     **iii** 25
   **b** 8 different sizes, total of 204 squares

## 10.2   Tessellations

**Exercise 10B**

**1** Check students' tessellations.

**2** Check students' tessellations.

**3** All quadrilaterals tessellate.

**4** The interior angle for each shape divides exactly into 360°.

**5** It is not true in general but it is impossible to tessellate a regular pentagon.

**6** Imagine rows of circles all sitting in perfect columns. The spaces between them all are the same curved four-pointed star shape.

**7** There will be many different correct answers, but do not accept bricks arranged in vertical columns as this would not give a strong design.

## 10.3   Translations

**Exercise 10C**

**1** Check students' translations.

**2** Check students' translations.

**3 a i** $\begin{pmatrix} 1 \\ 3 \end{pmatrix}$ **ii** $\begin{pmatrix} 4 \\ 2 \end{pmatrix}$ **iii** $\begin{pmatrix} 2 \\ -1 \end{pmatrix}$

**iv** $\begin{pmatrix} 5 \\ 1 \end{pmatrix}$ **v** $\begin{pmatrix} -1 \\ 6 \end{pmatrix}$ **vi** $\begin{pmatrix} 4 \\ 6 \end{pmatrix}$

**b i** $\begin{pmatrix} -1 \\ -3 \end{pmatrix}$ **ii** $\begin{pmatrix} 3 \\ -1 \end{pmatrix}$ **iii** $\begin{pmatrix} 1 \\ -4 \end{pmatrix}$

**iv** $\begin{pmatrix} 4 \\ -2 \end{pmatrix}$ **v** $\begin{pmatrix} -2 \\ 3 \end{pmatrix}$ **vi** $\begin{pmatrix} 3 \\ 3 \end{pmatrix}$

**c i** $\begin{pmatrix} -4 \\ -2 \end{pmatrix}$ **ii** $\begin{pmatrix} -3 \\ 1 \end{pmatrix}$ **iii** $\begin{pmatrix} -2 \\ -3 \end{pmatrix}$

**iv** $\begin{pmatrix} 1 \\ -1 \end{pmatrix}$ **v** $\begin{pmatrix} -5 \\ 4 \end{pmatrix}$ **vi** $\begin{pmatrix} 0 \\ 4 \end{pmatrix}$

**d i** $\begin{pmatrix} 3 \\ 2 \end{pmatrix}$ **ii** $\begin{pmatrix} -4 \\ 2 \end{pmatrix}$ **iii** $\begin{pmatrix} 5 \\ -4 \end{pmatrix}$

**iv** $\begin{pmatrix} -2 \\ -7 \end{pmatrix}$ **v** $\begin{pmatrix} 5 \\ 0 \end{pmatrix}$ **vi** $\begin{pmatrix} 1 \\ -5 \end{pmatrix}$

**4**

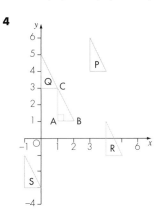

**5 a** $\begin{pmatrix} -3 \\ -1 \end{pmatrix}$ **b** $\begin{pmatrix} 4 \\ -4 \end{pmatrix}$ **c** $\begin{pmatrix} -5 \\ -2 \end{pmatrix}$ **d** $\begin{pmatrix} 4 \\ 7 \end{pmatrix}$

**e** $\begin{pmatrix} -1 \\ 5 \end{pmatrix}$ **f** $\begin{pmatrix} 1 \\ 6 \end{pmatrix}$ **g** $\begin{pmatrix} -4 \\ 4 \end{pmatrix}$ **h** $\begin{pmatrix} -4 \\ -7 \end{pmatrix}$

**6** $10 \times 10 = 100$ (including $\begin{pmatrix} 0 \\ 0 \end{pmatrix}$)

**7** Check students' designs for a Snakes and ladders board.

**8** $\begin{pmatrix} -x \\ -y \end{pmatrix}$

## 10.4 Reflections

**Exercise 10D**

**1 a** 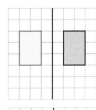 **b**

**c** **d**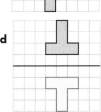

**2**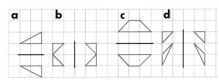

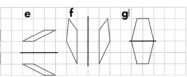

**3**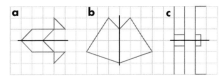

**4**

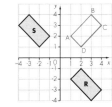

**c** congruent

**5 a–e**

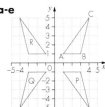

**f** reflection in $y$-axis

**6**

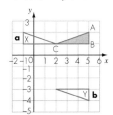

**7** a    b    c

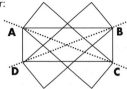

**8** a    b    c

**9** Possible answer:

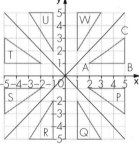

**10** Possible answer: Take the centre square as ABCD then reflect this square each time in the line, AB, then BC, then CD and finally AD.

**11** Possible answer: A reflection of a reflection in a line will always return to its starting position as each reflected point is the same perpendicular distance from the mirror line as the original.

**12** a–i

j A reflection in the line $y = x$.

**13** b yes    c yes

## 10.5   Rotations

**Exercise 10E**

**1** a    b    c    d

**2**

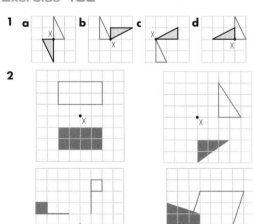

**3**

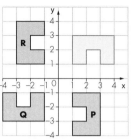

d 90° turn clockwise about O

**4** a   A(1, 2), B(3, 1), C(4, 3)     b   (2, −1), (1, −3), (3, −4)
   c   (−1, −2), (−3, −1), (−4, −3)
   d   (−2, 1), (−1, 3), (−3, 4)
   e   Corresponding vertices have same pairs of numbers switching round and changing signs.

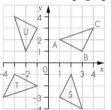

**5** a

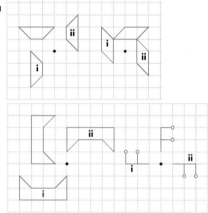

b Rotation 90° anticlockwise.
   Rotation 270° clockwise.

**6**

Centre point is C

**7** Possible answer: If ABCD is the centre square with A being bottom left and B bottom right, rotate about A 90° anticlockwise, rotate about new B 180°, now rotate about new C 180° and finally rotate about new D 180°.

**8** 4 × 90° is 360°, a complete turn brings the shape back to the original place.

**9** a, b

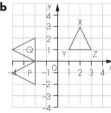

c a rotation of 90° about the point (0, −1)

**10** **a–c**

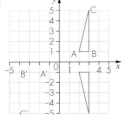

**d** rotation 180° about O     **e** yes     **f** yes

## 10.6    Enlargements

Exercise 10F
Exercise 10F

**1**

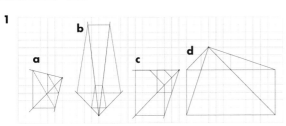

**2** **a**

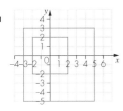

**c**

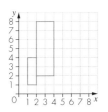

**3** **a**                    **b**

**4** **a-d** They are all congruent.

**5**

**6** No, it is false, congruent shapes must be identical in size.

**7** 9

**8**

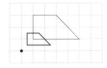

**9** **a**

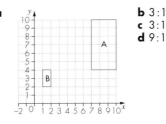

**b** 3 : 1
**c** 3 : 1
**d** 9 : 1

## Examination questions

**1** **a** E     **b** F and H

**2** **a** A and C
   **b** Check students' diagrams.

**3** **a** Rotation, clockwise 90° (or anticlockwise 270°), centre (1, 1)
   **b** Check students' diagrams. Ensure that centre is (0, 7).

**4** **a** Reflection in the line $x = 0$ (the $y$-axis).
   **b** Check students' diagrams.
   **c** Check students' diagrams. Ensure that centre is (0, 1).

**5** **a** Rotation through 90° anticlockwise (or 270° clockwise) about (0, 0).
   **b** Check students' diagrams. Ensure shape B is reflected in the line $y = -1$

**6** **a** Check students' diagrams.
   **b** Ensure shape B is reflected in the line $y = 1$
   **c** Check students' diagrams.

Answers to Chapter 11

## 11.1    Constructing triangles

Exercise 11A

**1** **a** BC = 2.9 cm, ∠B = 53°, ∠C = 92°
   **b** ∠E = 50°, EF = 7.4 cm, ED = 6.8 cm
   **c** ∠G = 105°, ∠H = 29°, ∠I = 46°
   **d** ∠J = 48°, ∠L = 32° JK = 4.3 cm
   **e** ∠N = 55°, ON = OM = 7 cm
   **f** ∠P = 51°, ∠R = 39°, QP = 5.7 cm

**2** **b** ∠ABC = 44°, ∠BCA = 79°, ∠CAB = 57°

**3** **a** 5.9 cm          **b** 18.8 cm²

**4** BC = 2.6 cm, 7.8 cm

**5** **a** 4.5 cm          **b** 10.8 cm²

**6** **a** 4.3 cm          **b** 34.5 cm²

**7** **a** A right-angled triangle constructed with sides 3, 4, 5 and scale marked 1 cm : 1 m.
   **b** A right-angled triangle constructed with sides that add to 12 cm.

**8** Even with all three angles, you need to know at least one length.

**9** An equilateral triangle of sides 4 cm.

## 11.2 Bisectors

**Exercise 11B**

**1–9** No answers required.

**10** Coventry or Leicester.

**11** The centre of the circle.

**12** Start with a base line AB, then construct a perpendicular to the line at point A. At the point B, construct an angle of 60°. Ensure that the line for this 60° angle crosses the perpendicular line; where they meet will be the final point C.

## 11.3 Loci

**Exercise 11C**

**1** Circle with radius    **a** 2 cm   **b** 4 cm   **c** 5 cm

**2 a**

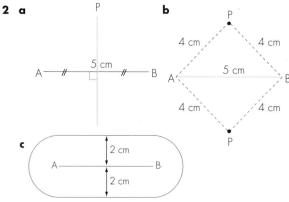

    **b**

**c**

**3 a** Circle with radius 4m     **b**

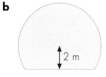

**4 a**   **b**   **c**   **d**   **e**   **f**

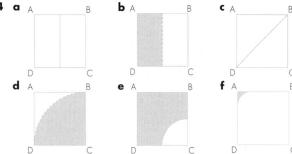

**5** Diagram **c**

**6** ─ ─ ─ ─ ─ ─ ─ ─ ─ ─ ─

**7 a** All points such that AP < PB.
    **b** The perpendicular bisector of the line BC.

**8** Start with a base line, AB, 3 cm long. At point A, draw a few points all 3 cm away from A towards the upper right side. Lightly join these dots with an arc. You can now find the point C that is 3 cm away from point B and draw your equilateral triangle.

**Exercise 11D**

**1**

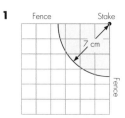

**2**

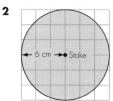

**3**

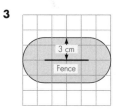

**4**

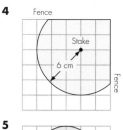

**5**

**6**

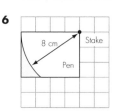

**7**

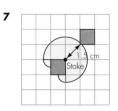

**8**

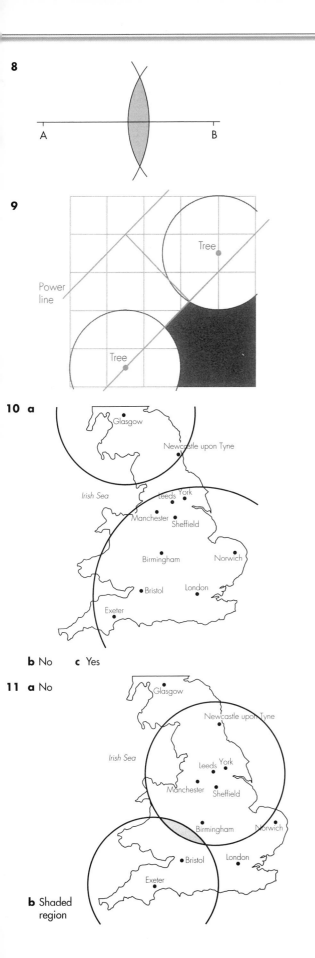

**9**

Power
line

Tree

Tree

**10 a**

Glasgow

Newcastle upon Tyne

Irish Sea

Leeds York
Manchester
Sheffield

Birmingham          Norwich

Bristol     London

Exeter

**b** No    **c** Yes

**11 a** No

Glasgow

Newcastle upon Tyne

Irish Sea

Leeds York
Manchester
Sheffield

Birmingham          Norwich

Bristol     London

Exeter

**b** Shaded
region

**12**

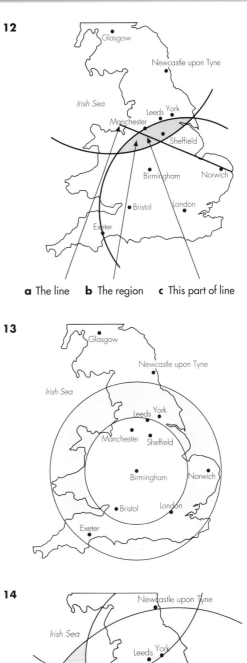

Glasgow

Newcastle upon Tyne

Irish Sea

Leeds York
Manchester
Sheffield

Birmingham          Norwich

Bristol     London

Exeter

**a** The line    **b** The region    **c** This part of line

**13**

Glasgow

Newcastle upon Tyne

Irish Sea

Leeds York
Manchester
Sheffield

Birmingham          Norwich

Bristol     London

Exeter

**14**

Newcastle upon Tyne

Irish Sea

Leeds York
Manchester
Sheffield

**15**

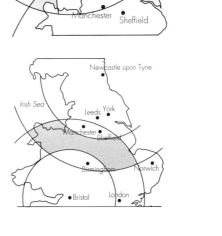

Newcastle upon Tyne

Irish Sea

Leeds York
Manchester Sheffield

Birmingham     Norwich

Bristol     London

**16**

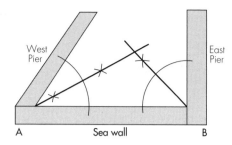

West Pier

East Pier

A      Sea wall      B

**17** Leeds

**18** On a map, draw a straight line from Newcastle to Bristol, construct the line bisector, then the search will be anywhere on the sea along than line.

## Examination questions

**1** Check students' diagrams.

**2 a**

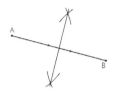

A

B

**b**

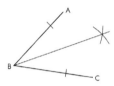

A

B

C

**3 a** Check students' diagrams.
  **b** 1.85 kg

**4 a**

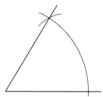

**b** Check students' diagrams. The diagram should comprise a circular arc with a radius of 6 km, with the centre at point A and another circular arc with a radius of 8 km, with the cetnre at point B. The intersection must be shaded.
Scale: 1 cm represents 1 km

**5 a** 20 km
  **b** Check students' diagrams.

**6** Check students' diagrams.

**7** Check students' diagrams.

**8**

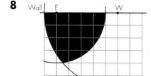

Wall   E     W

Answers to Chapter 12

## 12.1   Units of volume

**Exercise 12A**

**1 a** $12 \text{ cm}^3$       **b** $20 \text{ m}^3$
  **c** $23 \text{ cm}^3$       **d** $32 \text{ cm}^3$

**2** She reached this conclusion by multiplying 5 3 5 3 4.

**3** $65 \text{ cm}^2$

**4** 6

## 12.2   Surface area and volume of a cuboid

**Exercise 12B**

**1 a i** $198 \text{ cm}^3$     **ii** $234 \text{ cm}^2$
  **b i** $90 \text{ cm}^3$      **ii** $146 \text{ cm}^2$
  **c i** $1440 \text{ cm}^3$    **ii** $792 \text{ cm}^2$
  **d i** $525 \text{ cm}^3$     **ii** $470 \text{ cm}^2$

**2** 24 litres

**3 a** $160 \text{ cm}^3$     **b** $480 \text{ cm}^3$     **c** $150 \text{ cm}^3$

**4 a i** $64 \text{ cm}^3$     **ii** $96 \text{ cm}^2$
  **b i** $343 \text{ cm}^3$    **ii** $294 \text{ cm}^2$
  **c i** $1000 \text{ mm}^3$   **ii** $600 \text{ mm}^2$
  **d i** $125 \text{ m}^3$     **ii** $150 \text{ m}^2$
  **e i** $1728 \text{ m}^3$    **ii** $864 \text{ m}^2$

**5** 86

**6 a** $180 \text{ cm}^3$     **b** 5 cm     **c** 6 cm
  **d** 10 cm       **e** $81 \text{ cm}^3$

**7** 1.6 m

**8** $48 \text{ m}^2$

**9 a** 3 cm     **b** 5 m     **c** 2 mm
  **d** 1.2 m

**10 a** $148 \text{ cm}^3$     **b** $468 \text{ cm}^3$

**11** If this was a cube, the side length woud be 5 cm, so total surface area would be $5 \times 5 \times 6 = 150 \text{ cm}^2$; no this particular cuboid is not a cube.

**12** $600 \text{ cm}^2$

## 12.3 Surface area and volume of a prism

**Exercise 12C**

**1 a i a**

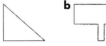

**b**

**c**

**d**

**e**      **f**

   **ii a** 21 cm$^2$     **b** 48 cm$^2$       **c** 36 m$^2$
     **d** 108 m$^2$     **e** 25 m$^2$       **f** 111 m$^2$
   **iii a** 63 cm$^3$    **b** 432 cm$^3$      **c** 324 m$^3$
     **d** 432 cm$^3$    **e** 225 cm$^3$      **f** 1332 m$^3$

**2 a i** 21 cm$^3$ **ii** 210 cm$^3$       **b i** 54 cm$^2$ **ii** 270 cm$^2$

**3** 525 000 litres

**4** solid **b** has greater volume (900 cm$^3$) than solid **a** (594 cm$^3$)

**5 a** 75 m$^3$         **b** 75 000 litres       **c** to be supplied

**6** 384 cm$^2$

**7** Multiply the volume by the weight of 1 cm$^3$ of the metal, then convert to kg.

## 12.4 Volume of a cylinder

**Exercise 12D**

**1 a** 251 cm$^3$   **b** 445 cm$^3$   **c** 2150 cm$^3$   **d** 25 m$^3$

**2 a** 226 cm$^3$   **b** 15 cm$^3$   **c** 346 cm$^3$   **d** 1060 cm$^3$

**3** £80

**4** 332 litres

**5** 366 ml

**6** 2827 cm$^3$

**7 a** 360$\pi$ cm$^3$         **b** 300$\pi$ cm$^3$

**8** 17.19 km

**9** Volume of A = $2^2 \times \pi \times 5 = 20\pi$, volume of B = $1^2 \times \pi \times 21$ = 21$\pi$, B has the larger volume.

## Examination questions

**1 a** 4 cm$^3$ **b** 18 cm$^2$

**2** 34 cm$^2$

**3** 3.75 cm

**4 a** $\frac{1}{2} \times \pi \times 1.4^2 = 3.1$ m$^2$     **b** $3.1 \times 0.5 = 1.5$ m$^3$

**5** $\pi r^2 h = \pi \times 8^2 \times 5 = 320\pi$ cm$^3$

**6 a** 200 cm$^2$         **b** 132 cm$^2$

## Answers to Chapter 13

### 13.1 Drawing quadratic graphs

**Exercise 13A**

**1** $x$: $-5, -4.5, -4, -3.5, -3, -2.5, -2, -1.5, -1, -0.5, 0$
   $y$: $25, 20.25, 16, 12.25, 9, 6.25, 4, 2.25, 1, 0.25, 0$

**2** $x$: $-3, -2, -1, 0, 1, 2, 3$
   $y$: $27, 12, 3, 0, 3, 12, 27$

**3** $x$: $-5, -4, -3, -2, -1, 0, 1, 2, 3, 4, 5$
   $y$: $27, 18, 11, 6, 3, 2, 3, 6, 11, 18, 27$

**4 a** $x$: $-5, -4, -3, -2, -1, 0, 1, 2, 3, 4, 5$
     $x^2$: $25, 16, 9, 4, 1, 0, 1, 4, 9, 16, 25$
    $-3x$: $15, 12, 9, 6, 3, 0, -3, -6, -9, -12, -15$
     $y$: $40, 28, 18, 10, 4, 0, -2, -2, 0, 4, 10$
  **b** 1.8     **c** $-1.2, 4.2$

**5 a** $x$: $-5, -4, -3, -2, -1, 0, 1, 2, 3, 4, 5$
     $x^2$: $25, 16, 9, 4, 1, 0, 1, 4, 9, 16, 25$
    $-2x$: $10, 8, 6, 4, 2, 0, -2, -4, -6, -8, -10$
    $-8$: $-8, -8, -8, -8, -8, -8, -8, -8, -8, -8, -8$
     $y$: $27, 16, 7, 0, -5, -8, -9, -8, -5, 0, 7$
  **b** $-7.9$   **c** $-2.5, 4.5$

**6 a** $x$: $-2, -1, 0, 1, 2, 3, 4, 5$
     $y$: $18, 10, 4, 0, -2, -2, 0, 4$
  **b** 6.8   **c** 0.2, 4.8

**7** Points plotted and joined should give parabolas

**8 a** 150 m
  **b**

| $t$ (s) | 1 | 2 | 3 | 4 | 5 | 6 | 7 | 8 | 9 | 10 |
|---|---|---|---|---|---|---|---|---|---|---|
| $v$ (m/s) | 27 | 24 | 21 | 18 | 15 | 12 | 9 | 6 | 3 | 0 |
| $s$ (m) | 28.5 | 54 | 76.5 | 96 | 112.5 | 126 | 136.5 | 138 | 148.5 | 150 |

  **c** Check students' graphs.     **d** 5.5

**9 a** $x$: $-3, -2, -1, 0, 1, 2, 3$
     $x^2$: $9, 4, 1, 0, 1, 4, 9$
   $+2x$: $-6, -4, -2, 0, 2, 4, 6$
    $-1$: $-1, -1, -1, -1, -1, -1, -1$
     $y$: $2, -1, -2, -1, 2, 7, 14$
  **b** 0.25 or 0.3     **c** $-2.7, 0.7$

**10 a** $x$: $-4, -3, -2, -1, 0, 1, 2, 3, 4$
     $y$: $12, 5, 0, -3, -4, -3, 0, 5, 12$
  **b** $x = \pm 2$       **c** $-1.8$       **d** $\pm 3.5$

**11 a**

| $x$ | $-5$ | $-4$ | $-3$ | $-2$ | $-1$ | 0 | 1 | 2 |
|---|---|---|---|---|---|---|---|---|
| $x^2$ | 25 | 16 | 9 | 4 | 1 | 0 | 1 | 4 |
| $+4x$ | $-20$ | $-16$ | $-12$ | $-8$ | $-4$ | 0 | 4 | 8 |
| $y$ | 5 | 0 | $-3$ | $-4$ | $-3$ | 0 | 5 | 12 |

  **b** $x = -4$ and 0
  **c** $-3.8$       **d** 0.6, $-4.6$

**12 a** $x$: $-1, 0, 1, 2, 3, 4, 5, 6, 7$
     $y$: $10, 3, -2, -5, -6, -5, -2, 3, 10$
  **b** $x = 0.5$ or 5.5   **c** $-5.8$       **d** $-0.3, 6.3$

**13 a** Check students' graphs.     **b** 150 m

## Examination questions

**1 a** −3, 7
   **b** Check students' graphs. Ensure following co-ordinates are used: (−2, 1), (−1, −3), (0, −5), (1, −5), (2, −3), (3, 1), (4, 7), x-axis from −2 to 4, y-axis from −3 to 4.
   **c** 2.8 and −1.8

**2 a** 6, 1
   **b** Check students' graphs. Ensure following co-ordinates are used: (−3, 6), (−2, 1), (−1, −2), (0, −3), (1, −2), (2, 1), (3, 5), x-axis from −3 to 3, y-axis from −4 to 7.
   **c** −1.7 and 1.7

**3 a** −2, 10
   **b** Check students' graphs. Ensure following co-ordinates are used: (−4, 4), (−3, 0), (−2, 2), (−1, −2), (0, 0), (1, 4), (2, 10), x-axis from −4 to 2, y-axis from −3 to 11.

## Answers to Chapter 14

## 14.1 Pythagoras' theorem

### Exercise 14A

**1 a** 10.3 cm   **b** 5.9 cm   **c** 8.5 cm
   **d** 20.6 cm   **e** 18.6 cm   **f** 17.5 cm
   **g** 32.2 cm   **h** 2.4 m   **i** 500 m
   **j** 5 cm   **k** 13 cm   **l** 10 cm

**2** 50 cm, 1.2 m and 1.3 m or 1.5 m, 2 m and 2.5 m

**3** 7.43 cm

**4** Because $6^2 + 7^2$ does not equal $10^3$.

## 14.2 Finding a shorter side

### Exercise 14B

**1 a** 15 cm   **b** 14.7 cm   **c** 6.3 cm
   **d** 18.3 cm   **e** 5.4 cm   **f** 217.9 m
   **g** 0.4 cm   **h** 8 m

**2 a** 20.8 m   **b** 15.5 cm   **c** 15.5 m
   **d** 12.4 cm   **e** 22.9 m   **f** 19.8 m
   **g** 7.1 m   **h** 0.64 m

**3 a** 5 m   **b** 6 m   **c** 3 m
   **d** 50 cm

**4 a** 3.53 m

**5** Many different combinations are possible, such as: 8 cm and 11.5 cm, 10 cm and 9.8 cm, 12 cm and 7.2 cm.

**6** Because $8^2 + 6^2 = 10^2$ or because the lengths are double those of a 3, 4, 5 triangle.

## 14.3 Solving problems using Pythagoras' theorem

### Exercise 14C

**1** 6.6 m

**2** 2.1 m

**3** 10.8 m

**4** 11.3 m

**5** 9.2 m

**6** 19.2 km

**7** 147 km

**8 a** 127 m   **b** 99.6 m   **c** 27.4 m

**9** 2.4 km

**10** 12 ft

**11 a** 3.9 m   **b** 1.7 m

**12** 3.2 m

**13** 13 units

**14 a** 4.7 m   **b** 4.5 m

**15** 16.5 cm$^2$

**16** 12.07 m

**17** Yes, $25^2 = 24^2 + 7^2$

**18** Yes, Pythagoras' theorem works in 3D, diagonal$^2 = a^2 + b^2 + c^2$.

**19** Check if the sum of the squares of the two smallest sides is equal to the square of the longest side

**20** In the triangle on the left, the hypotenuse is $\sqrt{(3^2 = 4^2)} = 5$. In the triangel on the right, the hypotenuse is $\sqrt{(12^2 + 13^2)} = 17.7$, so no, they will not match.

## Examination questions

**1** 10.8 cm

**2** 8 cm

**3** 16.7 cm (1 dp)

**4** 6.4 cm (1 dp)

**5** 4.7 m (1 dp)

**6** 13.17 cm or 13.2 cm (1 dp)

**7** 39.1 km (1 dp)

# GLOSSARY

**π (pronounced 'pie')** The numerical value of the ratio of the circumference of a circle to its diameter (approximately 3.14159).

**3D shape** A solid shape that has 3 dimensions (height, width, depth).

**acute angle** The space (usually measured in degrees °) between two intersecting lines or surfaces (planes). The amount of turn needed to move from one line or plane to the other.

**allied angles** When two parallel lines are cut by a third line (transversal), two pairs of allied angles are formed between the lines, each pair on one side of the transversal. Each pair of allied angles add up to 180°.

**alternate angles** When two parallel lines are cut by a third line (transversal), two pairs of alternate angles are formed between the lines. The alternate angles lie one on each side of the transversal. Alternate angles are of equal size.

**angle** The space (usually measured in degrees °) between two intersecting lines or surfaces (planes). The amount of turn needed to move from one line or plane to the other.

**angle bisector** A straight line or plane that divides an angle in half.

**angle of rotation** The angle turned through to move from one direction to another.

**angles in a triangle** The three interior (inside) angles of a triangle add up to 180°.

**angles around a point** The angles around a point add up to 360°.

**angles on a straight line** The angles on a straight line add up to 180°.

**anticlockwise** Turning in the opposite direction to the movement of the hands of a clock. (Opposite of clockwise.)

**arc** A curve forming part of the circumference of a circle.

**area** Measurement of the flat space a shape occupies. Usually measured in square units or hectares. (See also *surface area*.)

**average** A single number that represents or typifies a collection of values. The three commonly used averages are mode, mean, and median.

**axis (Plural: axes.)** A fixed line used for reference, along or from which distances or angles are measured. A pair of coordinate axes are shown.

**base** 1. A number on which a system of numeration is founded. For example, in the decimal system any value may be represented by the digits 0 to 9 and place value is increased as a sequence based on powers of 10. The binary system uses the digits 0 to 1 and place values based on the powers of 2.

**base** 2. A number that is raised to a power. For example, in the expression $3^4$, 4 is the power, index or exponent, and 3 is called the base.

**base** 3. The bottom of a shape or solid.

**bearing** The direction relative to a fixed point.

**best buy** A purchase that gives best value for money spent.

**better value** A purchase that costs less or buys a greater quantity than another.

**bisect** To divide into two equal parts. You can bisect a line or an angle.

**brackets** The symbols '(' and ')' which are used to separate part of an expression. This may be for clarity or to indicate a part to be worked out individually. When a number and/or value is placed immediately before an expression or value inside a pair of brackets, the two are to be multiplied together. For example, $6a(5b + c) = 30ab + 6ac$.

**calculator** An electronic device for working out mathematical operations. It is used by pressing keys and the results are shown on the screen.

**capacity** The volume of a liquid or gas.

**centilitre (cl)** A metric unit of volume or capacity. One hundredth of a litre. 100 cl = 1 litre.

**centimetre (cm)** A metric unit of length. One hundredth of a metre. 100 cm = 1 m.

**centre** The middle point. In a circle or sphere, it is the point equally distant from all points of the circumference or surface. In a regular polygon, it is the point equally distant from the vertices.

**centre of enlargement** The fixed point of an enlargement. The distance of each image point from the centre of enlargement is the distance of object point from centre of enlargement $x$ scale factor. (See also *scale factor*.)

**centre of rotation** The fixed point around which a shape is rotated or turned.

**chord (F)** A straight line joining two points that are on the circumference of a circle.

**circumference** The outline of a circle. The distance all the way around this outline.

**clockwise** Turning in the same direction as the movement of the hands of a clock. (Opposite of *anticlockwise*.)

**comment** A note whether a result in a trial and improvement problem is too high or too low.

**compasses** Also called a pair of compasses, an instrument used for drawing circles and measuring distances.

**compound shape** A shape made from two or more simpler shapes. For example, a floor plan could be made from a square and a rectangle joined together.

**congruent** Exactly alike in shape and size.

**construct** To draw angles, lines, or shapes accurately, according to given requirements.

**conversion factor** A number that is used to convert a measurement in one unit to another unit. For example, $\times \frac{5}{8}$ converts kilometres to miles.

**corresponding angles** When two parallel lines are cut by a third line (transversal), four pairs of corresponding angles are formed: $a$ and $e$, $b$ and $f$, $c$ and $g$, and $d$ and $h$. Corresponding angles are equal.

**cross-section** The shape of a slice through a solid. Depending on where the cut is made, the cross-section of a cone could be a circle, a triangle, an ellipse, or a parabola.

**cubic centimetre (cm³)** A unit of volume. A cube of side 1 cm has a volume of 1 cm³. $100 \times 100 \times 100$ cm³ = 1 m³.

**cubic metre (m³)** A unit of volume. A cube of side 1 metre has a volume of 1 m³.

**cubic millimetre (mm³)** A unit of volume. A cube of side 1 millimetre has a volume of 1 mm³. $10 \times 10 \times 10$ mm³ = 1 cm³.

**cylinder** A solid or hollow prism with circular ends and uniform (unchanging) cross-section. The shape of a can of baked beans or a length of drainpipe.

**decagon** A polygon with ten straight sides. The internal angles add up to 1440°.

**decimal place** Every digit in a number has a place value (hundreds, tens, ones, etc.). The places after (to the right of) the decimal point have place values of tenths, hundredths, etc. These place values are known as decimal places.

**denominator** The number below the line in a fraction. It tells you the denomination, name, or family of the fraction. For example, a denominator of 3 tells you are thinking about thirds; the whole thing has been divided into three parts. (See also *numerator*.)

**diameter** A straight line across a circle, from circumference to circumference and passing through the centre. It is the longest chord of a circle and two radii long. (See also *radius*.)

**direct proportion** Two values or measurements may vary in direct proportion. That is, if one increases, then so does the other.

**distance** The separation (usually along a straight line) of two points.

**divisions** The marks or partitions on a scale that break it into sections.

**do the same to both sides** To keep an equation balanced, you must do the same thing to both sides. If you add something to one side, you must add the same thing to the other side. If you double one side, you must double the other side, etc. If you are manipulating a fraction, you must do the same thing to the numerator and the denominator to keep the value of fraction unchanged. However, you can only multiply or divide the numbers. Adding or subtracting will alter the value of the fraction.

**edge** Two sides or faces of a solid join along an edge. A cube has 12 edges.

**elevation** An elevation is the view of a 3D shape when it is seen from the front or from another side.

**enlargement** A transformation of a plane figure or solid object that increases the size of the figure or object by a scale factor but leaves it the same shape.

**equals** The same as; on a calculator, the equals key indicates the end of the calculation and brings up the answer.

**equation** A number sentence where one side is equal to the other. An equation always contains an equals sign (=).

**equidistant** The same distance apart.

**equilateral triangle** A triangle with three equal sides, and three equal angles – all of which are 60°.

**estimate** (As a verb) to state or calculate a value close to the actual value by using experience to judge a distance, weight, etc. or by rounding numbers to make the calculation easier; (as a noun) the same as estimation.

**expand** Make bigger. Expanding brackets means you must multiply the terms inside a bracket by the number or letters outside. This will take more room to write, so you have 'expanded' the expression.

**expand and simplify** An expression involving brackets can be expanded (remove the brackets) and the resulting terms may contain like terms that can then be simplified.

**expression (F)** Collection of symbols representing a number. These can include numbers, variables ($x$, $y$, etc.), operations (+, ×, etc.), functions (squaring, etc.), but there will be no equals sign (=).

**exterior angle** The exterior angles of a polygon are outside the shape. They are formed when a side is produced (extended). An exterior angle and its adjacent interior angle add up to 180°.

**face** The flat surface of a solid shape. A cube has 6 faces.

**factor** A whole number that divides exactly into a given number.

**factorisation** Finding one or more factors of a given number.

**foot (ft)** An imperial measurement of length, about 15 cm long. 12 inches = 1 foot, 3 feet = 1 yard.

**formula** (Plural: formulae) an equation that enables you to convert or find a measurement from another known measurement or measurements. For example, the conversion formula from the Fahrenheit scale of temperature to the more common Celsius scale is: $C = \frac{5}{9}(F - 32)$ where C is the temperature on the Celsius scale and F is the temperature on the Fahrenheit scale.

**fraction** A fraction means 'part of something'. To give a fraction a name, such as 'fifths' we divide the whole amount into equal parts (in this case five equal parts). A 'proper' fraction represents an amount less than one. (The numerator is smaller than the denominator.) An 'improper' fraction describes when the numerator is more than or equal to the denominator. Any two numbers or expressions can be written as a fraction, i.e. they are written as a numerator and denominator. (See also *numerator* and *denominator*.)

**front elevation** The view of a 3D object when seen from the front.

**function key** Calculator key that is used for a specific task or function, for example, to enter a fraction or mixed number, or to find a trigonometric ratio, a square root or a cube root.

**gallon (gal)** An imperial measurement of volume and capacity. An average-sized bucket holds about 2 gallons. 8 pints = 1 gallon.

**gram (g)** A metric unit of mass. 1000 grams = 1 kilogram.

**guess** Using your mathematical knowledge, you can make an estimate of an answer and use this as a starting point in a trial and improvement problem.

**height** How tall something is. The linear measurement of a shape from top to bottom.

**heptagon** A polygon with seven sides. The sum of all the interior angles of a heptagon is 900°. A regular heptagon has sides of equal length.

**hexagon** A polygon with six sides. The sum of all the interior angles of a hexagon is 720°. A regular hexagon has sides of equal length and each of the interior angles is 120°.

**hypotenuse** The longest side of a right-angled triangle. The side opposite the right angle.

**image** In geometry the 'image' is the result of a transformation. In the diagram, triangle ABC is related to its image A'B'C' by reflection through the origin.

**imperial** The description of measurements used in the UK before metric units were introduced. They often have a long history (for example originating in Roman times) and are commonly based on units of twelve or 16 rather than ten used by the metric system.

**inch (in)** An imperial unit of length. One inch is about $2\frac{1}{2}$ cm long. 12 inches = 1 foot.

**interior angle** An angle between the sides inside a polygon. An internal angle.

**inverse operations** Operations that reverse or cancel out the effect of each other. For example, addition is the inverse of subtraction, division is the inverse of multiplication.

**isometric grid** Dots arranged on paper in a triangular pattern. The pattern makes it easier to draw shapes based on equilateral triangles, parallelograms, and trapeziums. It also makes it easier to draw three-dimensional diagrams.

**isosceles triangle** A triangle with two sides that are equal. It also has two equal angles.

**key** 1. A key is shown on a pictogram and stem and leaf diagram to explain what the symbols and numbers mean. A key may also be found on a dual bar chart to explain what the bars represent.

**key** 2. A button on a calculator.

**kilogram (kg)** A metric unit of mass. A bag of sugar has a mass of 1 kg. 1 kilogram = 1000 grams.

**kilometre (km)** A metric unit of distance. 1 kilometre = 1000 metres.

**kite** A quadrilateral with two pairs of adjacent sides that are equal. The diagonals on a kite are perpendicular, but only one of them bisects the kite.

**length** How long something is. We can talk about distances, such as the length of a table and also time, such as the length of a TV programme.

**like terms** Terms in algebra that are the same apart from their numerical coefficients. For example, $2ax^2$ and $5ax^2$ are a pair of like terms but $5x^2y$ and $7xy^2$ are not. Like terms can be combined by adding together their numerical coefficients so $2ax^2 + 5ax^2 = 7ax^2$.

**line bisector** A point, straight line, or plane that divides a line in half.

**line of symmetry** A mirror line. (See also *axis* and *symmetry*.)

**litre (l)** A metric measure of volume or capacity. 1 litre = 1000 millilitres = 1000 cubic centimetres.

**loci** See *locus*.

**locus** (Plural: loci) the locus of a point is the path taken by the point following a rule or rules. For example, the locus of a point that is always the same distance from another point is the shape of a circle.

**measurement** Finding the size, quantity or amount of an item expressed in appropriate units. In a geometric shape, you can measure lengths, area, volume, and angles which are shown in units such as metres, square centimetres, litres, and degrees. Linear measure indicates measurement of length; square measure indicates measurement of area, and cubic measure indicates measurement of volume.

**metre (m)** A metric unit of length. 1 metre is approximately the arm span of a man. 1 metre = 100 centimetres

**metric** A system of units of measurement where the sub-units are related by multiplying or dividing by ten. For example, for mass, 1 kilogram = 10 hectograms, 1 hectogram = 10 decagram, 1 decagram = 10 grams, 1 gram = 10 decigrams, 1 decigram = 10 centigrams, 1 centigram = 10 milligrams. The basic units of length and volume are metres and litres.

**mile (mile)** An imperial unit of length. One mile is almost 2 km. 1 mile = 1760 yards.

**millilitre (ml)** A metric unit of volume or capacity. One thousandth of a litre. 1000 ml = 1 litre.

**millimetre (mm)** A metric unit of length. One thousandth of a metre. 1000 mm = 1 metre.

**mirror line** A line where a shape is reflected exactly on the other side. (See also *line of symmetry*.)

**mixed number** A mixed number is made up of a whole number and a proper fraction.

**net** If a 3D shape is made from a sheet of card that can be unglued and folded down flat it will show a net of that solid. Any diagram that could be folded to make a 3D shape is a net of the shape.

**nonagon** A polygon with nine sides. All the sides of a regular nonagon are of equal length, and each of its interior angles measures 140°.

**numerator** The number above the line in a fraction. It tells you the number of parts you have. For example, $\frac{3}{5}$ means you have three of the five parts. (See also *denominator*.)

**object** You carry out a transformation on an object to form an image (in maths). The object is the original or starting shape, line, or point. (See *enlargement* for an example.)

**obtuse angle** An angle that is greater than 90° but less than 180°.

**octagon** A polygon that has eight sides. A regular octagon has all its sides of equal length, and each of its interior angles measures 135°.

**opposite angles (or vertically opposite angles)** When two straight lines cross, four angles are formed. The angles on the opposite side of the point of intersection are equal, so there are two pairs of equal opposite angles.

**order of rotational symmetry** A shape or pattern can be rotated about a fixed point. If it has to be turned through a full circle before the picture looks the same as when it started, it has an order of rotation of one. If it looks the same two or three times during that complete rotation it has an order of rotation of two or three.

**ounce (oz)** An imperial unit of mass. 1 ounce is about 25 grams. 16 ounces = 1 pound.

**parabola** The shape of a graph plotted from an equation such as $5x^2 - 7x + 2 = 0$. The equation will have an '$x^2$' term.

**parallelogram** A four-sided polygon with two pairs of equal and parallel opposite sides.

**pentagon** A polygon that has five sides. A regular pentagon has all its sides of equal length, and each of its interior angles measures 108°.

**perimeter** The outside edge of a shape. The distance around the edge. The perimeter of a circle is called the circumference.

**perpendicular bisector** A line drawn at a right angle to a line segment which also divides it into two equal parts.

**perpendicular height** The perpendicular height of a plane shape is the length of the perpendicular from one side, taken as the base, to the highest point relative to the base. In a triangle, it is the perpendicular distance from the base to the apex.

**pint (pt)** An imperial unit of volume or capacity. 1 pint is about half a litre. Milk is usually sold in 1-pint or 2-pint cartons. 8 pints = 1 gallon.

**plan** A drawing of a room or solid shape as if it is seen from directly overhead.

**polygon** A closed shape with three or more straight sides.

**pound (lb)** An imperial unit of mass. 1 ounce is about half a kilogram. 1 pound = 16 ounces, 14 pounds = 1 stone.

**prism** A 3D shape that has a uniform or constant cross-section; the shape of the slice formed by cutting perpendicular to its length is always the same.

**protractor** An instrument used for measuring angles.

**Pythagoras' theorem** The theorem states that the square on the hypotenuse of a right-angled triangle is equal to the sum of the squares on the other two sides.

**quadratic equation** An equation that includes an $x^2$ term. For example, $y = 5x^2 - 7x + 2$.

**quadratic graph** A graph plotted from a quadratic equation.

**quadrilateral** A polygon that has four sides. The square, rhombus, rectangle, parallelogram, kite, and trapezium are all special kinds of quadrilaterals.

**radius** (Plural: radii) the distance from the centre of a circle to its circumference.

**ratio** The ratio of A to B is a number found by dividing A by B. It is written as A : B. For example, the ratio of 1 m to 1 cm is written as 1 m : 1 cm = 100 : 1. Notice that the two quantities must both be in the same units if they are to be compared in this way.

**rearrangement** To change the arrangement of something. An equation can be rearranged using the rules of algebra to help you solve it. Data can be rearranged to help you analyse it.

**rectangle** A quadrilateral in which all the interior angles are 90°. The opposite sides are of equal length. A rectangle has two lines of symmetry and a rotational symmetry of order 2. The diagonals of a rectangle bisect each other and also bisect the rectangle itself.

**reflect** An operation that keeps all angles, lengths and areas the same, but reverses the object about a mirror line. (See also *mirror line*.)

**reflection** The image formed after being reflected. The process of reflecting an object.

**reflex angle** An angle that is greater than 180° and less than 360°.

**regular polygon** A polygon that has sides of equal length and angles of equal size.

**rhombus** A parallelogram that has sides of equal length. A rhombus has two lines of symmetry and a rotational symmetry of order 2. The diagonals of a rhombus bisect each other at right angles and they bisect the figure.

**right-angled triangle** A triangle with one angle equal to 90°.

**rotation** Turning. A geometrical transformation in which every point on a figure is rotated through the same angle.

**rotational symmetry** A shape which can be turned about a point so that it coincides exactly with its original position at least twice in a complete rotation.

**scalar** A quantity with magnitude only. (See also *vector*.)

**scale drawing** A accurate drawing where lengths are reduced from the real-life lengths to ones that can be drawn on paper. The reduction is by a given ratio each time.

**scale factor** The ratio by which a length or other measurement is increased or decreased.

**scales** 1. A scale on a diagram shows the scale factor used to make the drawing.

**scales** 2. An instrument used to find the mass or weight of something.

**sector** A region of a circle, like a slice of a pie, bounded by an arc and two radii.

**segment** A part of a circle between a chord and the circumference.

**shift key** This calculator key is used in conjunction with others, to access further functions such as reciprocals, inverse trigonometric functions or logarithms.

**side** 1. A straight line forming part of the perimeter of a polygon. For example, a triangle has three sides.

**side** 2. A face (usually a vertical face) of a 3D object, such as the side of a box.

**side elevation** The view of a 3D object when seen from a side.

**simplify** To make an equation or expression easier to work with or understand by combining like terms or cancelling down. For example, $4a - 2a + 5b + 2b = 2a + 7b$, $\frac{12}{18} = \frac{2}{3}$.

**solution** The result of solving a mathematical problem. Solutions are often given in equation form.

**speed** How fast something moves.

**stone (st)** An imperial unit of mass. 1 stone is about 6 kilograms. 1 stone = 14 pounds, 160 stone = 1 ton.

**substitute** When a letter in an equation, expression, or formula is replaced by a number, we have substituted the number for the letter. For example, if $a = b + 2x$, and we know $b = 9$ and $x = 6$, we can write $a = 9 + 2 \times 6$. So $a = 9 + 12 = 17$.

**substitution** When a letter in an equation, expression, or formula is replaced by a number, we have substituted the number for the letter. For example, if $a = b + 2x$, and we know $b = 9$ and $x = 6$, we can write $a = 9 + 2 \times 6$. So $a = 9 + 12 = 17$.

**surface area** The area of the surface of a 3D shape, such as a prism. The area of a net will be the same as the surface area of the shape.

**symmetry** A figure is said 'to have symmetry' if it remains unchanged under a transformation. For example, the letter T has one line of symmetry (a mirror down the middle would produce an identical reflection), the letter N has rotational symmetry of order two (a rotation of 180° would produce an image that looks like an N).

**tangent** 1. A straight line that touches the circumference of a circle at one point only.

**tangent** 2. The ratio of the opposite side to the adjacent side in a right-angled triangle.

**tessellation** A shape is said to tessellate if, when its image is translated and/or reflected and/or rotated, the shapes completely fill a space, leaving no gaps. A space filled in this way is said to form a tessellation.

**three-figure bearing** The angle of a bearing is given with three digits. The angle is less than 100°, a zero (or zeros) is placed in front, such as 045° for north-east.

**time** How long something takes. Time is measured in days, hours, seconds, etc.

**ton (t)** An imperial unit of mass. 1 ton is about 1 tonne. 1 ton = 160 stone.

**tonne (t)** A metric unit of mass. 1 tonne is about 1 ton. 1 tonne = 1000 kilograms.

**transformation** An action such as translation, reflection, or rotation.

**translation** A transformation in which all points of a plane figure are moved by the same amount and in the same direction.

**trapezium** A quadrilateral with one pair of parallel sides.

**trial and improvement** Some problems require a knowledge of mathematics beyond GCSE level but sometimes these can be solved or estimated by making an educated guess and then refining this to a more accurate answer. This is known as trial and improvement.

**triangle** A three-sided polygon. The interior angles add up to 180°. Triangles may be classified as: 1. scalene: no sides of the triangle are equal in length (and no angles are equal). 2. equilateral: all the sides of the triangles are equal in length (and all the angles are equal). 3. isosceles: two of the sides of the triangle are equal in length (and two angles are equal). 4. a right-angled triangle has an interior angle equal to 90°.

**unit cost** The cost of one unit of a commodity, such as the cost per kilogram.

**unitary method** A method of calculation where the value for one item is found before finding the value for several items.

**units** Ones, as in hundreds, tens, and units.

**value for money** See *best buy*.

**variable** A quantity that can have many values. These values may be discrete or continuous. They are often represented by $x$ and $y$ in an expression.

**vector** A quantity with magnitude and direction. (See also *scalar*.)

**vertex** 1. The points at which the sides of a polygon or the edges of a polyhedron meet.

**vertex** 2. The turning point (maximum or minimum) of a graph.

**vertical height** The perpendicular height from the base to the apex of a triangle, cone, or pyramid.

**volume** The amount of space occupied by a substance or object or enclosed within a container.

**weight** How heavy something is. An object's weight is measured on scales or on a balance.

**width** How wide something is. The linear measurement of a shape from side to side.

**yard (yd)** An imperial unit of length. 3 feet = 1 yard. In metric units, 1 yard is about 91 cm.

William Collins' dream of knowledge for all began with the publication of his first book in 1819. A self-educated mill worker, he not only enriched millions of lives, but also founded a flourishing publishing house. Today, staying true to this spirit, Collins books are packed with inspiration, innovation and practical expertise. They place you at the centre of a world of possibility and give you exactly what you need to explore it.

Collins. Freedom to teach.

Published by Collins
An imprint of HarperCollins*Publishers*
77–85 Fulham Palace Road
Hammersmith
London
W6 8JB

Browse the complete Collins catalogue at
www.collinseducation.com

10 9 8 7 6 5 4 3 2 1

ISBN-13 978-0-00-734006-4

Kevin Evans, Keith Gordon, Trevor Senior and Brian Speed assert their moral rights to be identified as the authors of this work

British Library Cataloguing in Publication Data
A Catalogue record for this publication is available from the British Library

Commissioned by Katie Sergeant
Project managed by Alexandra Riley
Edited and proofread by Brian Asbury, Joan Miller, Philippa Boxer, Margaret Shepherd and Karen Westall
Indexing by Michael Forder
Answer check by Amanda Dickson
Photo research by Jane Taylor
Cover design by Angela English
Content design by Nigel Jordan
Typesetting by Gray Publishing
Functional maths and problem-solving pages by EMC Design and Jerry Fowler
Production by Arjen Jansen
Printed and bound by L.E.G.O. S.p.A. Italy

AQA has checked that the content and level of this publication are appropriate for its GCSE Mathematics (4360) specification.

**Acknowledgements**

The publishers have sought permission from AQA to reproduce questions from past GCSE Mathematics papers.

The publishers wish to thank the following for permission to reproduce photographs. Every effort has been made to trace copyright holders and to obtain their permission for the use of copyright material. The publishers will gladly receive any information enabling them to rectify any error or omission at the first opportunity.

Talking heads throughout © René Mansi/iStockphoto.com; p.6 © Patricia Burch/iStockphoto.com, © Jaroslaw Wojcik/iStockphoto.com, © Terry Wilson/iStockphoto.com; p.54–55 © Peter Garbet/iStockphoto.com, © Iztok Grilc/iStockphoto.com, © Anastasia Pelikh/iStockphoto.com; p.56 © Anastazzo/Shutterstock Images LLC, © Kevin Gardner/Shutterstock Images LLC; p.70–71 © Caitlin Cahill/Dreamstime.com, © Aleksandar Kamasi/Dreamstime.com, © Orlando Florin Rosu/Dreamstime.com; p.72 © Collins Bartholomew Ltd 2009, © Martin Vegh/iStockphoto.com, © Branko Miokovic/iStockphoto.com, © Vasko Miokovic/iStockphoto.com, © Tomasz Pietryszek/iStockphoto.com; p.100–101 © Mrakos/Dreamstime.com, © Severija/Dreamstime.com, © Philip Lange/Dreamstime.com; p.102 © Andrew Howe/iStockphoto.com, © Darren Pearson/iStockphoto.com, © Graeme Purdy/iStockphoto.com, © Pete Saloutos/iStockphoto.com; p.118–119 © Martin Darley/Dreamstime.com, © Petar Neychev/Dreamstime.com, © Angelo Gilardelli/Dreamstime.com, © Jazzboo/Dreamstime.com, © Scott Karcich/Dreamstime.com; p.120 © Brent Wong/iStockphoto.com, © Alessandro Argentieri/iStockphoto.com; p.152 © Ludmilla Yilmaz/iStockphoto.com, © agoxa/iStockphoto.com, © Carmen Martinez Banus/iStockphoto.com, http://britton.disted.camosun.bc.ca/escher/pegasus.jpg, © Dirk Freder/iStockphoto.com, © Giorgio Fochesato/iStockphoto.com; p.166–167 © AVTG/iStockphoto.com, © Shana McCormick, © Stephen Pitts, © deepblue4you/iStockphoto.com, © ra-photos/iStockphoto.com, © stshank/iStockphoto.com; p.168 © Henryk Sadura/iStockphoto.com, © MB Birdy/iStockphoto.com; p.208–209 © Gvision/Dreamstime.com, © Dale Berman/Dreamstime.com; p.210 © Selahattin BAYRAM/iStockphoto.com, © valdis torms/iStockphoto.com; p.234–235 © Mark Fairey/Dreamstime.com, © Jaroslaw Grudzinski/Dreamstime.com, © Jonnycwh/Dreamstime.com; p.236 © Roberto Gennaro/iStockphoto.com, © Andrew Prokhorov/iStockphoto.com; p.270–271 © Michael Flippo/Dreamstime.com, © Subbotina/Dreamstime.com; p.272 © Sam Valtenbergs/iStockphoto.com; p.320 © Andreas Weber/iStockphoto.com, © Philip Beasley/iStockphoto.com; p.334 © HultonArchive/iStockphoto.com, © FotoVoyager/iStockphoto.com, © Monika Lewandowska/iStockphoto.com; p.350–351 © Jun Mu/Dreamstime.com, © Davidmartyn/Dreamstime.com, © Eric Simard/Dreamstime.com

With thanks to Samantha Burns, Claire Beckett, Chris Pearce, Anton Bush (Gloucester High School for Girls), Matthew Pennington (Wirral Grammar School for Girls), James Toyer (The Buckingham School), Gordon Starkey (Brockhill Park Performing Arts College), Laura Radford and Alan Rees (Wolfreton School) and Mark Foster (Sedgefield Community College).